$6.48
9-7

THE
ROYAL HOUSE OF PORTUGAL

Dom Manoel.
Ex. King of Portugal.

THE ROYAL HOUSE OF PORTUGAL

BY
FRANCIS GRIBBLE

KENNIKAT PRESS
Port Washington, N. Y./London

THE ROYAL HOUSE OF PORTUGAL

First published in 1915
Reissued in 1970 by Kennikat Press
Library of Congress Catalog Card No: 73-110904
SBN 8046-0887-3

Manufactured by Taylor Publishing Company   Dallas, Texas

PREFACE

PORTUGUESE history may be very dull or very amusing, as one prefers. It depends upon the line of approach, and the scenes which one stops to contemplate. One could easily bore the general reader to tears by leaning too heavily upon the Methuen Treaty or taking too much trouble to define the precise points at issue between the Chartists and the Septembrists. On the other hand, the history of the fortunes of that House of Braganza which, until the other day, controlled—or, at least, tried and affected to control—the destinies of Portugal, is sometimes diverting, and sometimes dramatic. And that whether one sees the picture as one of good men struggling with adversity or one of incompetent men aghast at the demand that they should accept the consequences of their incapacity and retire into private life.

It will be the purpose of the present work to consider which of these pictures is the true one, or whether there is not, perhaps, an element of truth in both pictures. The process of the Decline and Fall of the House of Braganza will, that is to say,

PREFACE

be reviewed in the light, not only of public events, but also of the private lives of Kings and Queens. The writer is perfectly well aware that some of his critics regard an interest in this branch of the inquiry as an indication of a frivolous mind; but he does not agree with them. National institutions are the product of national character; and the efficient working of those institutions depends upon the characters of individuals. Monarchical institutions furnish no exception to that rule. Where they fail, the causes of their failure are to be found, not only in the matters nominally at issue between Kings and Parliaments, but also in the inadequacy or inadaptability of the Kings themselves. Which is to say that their private proceedings, being the causes of their public misfortunes, are matters of public concern.

The misfortunes of the House of Braganza will here be studied upon that assumption. It failed flagrantly before the eyes of an astonished Europe, which could see no particular harm in its later Kings, but was disposed to attribute their overthrow to a double dose of original sin inherent in the bosoms of their Republican opponents. Those later Kings belonged, not only to the House of Braganza, but also to the House of Coburg; and the Coburgs were professional Kings who always did their best. What then, Europe demanded, except that double dose of original sin in Republican bosoms, could account for the assassination of one Coburg and the summary eviction of another? That is our problem. The desire to solve it is the natural outcome of a serious

PREFACE

curiosity; and the matters which have to be inquired into for the satisfaction of that curiosity—down to and including the sowing of Dom Manoel's wild oats—are serious in substance though sometimes entertaining in detail.

Such matters, it is obvious, cannot be reviewed without comment on the proceedings of persons still living prominently in the public eye; and the writer has discovered that the passing of such comments on such persons is apt to be reproved by some severe reviewers as an outrage on the proprieties. He ventures to rejoin that he would be more affected by such reproaches if he were conscious of having violated any rule, written or unwritten, which is normally observed by the editors of the very newspapers which sometimes exclaim against his candour. It is his habit, however, to read those newspapers; and as he sometimes remembers what he has read, he could quote precedents for his own freedom of criticism on living personages from the columns of any one of them. A few examples will not be out of place.

Charles Stewart Parnell was no more dead than Dom Manoel at the time when our leading journals gave, for political purposes, a publicity to the sowing of his wild oats which he himself would assuredly have preferred to avoid. Mr. Lloyd George and Mr. H. G. Wells are only two among many of our more valuable contemporaries who have been aspersed with poisonous oil by the editor who is always claiming that his opinions are those of " all right-minded persons." One of the newspapers

PREFACE

which admonished the present writer for discussing the *vie intime* of the Emperor Francis Joseph had himself, only a little while previously, been constrained by the stress of legal proceedings to apologise for publishing as "exclusive information" an unsupported charge of immorality against a Cabinet Minister. As for the commentaries which contemporary newspapers permit themselves to pass on the investments of the Chancellor of the Exchequer, and his trips in the motor-cars of his millionaire friends—but why continue? Enough has been said to show that a good many of the houses from which stones are apt to be thrown are built of glass.

The author gratefully acknowledges his indebtedness to the work of previous labourers in the field, and more particularly to *A Bride of Two Kings*, by Mr. E. B. d'Auvergne, *La République Portuguaise*, by M. Phileas Lebesgue, *La Révolution Portugaise*, by M. Alcide Guiffard, and *Souvenirs sur la Reine Amélie*, by M. Lucien Corpechot.

FRANCIS GRIBBLE.

CONTENTS

CHAPTER I

PAGE

The reason why the House of Braganza "ceased to reign"—The reasons why it is unlikely to be restored—The King and the Dancing Girl—The pleasures of immorality—Their cost and the reluctance of the Portuguese to pay for them   1

CHAPTER II

The beginnings of Portugal—Henry of Burgundy—Relations between the three Royal Houses of Burgundy, Avis, and Braganza—The story of Inez de Castro—The Newdigate Prize Poem on the subject   10

CHAPTER III

The Golden Age of Portugal—Henry the Navigator, Vasco da Gama, and others—The reasons why the rot set in—Dom Sebastiam and his Crusade against the Moors—Defeat and death of Dom Sebastiam at Alcacer-Kebir—Refusal of the Portuguese to believe that Dom Sebastiam was really dead—Importance of the legend of his survival in keeping the Portuguese spirit of nationality alive   17

CHAPTER IV

The tragic life of Camoens—The contrasts in it—His early opportunities and his unfortunate love affairs—His enrolment in the Colonial service—His difficulties with his official superiors—Imprisonment and shipwreck—"The Lusiads" saved from the sea—Return to Portugal—Poor reward for his services—Destitution of his last years   26

CHAPTER V

Genealogy of the House of Braganza—Conquest of Portugal by Philip II. of Spain—His corruption of the Portuguese notables—Disgust of the common people at foreign rule—Growth of the legend that Dom Sebastiam was still alive "biding his time"—Rise and overthrow of the four "false Dom Sebastiams"   34

CONTENTS

CHAPTER VI

PAGE

Claimants to the Portuguese throne—The Duchess of Braganza and Dom Antonio o Crato—Refusal of the Duchess to marry Philip II.—English expedition, under Drake and Norris, on behalf of Dom Antonio—Assertion of the claims of John Duke of Braganza—His great position in Portugal—His timidity—His wife's insistence that he should—Revolution which raised John Duke of Braganza to the throne 44

CHAPTER VII

Portugal in decadence—John the Mediocre—Affonso the Ill-conditioned—Pedro the Glum—Affonso's insane and violent proceedings—His grotesque appearance—His marriage—Conspiracy of his wife and brother to depose him—His long imprisonment at Cintra—His death in prison—The gleam of reason which came to him on his death-bed 56

CHAPTER VIII

Affonso's sister Catherine of Braganza—Her marriage to Charles II.—Her dowry and the haggling about it—Her resentment at the favour shown to Lady Castlemaine—Her reconciliation to Charles—Discomfort of her position after the accession of William of Orange—Her return to Portugal—Her proclamation as Queen Regent of Portugal 71

CHAPTER IX

Continued decadence of Portugal—Disastrous reign of John the Dilettante—His passion for building, for endowing monasteries, and for embracing nuns—Voltaire's estimate of his character—Accession of Dom Joseph—The Lisbon earthquake—Success of Pombal in repairing the effects of that disaster—Quarrel of Pombal with the Jesuits 80

CHAPTER X

Dom Joseph and Pombal—The philosopher King and his Minister—Attempt to assassinate Dom Joseph—The complicity of the Jesuits—Execution of the conspirators—The anti-clerical campaign—The justification for it—Pombal's other reforms—His fall on the death of Dom Joseph—Dom Joseph's successor—her incestuous marriage and her weak mind—Dom John VI. becomes Regent—Approach of the French Revolution and its problems 87

CONTENTS

CHAPTER XI

John VI.—Reasons for calling him John the Runaway—His weak mind and his superstitions—Invasion of Portugal by Junot—French scheme for partition of Portugal—Flight of Dom John to Brazil—Southey's description of the Scene—The House of Braganza disgraced 100

CHAPTER XII

The Peninsular War—Residence of John the Runaway in Brazil—Reforms which he introduced there—The bank which he founded—Its peculiar constitution and methods—The first Brazilian financial crisis—Return of Dom John to Portugal—His farewell speech to his son—Dom Pedro I. crowned Emperor of Brazil 111

CHAPTER XIII

Personal appearance and character of John VI.—His acceptance of a Portuguese Constitution—Objections of his wife and younger son, Dom Miguel—Dom Miguel's revolt against his father—The intervention of the Ambassadors—Their collective visit to the Palace—Description of the scene by Hyde de Neuville—The Infant cowed for the moment but still rebellious—Dom John takes refuge on the *Windsor Castle* 121

CHAPTER XIV

Dom Miguel summoned to the *Windsor Castle*—Reproaches and penitence—The Ambassador's assert themselves—Proposal to banish the Queen—Her refusal to go—Dom Miguel sent on his travels—His reception in Paris and Vienna—Proposal to marry him to his niece, Maria da Gloria—Death of Dom John—Metternich's opinion of Dom Miguel—The Duke of Wellington's opinion—Dom Miguel, instead of marrying Maria da Gloria, usurps her throne 133

CHAPTER XV

Dom Miguel burns the Charter which he has sworn to observe—Doubts as to his parentage—Anecdotes illustrative of his character—Victor Hugo's hopes for him—That he would be hanged upside down—Dom Miguel's reign of terror—Anecdote illustrative of the state of the prisons—Dom Pedro's decision to come to his daughter's help—The rally in the Azores and the swoop on Oporto 145

CONTENTS

CHAPTER XVI

Dom Pedro's "cause"—Constitutional government and consanguineous marriage—English view of the rivals—The siege of Oporto by Dom Miguel—Dom Pedro's neglect to pay his troops—Precarious position of Dom Pedro—Saldanha to the rescue—Lisbon seized and defended against Dom Miguel—Final triumph of Dom Pedro—His early death 156

CHAPTER XVII

Dom Pedro II. Emperor of Brazil—A scholar—A poet—Specimen of his poetry—Descriptions of his Court by various visitors—By Prince Adalbert of Prussia—By Agassiz—By Messrs. Fletcher and Kidder—Dom Pedro as patron of literature—His great admiration for Longfellow 167

CHAPTER XVIII

A day in Dom Pedro's life—Testimonials to his merits—By Mme. Ristori—By Gladstone—By Darwin—His visits to France—Interview with Mistral—Conversation with Arsène Houssaye—Flattery from Lamartine—Exchange of civilities with Victor Hugo 179

CHAPTER XIX

Causes of the revolution in Brazil—The Cave of Adullam—Unpopularity of Princess Isabel and her husband, the Comte d'Eu—Story of the marriage of Princess Isabel and her sister—Character of the Comte d'Eu—Sudden decision of the Brazilians to have a Republic—The provisional government—It deports Dom Pedro, giving him twenty-four hours to pack 190

CHAPTER XX

Departure of Dom Pedro from Brazil—Incidents of the voyage—Arrival at Lisbon—The initiation into private life—Dom Pedro in Paris—Visit to M. Flammarion's Observatory—Last years and death—Wrangle at the funeral 200

CHAPTER XXI

Reign of Maria da Gloria—Her visit to England as a child—Impressions then formed of her—Her first marriage to the Duc de Leuchtenberg—His death—Her second marriage to Ferdinand of Saxe-Coburg—General characteristics of the Coburgs—Belgian Minister's impression of the situation in Portugal 207

CONTENTS

CHAPTER XXII

PAGE

Scenes in the life of Maria da Gloria—Fourteen revolutions in fifteen years—Battle for Court influence between Herr Dietz and Father Marcos—Visit to Lisbon by Duke Ernest of Saxe-Coburg—His description of Palace life there—Dumplings for dinner—Marshal Saldanha's revolution—The Queen's reconciliation to him—Her domestic virtues and her death 217

CHAPTER XXIII

Ferdinand of Saxe-Coburg as Regent—His son, Dom Pedro—Queen Victoria's attempt to marry Pedro to Princess Charlotte of Belgium—His marriage to Princess Stéphanie of Hohenzollern-Sigmaringen—Death of Stéphanie—Death of Pedro—Uncertainty as to his abilities 229

CHAPTER XXIV

Later life of Ferdinand—His refusal of Kingly Crowns—An Opera artiste consoles him for the loss of his wife—His marriage to her—Rudeness of the Portuguese Court to her—Domestic life at Cintra—The gardens and the parrot—A visit from General and Mrs. Grant 237

CHAPTER XXV

Queen Victoria's praise of Stéphanie of Hohenzollern—And of Dom Luiz—Simple character of Dom Luiz—His marriage to Maria Pia, daughter of Victor Emmanuel—Anti-Clericalism of Dom Luiz—His failure to govern Portugal—Saldanha's last revolution—His treatment of Maria Pia—Her severe rebuke—Death of Dom Luiz and accession of Dom Carlos—The problem which faced Dom Carlos 246

CHAPTER XXVI

Anecdotes of Dom Carlos's boyhood—His achievements as artist, sportsman, and athlete—His feats in the Mall and in the bull-ring—His search for a wife—Incidents of his courtship—Anecdotes of the wedding—Great qualities of his wife, Princess Amélie—Her rescue of a fisherman from drowning—Dom Carlos as a reformer—His desire to be a benevolent dictator—His failure to conciliate the rival reformers of Coimbra 255

CONTENTS

CHAPTER XXVII

The rise of the Coimbra School—Attempt to define their philosophical standpoint—Their anti-clericalism and their "Sebastiamism"—Their Republican aspirations develop into a Republican policy—Dictatorship of Joao Franco—Franco's devices for extricating Dom Carlos from financial embarrassments—"Suspicious" transactions—Dom Carlos's touching faith in France—His premonition of catastrophe 268

CHAPTER XXVIII

Warnings—Queen Amélie's pessimism—Her French friends' fears for her—Franco becomes an oppressor—Frustrated plot to declare a Republic—Assassination of Dom Carlos and the Crown Prince—Were the Republicans implicated?—Utterances of representative Republicans—Repudiation of Franco by the royal family—Attitude of Queen Amélie—Accession of Dom Manoel—His hopeless prospects 280

CHAPTER XXIX

The royal point of view of monarchy—Queen Amélie's approval of the institution—Extracts from her letters—Her programme for Dom Manoel—His inability to execute it—His trip to Paris—The sowing of wild oats—The King and the dancing-girl—How the friendship helped the lady—How it harmed the King—Increasing power of the Republicans—Their mysterious conspiracy 291

CHAPTER XXX

Conspiracy and constitutional opposition—Their points of contact—Denunciation of the House of Braganza by Théophilo Braga—The writing on the wall—Queen Amélie's hopes and fears—Intricate organisation of the conspiracy—Impossibility of discovering who belonged to it and who did not 302

CHAPTER XXXI

The collapse of the House of Braganza—Shelling of the Necessidades Palace—Plans of resistance—Their impossibility—Flight of the royal family—The dancing-girl held responsible—What she said to the reporter—Dom Manoel at Richmond 311

INDEX 321

LIST OF ILLUSTRATIONS

DOM MANOEL, EX-KING OF PORTUGAL . . *Frontispiece*

CATHERINE OF BRAGANZA . . . . . *To face p.* 74

QUEEN MARIA DA GLORIA . . . . . ,, 140

PRINCESS STÉPHANIE OF
    HOHENZOLLERN-SIGMARINGEN . . . ,, 234

QUEEN MARIA PIA . . . . ,, 248

QUEEN AMÉLIE AND THE LATE KING CARLOS . ,, 264

THE
ROYAL HOUSE OF PORTUGAL

CHAPTER I

The reason why the House of Braganza "ceased to reign"—The reasons why it is unlikely to be restored—The King and the Dancing Girl—The pleasures of immorality—Their cost and the reluctance of the Portuguese to pay for them.

THE House of Braganza "ceased to reign" for the third time in October, 1910; and one may hazard the prophecy that this third cessation will prove to be definite. Dom Manoel, now of Richmond,—the boy King who loved the dancing-girl who boasted to the newspaper reporter that her salary was larger than his Civil list—does not impress one as likely to regild its tarnished glories. Perhaps he does not want to, but really prefers to take his ease in those suburban picture palaces of which he is said to be a frequent patron. In any case, there are many obstacles on the road to restoration; and the dancing-girl—or the memory of the dancing-girl—is not the least of them.

It may be that he has ceased to love her, or has been reduced to loving her in vain that is his private business; but the recollection of the episode which made her conspicuous remains one of the factors determining the attitude of the Portuguese towards monarchical institutions. There have been times and circumstances in which such episodes have not mattered; but they do matter nowadays, and they tend to matter more and more as political power passes into the hands of middle-class people with middle-class moral standards, and the journalists of all nations turn the hose of ridicule on the *amours* of Kings. They mattered in Spain when Isabella II. advertised her passion for the son of a cook; and they mattered in Bavaria when Ludwig I. squandered the substance of the taxpayers on Lola Montez. All the indications point to their now mattering in Portugal.

Not solely on high moral grounds, though a high moral tone has been taken, but on economic grounds as well. There is no warrant for the assumption that the Portuguese are a specially Puritanical people for whom the pleasures of immorality have no attraction. But they are, at any rate, a poor people—underpaid and over-taxed; and the incident of the dancing-girl, adroitly handled by politicians and publicists, has brought home to them a fact to which their poverty compels them to attach importance: the fact that the pleasures of immorality cost money, and, in the case of Kings, cost a great deal of money.

Moreover, the money which these pleasures cost is not theirs but the taxpayers'—a trust fund, as it were, committed to them to be expended on legiti-

FALL OF THE HOUSE OF BRAGANZA

mate *frais de représentation* for the greater dignity of the country; and it is—so the advanced thinkers in Portugal have taken to maintaining—no more essential to the pride of Portugal than to the pride of England or Germany that its sovereign should entertain a dancing-girl in the royal palace for the week-end, and present her with diamond necklaces and ropes of pearls, to say nothing of jewelled garters. They were already inclining to that view of the matter when the late Dom Carlos presented a distinguished French actress with four cream-coloured mules. The King, they reflected, must have got something, if only a smile, in return for the gift; whereas his subjects, whose money paid for it, got nothing. That seemed to them not only unsatisfactory, but unjust; and there has been nothing in the conduct of Dom Manoel to induce them to change their opinion.

There are cynics who write as if such Puritanical reflections had no practical bearing on politics; but they have. History shows that they had in the cases of Isabella of Spain and Ludwig of Bavaria; but we need not dwell upon those precedents. It suffices to invite the cynic to imagine the probable attitude of the Swiss people towards a proposal that the President of the Swiss Confederation should be authorised to indulge in the pleasures of immorality at the public cost—or even, to leave immorality out of the question, should be voted an entertainment allowance to be expended in endowing actresses with equipages and *figurantes* with precious stones. The cynic knows as well as the

THE ROYAL HOUSE OF PORTUGAL

Puritan that the Swiss, in such a case, would button up their pockets and make gestures expressive of virtuous indignation; and it is hard to discover any good reason why the Portuguese, who are poorer than the Swiss, and more heavily taxed, should take a more genial view than they of a demand that they should find the money to pay for the bought kisses of public functionaries.

It avails nothing to scoff at such objections as paltry and characteristic of small tradespeople. They are, in Portugal, the objections not only of small tradespeople, but also of University men—the class which made the Revolution. These men being in power, an estimate of the probabilities of the case must take cognisance of their doctrines, instead of laughing at them because they are inconvenient to the immoral. The doctrines can be reconciled with monarchy when the monarch recognises his subjects as the source of his power, and rules, not over them, but through them, as the chosen incarnation of the national will—the position, for example, of King Haakon of Norway and King Constantine of Greece. They cannot be reconciled with it when the sovereign claims more rights than the subjects of their own free will bestow, and looks upon his *amours* as enterprises to be supported by votes on account and supplementary estimates.

They cannot be reconciled with it, that is to say, in the case of Dom Manoel; and it only remains to inquire whether, as the door has been slammed in his face, and is unlikely to be re-opened to him,

FALL OF THE HOUSE OF BRAGANZA

there is any real prospect of his forcing it, with the help of aristocratic royalists and clerical fanatics.

There is always, of course, the doctrine of divine right, for those who believe in it, and for what it may be worth; but that faith seems, in this instance, for two reasons, a broken reed to lean upon. The people who conscientiously hold the creed in this year of grace can hardly be more numerous than, let us say, the Plymouth Brethren or the Swedenborgians; and those who do hold it cannot very well apply it to the claims of Manoel, for it is not he, but the Pretender, Dom Miguel, whom the strict adherents of the principle recognise as the legitimate King of Portugal. The royalists who support him, therefore, are merely royalists with axes to grind; and the Portuguese people know it, and have seen, and heard, quite enough of the grinding of their axes in the recent past.

The clerical interest may be more formidable, because fanaticism is always formidable; and the interested and disinterested fanatics are at one in their eagerness to strike a corrupt bargain: the King to be empowered to take money away from peasants and shop-keepers and give it to dancing-girls, on condition that he also takes money away from laymen and gives it to clergymen. Bargains of that sort have long been the mainspring of clerical policy in the Peninsula; and it was mainly on account of her readiness to conclude them that Pius IX. sent Isabella II. a Mystic Rose blessed with his own hands—a distinction reserved for ladies who were " patterns of all feminine virtues "—at the time when the cook's son was known to be enjoying her favours. There would not, therefore, be any grave departure from precedent if the present Pope should accord his moral support to the young man who entertained the Music Hall performer in the Necessidades Palace—just as an earlier Pope accorded it to that Dom Miguel who used to amuse himself by tossing sucking-pigs into the air and catching them on the point of his sword.

But the probable value of that moral support is another matter. Whether religion is gaining or losing ground in the world is a doubtful question, not to be settled until religion has been defined; but all the available evidence goes to show that clericalism—which some people identify with religion—is everywhere losing ground. It retains a certain hold on the bucolic mind; but it is losing its grip in the towns, where people read the newspapers and talk politics in cafés. The tendency in intelligent circles, however religiously inclined, is to keep the priest to his ritual routine, and treat him as a suspected person when he departs from it.

It is true, of course, that the appeal of clericalism is not to the intelligent, but to the ignorant, and that the ignorant are numerous in Portugal; but little hope can legitimately be based upon those considerations. There will be no concerted response to the call, because there will be no facilities for the concerted preaching of the crusade; while the glories of the House of Braganza—such as they have been—are too remote for the memory of them to evoke spontaneous enthusiasm. As well might

FALL OF THE HOUSE OF BRAGANZA

one expect the memories of the Elizabethan age to influence the votes of our own agricultural labourers. These things are history, not politics, and mean nothing to the man who has a garden or a vineyard which he wants to cultivate in peace. Whence it follows that the fall of the House of Braganza will indeed, in all likelihood, prove to be as final as the fall of Lucifer.

One may feel sorry for Dom Manoel—or, at all events, one need not be too hard on him. His performances, when one weighs them solemnly in the balance, seem, after all, to have been no worse than the pranks of many an undergraduate who "goes the pace" because he has more money than sense. He was no older than the average undergraduate when he indulged in those pranks; assuredly he had no idea that so much would come of them, or that so much importance would be attached to them. He was only following an example which many ancestors had set him; he simply did not understand that light-hearted irresponsibility such as his was out of date for people in his position; and he was not frightened, but only amused, when Ferdinand of Bulgaria, who had just kept up his reputation by falling off his horse, said to him:

"Very well, young man! Laugh, if you like; but bear this in mind: My seat on the saddle may not be very secure, but it is a good deal safer than your seat on your throne."

But though Dom Manoel laughed, King Ferdinand was right; the difference between them being that he performed functions recognised as of national utility, whereas Dom Manoel did not. It is quite possible, indeed, that Ferdinand would have kept his throne if he had been King of Portugal, and that Dom Manoel would have lost his throne if he had been the ruler of Bulgaria. In modern conditions, personality is apt to make such differences. In any case, Dom Manoel failed—partly because his personality was inadequate to the situation in which he found himself, and partly because he clung, in spite of his constitutionalism, to the old Braganza notion that the country was an estate which belonged to the King, and might properly be exploited by him. Consequently he had to depart in a hurry, pursued by the contemptuous indignation of a people who, whatever their attitude towards monarchical institutions in the abstract, had no use whatever for a crowned young man about town who squandered the substance of the taxpayers on the sowing of his wild oats.

Truly it is an ignominious end for a House which was once veritably great and glorious—the House of Henry the Navigator, John the Constable, and Ferdinand the Saint—a House closely associated with our own sovereign Houses by many links, both matrimonial and political. But though the end came suddenly, amid a riot of street fighting and a roar of guns, it came as the culmination of a continuous and protracted process of decline. Portugal had long been a little country ruled over by little men—little in the physical sense even when they

FALL OF THE HOUSE OF BRAGANZA

were physically fat—who clung to the old ideas while their subjects were developing new ones. Our story of the Decline and Fall of the House of Braganza will exhibit the part played by their inadequate personalities—their weaknesses, their pride, their prejudices, their timidities, and their scandals—in the gradual evolution of the great historical drama.

CHAPTER II

The beginnings of Portugal—Henry of Burgundy—Relations between the three Royal Houses of Burgundy, Avis, and Braganza—The story of Inez de Castro—The Newdigate Prize Poem on the Subject.

IT was not as King of Portugal only that Dom Manoel used to figure in the Almanach de Gotha. His full description—too long for him to be announced by it at even the most ceremonious of Court functions—was as follows:—

"King of Portugal and of the Algarves, on this side, and also on the other side of the Sea in Africa, Lord of the conquest, navigation, and trade of Guinea, Ethiopia, Arabia, Persia, India," &c.

The enumeration of titles has a majestically impressive ring, whether one knows, or does not know, that the Algarves are merely the southernmost provinces of Portugal. A gorgeous pageant seems to pass as the phrases roll off the tongue: a pageant the more imposing through its contrast with the present condition of the young man in whom so much of the pomp and glory of the world was until lately concentrated. And all the phrases meant something; there had once been solid sub-

BEGINNINGS OF PORTUGAL

stance behind them, even if, at the last, little more than the shadow remained. They magnetised the imagination, and drew it back to the days when the smallest country in Europe held her own with the greatest, treated with them on equal terms, and showed them the way across the ocean to Brazil, and round the Cape of Storms—not yet the Cape of Good Hope—to India and China and the Philippines and Japan. We will occupy ourselves for a moment with the dawn of that Golden Age.

We need not go too far back. At a time when our own history is already consecutive and precise, the history of the Iberian Peninsula is still vague: the history of the fluctuating fortunes of the long struggle of Christendom to shake off the dominion of the Moors. There was not in those days a definite Portugal, or even a definite Spain. The ultimate Kingdom of Spain was the amalgam of certain other kingdoms—Leon, and Galicia, and Arragon, and Castile, and the rest. The eventual Kingdom of Portugal was originally a fief of the Kingdom of Galicia. It might very easily have formed part of the amalgam, but, mainly for geographical reasons, failed to do so. The fief was given to Count Henry of Burgundy when he married the natural daughter of the King of Galicia, in 1095. It was only a small strip of territory, but he was to add to it whatever he could conquer from the Moors. He, and his son Affonso Henriques after him, not only fought the Moors, but also fought their Galician relatives, with the result that, in 1140, Portugal was recognised as an independent State.

THE ROYAL HOUSE OF PORTUGAL

The Portugal so recognised, however, was only a fragment of the Portugal of to-day. Lisbon itself was not taken from the Moors until 1147, and the power of the Moors was not finally broken until 1249. It was not, that is to say, until towards the end of the reign of our own Henry III. that the Portuguese made their title to Portugal good against the Africans; and it was not until the middle of the reign of our Richard II. that they made it good against Spanish claims to over-lordship—helped to do so by Richard himself, who lent both money and troops. The battle in which they prevailed was that of Aljubarrota, fought in 1385—a date which may be called the Portuguese Hegira; and the Anglo-Portuguese alliance was, in the following year, cemented by the famous Treaty of Windsor.

That is our historical starting-point, and we may pass at once from it to the genealogy of the dynasties. There have been three of them in all, that of Braganza being the third and last; but the three are, in a sense, one, though the line of descent has been neither legitimate nor direct. We have to distinguish, and also to show the connection, between:—

1. The House of Burgundy.
2. The House of Avis.
3. The House of Braganza.

The House of Burgundy, under which Portugal was carved out as a separate country, came to an end when Dom Ferdinand was succeeded by his illegitimate brother, Dom John the Bastard, who reigned as John I. He was Master of the Knights of St. Benedict of Avis, the great Portuguese Order of Chivalry founded by Affonso Henriques, whence the new dynasty derived its name. It was he who, after his election by the Cortes, defeated his enemies, with English help, to the cry of "Portugal and St. George," at Aljubarrota; and he forged a further link with England by marrying Philippa of Lancaster, daughter of John of Gaunt. His reign, which lasted for nearly fifty years, was the Portuguese Golden Age—the Portuguese equivalent of our own Elizabethan Age—the period when the Portuguese mariners made their greatest discoveries and the Portuguese poets wrote their greatest works. He was the father of that great man, Henry the Navigator.

The years passed, however, and the lineage proved unworthy of its heroic ancestor. The glories gradually dwindled, and decadence gradually set in; the last King of the line being Cardinal Henry —a feeble old man who did not realise the world about him, but had to be fed, like a baby, from a spoon. When he died, childless, in 1580, there were many claimants to the throne, including our own Queen Elizabeth, and Philip II. of Spain; and while the other claimants were disputing, Philip bribed the Portuguese leaders, sent an army across the frontier, had himself proclaimed King, and so inaugurated the period which the Portuguese call "the sixty years' captivity." At the end of those sixty years came the revolution which turned the Spaniards out and bestowed the crown on the eighth

THE ROYAL HOUSE OF PORTUGAL

Duke of Braganza—a lineal descendant of the bastard son of the illustrious John I., and the ancestor of the Dom Luis, the Dom Carlos, the Dom Manoel, and the Dom Miguel, whom we remember or know.

Obviously the three Houses may be treated as one if the historian wishes. Our business in these pages will be mainly with the House of Braganza strictly and properly so called; but the moments of transition from House to House are marked by stories of dramatic intensity, some of which are famous. Notably there is the dramatic story of Inez de Castro—the mother of the great Dom John—which, after furnishing a theme for the novelists and playwrights of all countries, was the topic appointed for the Newdigate Prize Poem at Oxford in 1882. One may pause, even at the risk of digression, to recall it.

Dom Pedro, the King's son—so the story goes—loved Inez, and for her sake refused to marry any of the royal princesses proposed to him by his royal father. In the King's eyes she was an obstacle to be got out of the way—no matter how, but the more barbarously the better. He threw out a hint, therefore, as Henry II. did in the case of Thomas Becket, and three complacent courtiers fell upon her in the streets of Coimbra, and there hacked her to pieces. It is a story, so far, of a fairly commonplace mediæval atrocity, or one only lifted out of the commonplace by Donna Inez's fame for beauty. What was not commonplace, but served to keep the memory of the crime alive, was the patience with

INEZ DE CASTRO

which Dom Pedro bided his time and exacted signal and spectacular reparation for the wrong.

It was not until after the lapse of many years that he succeeded to the throne, but then his first thought was of his murdered mistress and her murderers. Those murderers, fearing his vengeance, had fled; but Dom Pedro obtained their extradition, and had them tortured—sitting ostentatiously at dinner while they were slowly done to death before his eyes. He also had Inez's body exhumed, and taken from Coimbra to the Convent of Alcobaça, there to be solemnly crowned, and then buried in state. That crowning of the skeleton of an old love—all beauty gone from it save the glory of such golden hair as the world seldom sees—is the culminating and astounding scene on which the imagination of the poets dwells. One has sufficient choice if one desires to quote; and one might do worse than rescue some lines from the British Museum's uncut copy—left uncut for more than thirty years—of Mr. John Bower Buchanan Nichols's Newdigate :—

> A great cathedral thronged in festal wise,
> Hung thick with cloth of gold and tapestries;
> The strong Te Deum thrills all hearts and ears,
> The organ's voice, triumphant unto tears,
> Floods the aerial space from roof to ground,
> And dies in eddies of dissolving sound;
> But when the singing leaves the silence bare,
> A hush of awe falls on the throbbing air;
> And each man turns and sees his fellow's face
> White like his own, as though in that same place
> With shuddering vision both had seen appear
> The very features of incarnate fear. . . .
> This only left of her that was so fair:
> The exceeding glory of her golden hair.

THE ROYAL HOUSE OF PORTUGAL

That was how Mr. Nichols, of Balliol, conjured up the spectacle; and two other poets, both of them of Balliol, and both of them well-known men—H. C. B. being identifiable as Canon Beeching, and J. W. M. as Mr. Mackail, of the Education Office—supported him with introductory and valedictory lines. "Could song," wrote Mr. Mackail:—

> Could song repass the portal
>   Where silent feet are led;
> Could loving lips of mortal
>   Praise duly loves long dead,
> Or catch that golden glory
>   The mists of time make dim,
> No sadder, sweeter story
>   Than this were told by him.
>
> Love wrought her life and shattered;
>   Death found and left her fair:
> Five hundred years have scattered
>   The marvel of her hair.
> Such gifts to them that know him
>   Love gives at last to keep:
> Remembrance in a poem,
>   Forgetfulness in sleep.

Perhaps Mr. Mackail wrote in those days as if he were "deputising" for another Balliol man—Algernon Charles Swinburne, to wit; but if Swinburne raised no objection, we need not. The purpose of the quotation is only to show how long and how vividly the tale has lingered in the recollections of the impressionable. More important things have happened in the early period of Portuguese history, but nothing has happened which made a more wonderfully human appeal. One could not resist the temptation to tell the story; but, having told it, one must hurry on.

CHAPTER III

The Golden Age of Portugal—Henry the Navigator, Vasco da Gama, and others—The reasons why the rot set in—Dom Sebastiam and his Crusade against the Moors—Defeat and death of Dom Sebastiam at Alcacer-Kebir—Refusal of the Portuguese to believe that Dom Sebastiam was really dead—Importance of the legend of his survival in keeping the Portuguese spirit of nationality alive.

WE come—or return—to the Golden Age which began with the reign of John I. The great names known to all the world are those of Henry the Navigator, Vasco da Gama, Magellan, Tristan d'Acunha, Francisco d'Almeida, and Albuquerque. The Portuguese soldiers and sailors were then reputed the best in Europe. The Portuguese flag was carried to the ends of the earth, and trade followed the flag. A great colonial Empire was acquired—an Empire of which there still remain such settlements as those of Goa, Macao, and Mozambique to keep the memory of the great days alive.

But it was all over in little more than a century and a half. The rot, setting in at the centre, spread to the extremities. The politicians at home were

THE ROYAL HOUSE OF PORTUGAL

jealous of the Proconsuls abroad; they recalled them, and imprisoned them—a goodly number of them dying in prison. The Empire comprised thirty-two foreign kingdoms and four hundred and thirty-three garrison towns; but no fewer than nine of the Governors of India alone were placed under arrest. Even the great Albuquerque himself was dismissed from his post, and died a broken-hearted man—died actually, some of his biographers tell us, "of a broken heart."

He had governed well and endeared himself to his Indian subjects, making a reputation like that which John Nicholson was afterwards to make in the Punjaub. Both Hindus and Mohammedans are said, after his death, to have worshipped him as a God, "going to Goa, to his tomb, and making offerings of flowers and oil for his lamp, and praying him to cause justice to be done in their suits." But his sympathies had cost him his post and the royal favour; and his death-bed speech is famous:—

"In bad repute with men because of the King, and in bad repute with the King because of the men, it were well that I was gone."

He went; and his successors were mostly men in whose eyes the colonial possessions of Portugal were merely treasure-houses to be plundered—treasure-houses destined, in many cases, soon to be wrested from them by the Dutch.

Meanwhile there was decadence at home and trouble of various kinds—notably civil wars and religious persecutions. To one of the civil wars

END OF GOLDEN AGE

we shall have to return because a Duke of Braganza forfeited his life in it; but the persecutions are more important for the moment, because of the evidence which they furnish of the new spirit coming over the Kings and people. They who had once been Crusaders now became Inquisitors, bent not on the slaying of the infidel, but on the extirpation of the heretic. The Jesuits were brought in, and the Jews were hunted out. Manoel the Fortunate decreed that every Jewish child under the age of fourteen should be taken away from its parents and brought up as a Christian; and there are stories of Jewish mothers throwing their babies down the wells in order to save them from this fate. The Jews, too, because they enjoyed comparative immunity from an epidemic of the plague, were held responsible for the dissemination of the disease among the Christians, and were burned, and hanged, and chopped in pieces.

That that sort of thing—together with the constant drain on the population for the control of so vast an Empire—heralded, and was sure to bring, decline, was, however, a fact which the wisest hardly realised at the time. We, looking backwards, can see that it was bound to be so; but to them the collapse was almost as sudden and surprising as a great convulsion of Nature—a catastrophe almost comparable to that great earthquake by which Lisbon was presently to be destroyed. It came, by one of the curious ironies of history, in the reign of a King who seemed to have inherited, not from his father, but from some remote ancestor, a double

THE ROYAL HOUSE OF PORTUGAL

portion of the crusading spirit, and dreamed of reviving old glories by attempting heroic deeds for which the time and the circumstances were inappropriate. It came, in short, because Dom Sebastiam was a visionary, weak but self-willed, who cherished a great aim, but turned a deaf ear to those who warned him that his means were inadequate to his end.

From different sources one gets contradictory accounts of him. There was Habsburg blood in his veins, and he had the pendant Habsburg jaw, and the blue eyes and fair hair of a German or Scandinavian. He delighted in hunting and jousting, and in long, solitary rambles in the forests. The priests had brought him up and made him their man, so that the obligations of religion and chivalry were confounded in his mind. He chose for himself a noble motto, taken from Petrarch:

Un bel morir tutta la vita honora.

That is what his friends tell us; but his detractors supplement the picture. Dr. Galippe, in his great work on the signs of that moral and physical degeneracy which has wiped out so many royal houses, sums up his symptoms thus:—

"He was mad, dangerous, passionate, and had an unconquerable horror of women. Apparently he suffered from some anatomical abnormality which made it easy for him to be chaste. Philip II. of Spain sent his own physician, Dr. Almazan, to him, to attempt a cure which could not possibly be effected."

Such, in so far as it is possible to know him, was

DOM SEBASTIAM

the youth who declared that he would and must go crusading at a time when crusades were out of date, and even the Pope was disposed to leave the heathen Turk in peace while he directed his thunders against such domestic heretics as Luther and Calvin. His forefathers had crossed the seas to fight the Moors in their own Morocco—why should not he do the same?

There were, in fact, many reasons why he should not, and many men—and even women—to formulate them. "Let not the King cross over to Africa," were his mother's last words on her death-bed; and when it was found that the King meant to take no heed of her dying entreaties, the statesmen spoke out in their turn. One of them advised Dom Sebastiam to be sure to take with him "a winding-sheet to bury his kingdom in"—only to be called a coward for his pains. Another exclaimed, in the royal palace, that as it was the custom of the country to place lunatics under restraint, he wondered why the King was left at large. But Dom Sebastiam persisted, encouraged only by the King of Spain, who had his own reasons for wishing to lure him to destruction. Not only would he cross over to Africa, he said, but he would take with him the crown which he proposed to wear as the first Christian Emperor of Morocco.

So—none being able to stop him—he set out in the year 1578. All his best troops were in the Indies; but he raised an army of a kind—a miscellaneous mob of 17,000 strong—and placed his courtiers in command of it. The courtiers, it

THE ROYAL HOUSE OF PORTUGAL

is said, took court suits with them instead of armour; and one of them delighted the ladies by boasting of his intention to cut off the ears of the Emperor of Morocco, and fry them, and eat them with oil and vinegar. But that was not at all how things fell out.

The end came quickly. There was only one battle—the terrible battle of Alcacer-Kebir. On that field, on August 4th, 1578, the Moors, anticipating the tactics of Isandula, enveloped the Portuguese army and destroyed it. The King himself fell fighting—for he was brave enough, if he had no other attribute of greatness—and of the whole host which had landed in Morocco, only about fifty ever got back to Portugal. And that disaster—the inevitable culmination of a gallant but silly fanatic's dream—was, for the time being, the end of Portugal. In a sense, indeed, it was a blow from which Portugal has not yet recovered, and the effects at the moment were tremendous. Philip II. was waiting for his chance, and he had now only a little while to wait for it. When the dispute arose about the succession, less than two months later, he would have little to do except to march in.

So that the Golden Age of Portugal—a Golden Age which had already become a Silver Age unperceived by contemporary eyes—was succeeded by the sixty years' captivity, almost without a pause. The brief reign of Cardinal Henry which intervened was the reign of an old man in his second childhood. The old man was aware of the dispute about the succession which was already raging round his death-bed, but he neither dictated, nor even proposed, a settlement of it. He "cited" the several candidates, but expressed no preference for any one of them in particular; and even his will reflected the muddled condition of his dissolving mind. As the anonymous author of an old work on *The Revolutions of Portugal* puts it:—

"In the midst of these disputes Henry died, on January 31st, at midnight, regretted by none, and leaving by will his crown to the next heir, without naming any person."

With the result that, when Philip II. of Spain named himself, no rival was in a position to oppose him effectively.

It seemed to the people a condition of things which ought neither to have been nor to be; and as it was impossible for them to regret Dom Henry, they began to regret Dom Sebastiam. If he had been a fool, at least he had been a romantic and gallant fool; so that the vulgar at least forgot his ghastly blunder for the sake of his glorious dream. He first passed into legend as "the Regretted"; and then another legend grew up around his name. He was too young and bright and beautiful and heroic to be really dead—God would not have let him die. The corpse shown as his must have been the corpse of some gaudy courtier mistaken for him. He himself must be in hiding somewhere—biding the auspicious time, intending to return.

THE ROYAL HOUSE OF PORTUGAL

It is the sort of legend which is common enough in superstitious times, and not confined to them. Long after the execution of Maximilian of Mexico the belief lingered at Trieste that the Emperor still lived in a Mexican prison, with three jailers—captains in the British, French, and Austrian navies—keeping ward over him; and there are also those at the present day in Austria who still insist that "John Orth" was not really drowned at sea, but will come home when Austria needs his services to save her from dismemberment. A belief of the kind generally preludes—and doubtless helps to bring about—the appearance of Pretenders; and it was so in Portugal. Just as in Russia there was more than one "false Demetrius," so in Portugal there was more than one "false Sebastiam."

These served their purpose by keeping the Portuguese spirit of nationality alive; and we will glance at their meteoric careers in a moment. Before we come to them, however, we have to say our farewell to the Heroic Age, and we cannot end our review of it better than by a cursory survey of the career of the national poet Camoens, who shared its glories, and sang of them, and lived to see them pass—perishing with them in a misery which is infinitely more pathetic than foolish Dom Sebastiam's death in futile battle with the Moors

"I saw him die," said the Carmelite Friar Joseph Indeo, "in a hospital in Lisbon, without a sheet or shroud to cover him, after having triumphed in the East and sailed five thousand leagues. What a

CAMOENS

lamentable thing to see so great a genius so ill-rewarded!"

" I die," he himself wrote to Francisco d'Almeida, "not only *in* my fatherland, but *with* my fatherland." So that his life is, in a way, a symbol; and we must give a chapter to it.

CHAPTER IV

The tragic life of Camoens—The contrasts in it—His early opportunities and his unfortunate love affairs—His enrolment in the Colonial service—His difficulties with his official superiors—Imprisonment and shipwreck—"The Lusiads" saved from the sea—Return to Portugal—Poor reward for his services—Destitution of his last years.

THE contrasts in the life of Camoens are terrible. He, who was to die a pauper, was born, it must have seemed, with all the chances in his favour—poor, indeed, but a gentleman, with friends, in an age in which gentlemen with friends had swords put into their hands and were told that the world was their oyster which they might open. He was of the family of Vasco da Gama, and had an uncle who was General of the Order of the Holy Cross; he received a University education at Coimbra. It only rested with him to say whether he would have a sinecure as a "buzzing monk" or an opportunity of achievement as an Empire-builder: a case like that of numbers of the "younger sons" who every year leave Oxford and Cambridge with light-hearted confidence in their ability to make their way.

He did not want to be a buzzing monk, not so

much because he lacked superstition as because he aspired to live his life. Why pace the cloister when the Court was open to him? Though his immediate fortune was only a distinguished manner and a fine suit of clothes, these things might suffice to launch him on a great and glorious career. So to Court he went; and patrons smiled on him—the Duke of Braganza and his brother Constantine, afterwards Indian Viceroy, among others; and all went well until he fell in love with Doña Catharina d'Athäide, a sister of one of the Queen's Maids of Honour.

In doing that he had presumed too far: he was a "detrimental" suitor, and the lady's relatives were influential. The decree went forth that he must not see her, and he defied it, entering the Palace secretly to urge his suit; and those were days when such offences carried heavy penalties—especially heavy if the offender committed them by night. One of the courtiers of John I. was burnt alive for such a fault, and one of the courtiers of Affonso V. was beheaded for it. John III., though of milder manners than these predecessors of his, had earned the sobriquet of "the Pious," and lived up to it. He banished Camoens; and when Camoens repeated his offence, returning from his exile without leave, he banished him yet again—this time to Africa, where he lost his right eye in a fight with "Sallee rovers."

He was very young when these calamities befell him; and his disgrace was the sort of disgrace which a man, as a rule, lives down, and comes to treasure in his honoured age as a romantic memory. Camoens

THE ROYAL HOUSE OF PORTUGAL

failed to do so, for reasons nowhere given, but not very hard to guess: because his enemies were very powerful, and because he himself was very much in love and not of a very accommodating temper. When he returned to Lisbon he got into trouble for the third time, and served a term of imprisonment for drawing his sword on a Palace servant in a street brawl. He was only released from prison on condition that he volunteered for the East; and the temper in which he sought the East is shown by the story that, as he boarded the vessel which was to take him there, he quoted the words of Scipio Africanus: "Ungrateful country, thou shalt not possess my bones!" And he further uttered the bitter complaint that "Sins worth three days of purgatory had cost him three thousand of biting tongues, envy, hatred, and malice."

Even so, however, there was nothing in either the fault or the punishment which he might not have lived down if the career to which he went had been the career for which he was fitted. It must have seemed, indeed, to others—and perhaps also to himself—that he was living it down, and slowly climbing the respectable ladder of the Portuguese Colonial Service, at the time when he was appointed to the office of Commissary for the Effects of the Defunct and Absent at one of the settlements in China. But Camoens was not of the stuff of which such Commissaries are made. He was living the life which would enable him to write his great poem on the glories of Portugal—he was writing the poem, in fact, at the very time when he was living the life;

CAMOENS

but he was not living the life in the way which brings preferment to public functionaries. He had not the Civil Service manner or the Civil Service discretion.

He was poet, dreamer, satirist, and critic: things which it was then, as it is now, very perilous for a Civil Servant to be. His very accomplishments made him fresh enemies wherever he went among fellow-countrymen corrupted by hot climates and given over to the enjoyment of the forbidden fruit which they shook from the pagoda tree—enemies who were generally powerful enough to make him pay for the annoyance which he caused them. No doubt it was necessary for him to suffer what he suffered in order that he might sing as he sang; for the greatest poetry, like the greatest music, is the outcome of great tribulation—never produced by those whose lives have been a matter of laughing, and growing fat, and laying up treasure, and adding field to field. But that is a trite reflection, and one which leaves the pathos of the story where it was.

We must picture Camoens as a man of genius thrown among gentlemen adventurers who had no use for men of genius. He looked at their emprises with other eyes than theirs, saw more in them, and therefore was able to make them immortal. "The conqueror," wrote a patriot of a later age, "who shall ever attempt to subjugate our beloved Country must first tear in pieces every page of the Immortal Lusiads." But the material reward which the Immortal Lusiads gained their author during his lifetime was a pension of £3 8s.; and, in the meantime, in the Indies, he seems to have been regarded as a nuisance to be suppressed. Such intermittent glimpses as we get at him show him, every now and again, in prison—sometimes as a debtor, and sometimes on false charges of malversation. On one occasion, indeed, he was not only in prison, but in chains.

Nor was it only with his enemies that he had to contend—the luck, too, was against him. When he did succeed—one does not know exactly how—in amassing a little property, the ship on which he had hoped to take it home was wrecked. He had to swim ashore, saving nothing but his life and his manuscript, which he held aloft in one hand while with the other he battled with the waves. It is one of the most famous incidents in the history of literature, and it meant, of course, the prolongation of his exile. He did not sigh the less for home because his friend Constantine of Braganza made him an Inspector of Public Works. Office was merely an enchaining servitude for a man conscious of a call to other tasks—the call to express himself and his country's Heroic Age; so he threw up his appointment and came home, bringing his sheaves with him.

The catastrophic end of the Heroic Age was nearing; and Camoens himself was, in some degree, unwittingly an instrument in bringing it about. In Portugal, as in the East, he saw the world about him with the eyes, not of a practical man, but of a poet—and that in the years in which Dom Sebastiam was meditating his disastrous *coup*. The practical men could see that Portugal was enfeebled, not only by the drain of men for Empire-building enterprises, but also by the consequences of recent floods, earthquakes, plagues, and famines, and that Dom Sebastiam was only a fanatical young fool. The dreamer only saw the dream; and mortal men of less than average worth were transfigured by his fancy into heroes.

It may have been easy for a man who lived in a dream to idealise Dom Sebastiam—especially easy for a dreamer who was drawing a pension, though but a small one, from his privy purse. The lavish festivities with which he celebrated the Massacre of St. Bartholomew may have seemed a proof of the sincerity of his convictions; and there may have been a good deal to be said—by a dreamer—in defence of his sumptuary laws. The sagacious declared that these—distinguishing, as they did, between permitted and forbidden meats, prescribing how every man should spend his money, and prohibiting the use of practically all imported goods, whether luxuries or necessaries—demonstrated that churchmen were as unfit to control temporal affairs as were civil magistrates to superintend the spiritual life: a view of the matter put on record by a Genoese employee in the Portuguese Customs Service. The dreamer doubtless regarded them as the religious regard the Lenten fast, and believed that the path to regeneration was paved with salt fish and could be best pursued in sack-cloth.

Be that as it may, Camoens did indubitably idealise Dom Sebastiam, and gave his policy such

THE ROYAL HOUSE OF PORTUGAL

support as a poet could, writing as his Tyrtæus, his Kipling—one is almost tempted to say his Great MacDermott. It was a part of his dream, it is said, to be allowed to accompany the expedition in the capacity of Sacred Bard; and it may only have been on account of his age and infirmities that a younger bard was preferred to him. One could wish that he had gone—a soldier-poet like Æschylus—and perished sword in hand. Such a death would have been infinitely better than to live on and be neglected after the blow had fallen and the glorious dream had been dissolved.

But there was to be no consolation for him; and the few details which we have of his last years are all distressing. Even his poor pension of £3 8s. was not paid: the royal almoner, he said, ought to receive 15,000 lashes—a lash for every coin which he had omitted to disburse. He was now a cripple who hobbled about on crutches. His home was a garret in which he lived on charity—alms begged for him in the street by a faithful Javanese servant. After his death even his winding-sheet had to be supplied by charity. He—the greatest Portuguese genius of his age—was buried "poorly and in plebeian fashion"; and it was sixteen years before it occurred to anyone to erect a monument to his memory.

Nor was that all. The first tribute paid to him after his death was not paid by grateful countrymen, but by the enemy of his country. Philip II., when he marched in triumph into Madrid, called at once for Camoens. Told that the poet was dead, he sent for his mother, and showed her some small

CAMOENS

kindness—little enough, but more, at any rate, than was shown by any of her compatriots. It is one of the few good actions—perhaps the only one—which history chronicles to the credit of the moody husband of our Bloody Mary; one may hope that the Recording Angel has taken note of it.

But Portugal and her greatest poet had, as the poet said, "died together"; and we come to those "sixty years' captivity" at the end of which the House of Braganza was enthroned.

CHAPTER V

Genealogy of the House of Braganza—Conquest of Portugal by Philip II. of Spain—His corruption of the Portuguese notables—Disgust of the common people at foreign rule—Growth of the legend that Dom Sebastiam was still alive "biding his time"—Rise and overthrow of the four "false Dom Sebastiams."

THE illegitimate roots of the House of Braganza reach down to remote antiquity. Henry of Burgundy, to whom we have already traced it, was the son of Robert I. of Burgundy, who was the son of Henri I. of France, who descended in the direct line from Hugues Capet. The title, however, only dates from 1442, when Affonso of Portugal, Count of Barcellos, natural son of John I. and Inez Perez, was created Duke of Braganza by Pedro of Portugal, Duke of Coimbra and Regent during the minority of Affonso V. The line was continued by his second son, Ferdinard I., Duke of Braganza; and the subsequent Dukes, up to the time when the House became the Royal House of Portugal, were:—

> Ferdinand II.,
> James,
> Theodosius I.,
> John I.,
> Theodosius II.,
> John II., who became King of Portugal under the title of John IV.

THE HOUSE OF BRAGANZA

By no means all of them have left their mark on history; but Ferdinand II. stands out in a *rôle* akin to that of our own Barons when they compelled King John to sign Magna Charta. He stood, not for the rights of man, of which no one in those days dreamed, but for the rights of feudal lords. John II. had threatened to infringe those rights by calling upon all nobles to return to him the letters patent by which previous Kings had granted them their estates; his evident purpose being to purge the ranks of the nobility, despoil such lords as he distrusted, and acquire something for himself in the process. History has preserved the speech in which Ferdinand II., Duke of Braganza, respectfully objected :—

"Deign, your Majesty, to listen to our remonstrances, for they are reasonable. Withdraw an unjust decree; restore us your confidence; give us back the privileges which have been taken from us."

But Ferdinand II. did not content himself with remonstrating; he also engaged in treasonable correspondence with the King of Arragon and Castile. He was found out; and though he was the husband of the Queen's sister, he was beheaded. His offence, however, was recognised as personal, and his family remained in favour. James, Duke of Braganza, was in very high favour with Manoel the Fortunate, who even designated him as his successor in the event of his dying without heirs— which he did not. Constantine of Braganza, the

THE ROYAL HOUSE OF PORTUGAL

brother of Theodosius I., Duke of Braganza, distinguished himself in many high offices. We have seen him already, as Viceroy of the Indies, befriending Camoens; and he was also Chamberlain to John III. and Portuguese Ambassador to France. And then we come to John I., whose wife we have met already, as one of the candidates for the disputed succession —" cited," but not selected, by the dying Cardinal Henry.

It cannot be said that he cuts a very heroic figure in the dispute. Philip II. of Spain, as has already been mentioned, owed his triumph over his rivals as much to bribery and corruption as to martial prowess; and it has to be added that he failed to distribute bribes as lavishly as he had promised them, and so sowed the seeds of discontent among those whom he might otherwise have relied upon for support. The applicants for his bounty thronged around him, hungry for office, preferment, Orders, and estates; and it was said that, in order to satisfy them all, he would have had to take everything away from everybody and give it to somebody else. However that may be, he failed to give satisfaction to John, Duke of Braganza, who appears before the bar of history as a man who first sold his birthright for a mess of pottage and then complained that the pottage did not come up to his expectations.

He had been promised Brazil, and the title of Emperor of Brazil, and a royal Prince as his daughter's husband; he was put off with the office of Constable and the Order of the Golden Fleece.

THE CAPTIVITY

Naturally, he became Philip's enemy, and fomented the general discontent for which there was considerable cause. It was the settled aim of the Spaniards indeed to "tear up every page of the Lusiads" and de-nationalise the Portuguese, much as the Germans of to-day try to de-nationalise the Alsatians and the Poles. One of the measures proposed was to close the University of Coimbra, so that the Portuguese students, compelled to repair to Spanish seats of learning, might acquire Spanish culture, and extinguish Portuguese culture with it when they returned. But that Philip forbade. It may have been, as his treatment of Camoens seems to indicate, that he had a sneaking sympathy with Portuguese culture; it may merely have been that he feared the consequences of that extreme outrage on national aspirations.

In any case, the dissatisfaction with his rule was widespread and deep. Portugal never accepted him. He only ruled as a conqueror—only ruled, in fact, in the towns which he garrisoned and the parts of the country in which his armies were encamped. Vivonne de Saint Goard, the French Ambassador, intrigued against him, and besought Henri III. to land troops on the coast—twelve hundred men, he said, would be enough—and seek advantage for France out of the general rising which would infallibly ensue. Henri III. did not see his way—or perhaps mistrusted the information; but his Ambassador had gauged Portuguese opinion rightly. The country was always simmering, always ready to boil over; and it was because of this condition

THE ROYAL HOUSE OF PORTUGAL

of things that the Portuguese people—not the common people only—lent a ready ear to the rumour about Dom Sebastiam: that he was not really dead; that he was biding his time, and would return to deliver his country from the foreign yoke; that he had bided sufficient time, and had now come back to reconquer his kingdom with the help of his loyal subjects.

The report that Dom Sebastiam was still alive, and was on board one of the ships which had returned from Morocco to Portugal, seems first to have been circulated for the purpose of diverting popular anger from the promoters of the disastrous expedition. It was not widely believed, and attracted little attention as long as there seemed a chance that the natural leaders of Portugal could be relied upon to organise rebellion against the invader. But that hope proved illusory; and then the instinctive feeling spread among the people that as there was no help for them from men, they must look for help from miracles. So, after having been forgotten, the legend that Dom Sebastiam had been miraculously preserved from death was once again remembered. The credulous whispered it to each other till they came to believe it; and the way was clear for any adventurer or enthusiast who might arise and say: "Behold! I am Dom Sebastiam! I have been biding my time; and now my hour has come."

Or it might be that the people themselves would take the initiative, and invoke the memory to explain the proceedings of an eccentric, saying:

THE FALSE SEBASTIAMS

"This, clearly, is no ordinary man; he is not what he seems. He must be Someone in Particular, going about in disguise. Who can he be except Dom Sebastiam, biding his time, and about, with our help, to come into his own again?" And when the people talked like that the eccentric would agree with them if he was half-witted, or pretend to agree with them if he was deep. Things happened thus four several times in the course of the sixty years' captivity.

The first case was that of a queer youth of humble birth whose real name no historian has been able to discover: the son of a potter who had begun life by peddling rosaries. He left his trade in order to become a monk, and then quitted his monastery in order to instal himself in a vacant hermitage at Albuquerque, near the Spanish frontier. It was a way of begging without being classed with beggars, and the hermit prospered in the occupation. A devout woman with large revenues accorded him her protection; and he then became less ascetic in his way of life, took to singing amorous songs to the accompaniment of the guitar, and boasted of imaginary adventures in Africa.

The local parish priest thought his proceedings unedifying, and besought him to move on; but the common people were impressed, and began to talk. "This," they said, "must be Dom Sebastiam, who has been condemned to seven years' penance for losing the battle of Alcacer-Kebir." He accepted that view of the matter, and formed a Court at Penamaçor—whence his title of King of Penamaçor

—and obtained gratuitous hospitality at the inns by telling the innkeepers, in strict confidence, who he was. Everybody being thus pledged to secrecy, everybody, of course, talked; so that the Spanish Government, getting wind of what was happening, sent soldiers to arrest the adventurer, paraded him through the streets of Lisbon on an ass, and then sent him to the galleys. He was compelled to serve in some menial capacity on one of the ships of the Invincible Armada; but he escaped to France, and there disappeared from view.

The date of his brief reign was 1584; and in 1585 the son of a potter was succeeded by the son of a mason—a certain Matheus Alvares. He, too, was a monastic novice who became a hermit—at Ericeira, near the mouth of the Tagus; but he differed from his predecessor in that he lived austerely. The story spread that he had been heard scourging himself in the watches of the night, and chaunting as he did so:—

"Portugal! Portugal! What sorrowful mourning is thine! I alone am the cause of the misfortunes which overwhelm thee. Wretched Sebastiam! Would that a life of poverty, penitence, and tears might suffice to expiate my faults!"

In personal appearance he was not unlike Dom Sebastiam, being of the same age and similarly bearded and blonde; so influential people professed to recognise him, and a certain local leader—the farmer Pedro Affonso—promised him his support without troubling about his identity.

THE FALSE SEBASTIAMS

"I care not," said Pedro Affonso, "whether he be Dom Sebastiam or not. Whoever he be, he shall be King of Portugal before the Feast of St. John."

It was the voice of a patriot in whom the national spirit was alive, and for whom any stick was good enough to beat the Spaniards with. So Pedro Affonso raised an army of eight hundred men, and proclaimed the Pretender King at Ericeira, and crowned him with a diadem taken from a statue of the Virgin, and married his daughter to him, and accepted for himself the title of Marquis of Torres Vedras and the office of Governor of Lisbon. He also seized the Magistrate who came from Ericeira to his camp to make inquiries, and had him hurled over a high cliff into the sea; and he made a fair show of fight when the King's army marched against him.

The King's army prevailed, however, without much trouble; and the so-called King of Ericeira was taken prisoner and hanged, after his right hand had been cut off, and Pedro Affonso shared his fate. But the Pretender's confession shows us in what spirit the adventure had been undertaken. He had had no personal ambitions, he said, and no design of keeping up the false pretence after he had got possession of Lisbon, but had then meant to tell the truth, saying:

"I am not Dom Sebastiam; but I have freed you from Spain. Now it is open to you to choose what King you will."

Next, after the failure of the potter's and the

mason's sons, it was the turn of Gabriel de Espinosa, the confectioner; but he never unfurled his banner. His designs, in so far as he had any—for he was really an instrument in the hands of others—were brought to light by the accidental discovery that he was in possession of valuable jewels which a mere confectioner was unlikely to have come by honestly. Questions were asked, and the unsatisfactory answers given to them put the police on the track of the plot. Donna Anna, the daughter of Don John of Austria, the hero of Lepanto, was somehow mixed up in it—genuinely deceived, it appears, by an imposture devised by a priest of the Order of Jesus; and when the Jesuit and the false Dom Sebastiam had been hanged, she was punished for her gullibility by religious discipline. Philip sent her to a convent, with strict orders that she was never to leave her cell except to attend divine service, and that her fare on Fridays was to be limited to bread and water: a lugubrious life which she lived for many years.

Finally there was the case of Marco Tullio—a Calabrian peasant who could not even speak Portuguese, but nevertheless told a most circumstantial story. He had escaped death, he said, on the battlefield by feigning to be dead, and had afterwards, on his return to Portugal, been threatened with death by Dom Henry, and had then gone back to Africa rather than stir up civil strife, and had lived as a hermit in Sicily, whence he had found his way to Venice. Presumably there was someone behind him, prompting him; but the source of his inspira-

THE FALSE SEBASTIAMS

tion is a mystery which no investigator has solved. Some of the Portuguese residents at Venice appear to have believed in him; a good many people who did not believe in him were disposed to support him in order to embarrass Philip III.

Even the Prince of Orange took an interest in him, and sent a representative to make inquiries; and polite requests for his extradition were at first met with a polite refusal. He made the mistake, however, of going to Padua in the disguise of a monk; and there the Duke of Tuscany arrested and surrendered him. Sent to the galleys, he still found adherents in penal servitude; and so it seemed that there was nothing for it but to put him to death. The belief that Dom Sebastiam would come again did not die with him; but he was nevertheless the last of the Pretenders. Their appearance was an indication that the spirit of nationality still lived in Portugal, and the talk which centred round them helped to keep it alive; but it seemed that if Portugal was to rise effectively she needed an authentic leader to rally round.

In 1640 the House of Braganza furnished one.

CHAPTER VI

Claimants to the Portuguese throne—The Duchess of Braganza and Dom Antonio o Crato—Refusal of the Duchess to marry Philip II.—English expedition, under Drake and Norris, on behalf of Dom Antonio—Assertion of the claims of John Duke of Braganza—His great position in Portugal—His timidity—His wife's insistence that he should—Revolution which raised John Duke of Braganza to the throne.

It has been written of more than one of the women of the House of Braganza that she was "the man of the family." The claim was quite lately made for Queen Amélie; and it might have been made, with equal justice, for the Duchess of Braganza who alleged a title to the throne in 1580.

She did not fight. It was another candidate—Dom Antonio o Crato—who waged guerilla war against Philip in the mountains. Handicapped by a husband who had first sold his birthright and then haggled about the pottage, she might have found it difficult to do that. But she struck the right note when she was left a widow, and Philip, who was a widower, made her an offer of marriage—not because he loved her, but in order to strengthen his grip on the conquered country.

DOM ANTONIO O CRATO

"No," she said to him. "I do not care to exchange my memory of the Duke of Braganza for the pomp and glory of the crown of Spain. Nothing shall induce me to take any step which would compromise the claims of my son, Prince Theodosius. Indeed, his Catholic Majesty would have nothing to gain by marrying me; for, in spite of the marriage, the rights of the Prince would remain intact, and King Philip, on his part, could not salve the scruples of his conscience by buying that which cannot be sold to him."

That speech gives the Duchess her niche in the temple, though her pedestal is not a high one. It served, as the false pretences of the false Dom Sebastiams served, to keep the consciousness of nationality alive in Portugal; but that is all that one can say. In the fighting, far from being the leader, the Duchess was not even the figure-head. It was not her cause, but that of Dom Antonio, which England espoused in the year after the defeat of the Armada.

The expedition is an inglorious and forgotten episode of our history, ignored by most of our historians, and yet rather a big expedition of its kind: a serious attempt made by Drake and Norris, with an army of 15,000 men, to take Lisbon and make Dom Antonio King of Portugal. It seems to have failed, partly because Drake was in too great a hurry to go looting, and partly because the Portuguese were apathetic. Some of them doubted whether it became Catholics to accept help from Protestants; others hung back because they got no lead from their own nobility, who either had been

THE ROYAL HOUSE OF PORTUGAL

bribed by Philip or were afraid of him. So they hid in their cellars until Drake sailed home again—holding up many treasure-ships laden with doubloons, but leaving Portugal to another fifty-one years of servitude. The proof was clear that, if the Spanish yoke was to be thrown off, the Portuguese aristocracy must start the movement against it.

The years passed, and then, at last, they did start it, acting in the name of the most illustrious of their number, John Duke of Braganza, of whom we may as well say at once that he was not a great man, but merely a man who occupied a great position, and admitted, under the pressure of argument, that something was due to it, and that, if there was to be a great, patriotic movement, it must be his and not another's.

The position of the House of Braganza in Portugal, indeed, was such as no noble house holds today in any country. If we could imagine the Duke of Norfolk, the Duke of Westminster, Earl Kitchener, and Earl Curzon, rolled into one, we might begin to gather a faint idea of it; but it will be better to give a few exact particulars. To begin with, the House had ten titles attached to it: three dukedoms, a marquisate, and six earldoms. It owned twenty-five towns, about three hundred estates, and innumerable convents and ecclesiastical benefices. The number of its vassals was computed at 80,000. Just like a royal house, it included among its retainers heralds, mace-bearers, knights, and chamberlains. It had a chapel invested with all the privileges of a royal chapel. The etiquette of its palaces was

JOHN DUKE OF BRAGANZA

like the etiquette of royal palaces—one palace alone accommodating no fewer than 480 nobles and servants; and its Dukes were dispensed even from the obligation of kissing the King's hand.

In so small a country there obviously was only room for one House so great as that; and it is not less obvious that the Head of the House was the man of all others whom it behoved to speak with his country's enemies in the gate. With his help almost anything might be done, whereas hardly anything could be done without it. Others, indeed, might provide the brains, and the energy, and take the risks; but the Duke of Braganza himself must at least lend the conspirators his name, and allow it to be understood that they were conspiring with his countenance, on his behalf, and for his greater glory. If he did not spontaneously take that view of the matter, then the conspirators must hustle him until he did take it.

He showed no disposition to take it; and no one had any illusions about him. He was a quiet man who loved a quiet life, and would have preferred to leave politics alone, and enjoy himself in his country seat at Villa-Viçosa, devoting his days to hunting and his evenings to chamber music. But that was not to be. The Spaniards, on their part, thought to keep him out of mischief by employing him in a public capacity as military governor of Portugal. The conspirators, on theirs, tried to hustle him into using his position in the Spanish service for Portuguese purposes; and when they found him reluctant, they induced his wife—the second Duchess

THE ROYAL HOUSE OF PORTUGAL

of Braganza, who proved herself the best man in the family—to hustle him on their behalf.

She was a Spaniard—Donna Luiza de Gusman, daughter of the Duke of Medina Sidonia. It need not be assumed that the interests of the Portuguese people were a matter of very deep concern to her; but she was ambitious. She wished to be a Queen instead of a Duchess; and, therefore, she cast her influence into the scale. Her advice was asked when her husband was summoned to Madrid, and was doubting whether to obey the summons or ignore it; and this was her reply :—

"That there was no room to hesitate, for he had no other party to take: he must of necessity go either to Madrid or Lisbon: That he must resolve to die either ingloriously in the former place, or honourably in the latter. That, in the first party he had no other chance, but had a fair probability of gaining a crown by the latter resolution."

It was a fine pronouncement, to whatever motive we ascribe it; and Dom John had, indeed, as weak men are apt to do, allowed things to drift to such a pass that he must go on because it was no longer safe to go back.

The Spaniards had not made him Military Governor of Portugal for the purpose of putting power in his hands, but for the purpose of keeping him under observation. They knew that he was a fool, and expected that he would be in the hands of his staff, whom they had chosen for him; and when they saw reason to believe that he was not in the hands of his staff, but in the hands of disaffected

THE RESTORATION

Portuguese noblemen, they laid plans for kidnapping him and carrying him off to Spain. He was invited to an entertainment on board a Spanish ship of war, which was to have sailed away with him; but he regretted that a previous engagement obliged him to decline the polite invitation. He was to have been detained in one of the fortresses which it was his duty to inspect; but he brought so many of his vassals to inspect them with him that it could not be done. He was to have been arrested in Madrid, when he arrived there to report in person to the King; but he did not arrive there.

That was the stage of the proceedings at which Dom John yielded to the pressure of the conspirators and his wife. Alike with them and with Philip IV. he temporised as long as he could. To the latter he wrote letters inquiring as to the dignity of the reception which would be accorded to him in the capital—would he be invited to sit under the same canopy as His Catholic Majesty, etc.? To the former he represented that he wanted to go hunting, and must have more time for reflection before definitely pledging himself to a policy. At last, however, his secretary, Antonio Paes Viegas, brought him to the point. This is the dialogue which is reported to have passed between them:—

"If the conspirators should form a Republic, would Your Excellency side with Castile or with Portugal?"
"I would follow the Portuguese."
"In that case it will be better to risk all things

THE ROYAL HOUSE OF PORTUGAL

in order to reign than to lose everything and remain a vassal."

"But the difficulties—the dangers—"

"A Prince who defends legitimate rights can find no better death-bed than on the field of battle."

Then Dom John consulted his wife, who exhorted him, as we have seen, to be a man instead of a sportsman and a *dilettante*; and he promised to do his best. He would raise no troops, indeed, and he would draw no sword; but he would lead the conspiracy from the rear, waiting quietly at Villa-Viçosa to learn the result of the rising, and would make any suggestions which occurred to him, and accept the crown if the revolutionists should find themselves in a position to offer it to him. So it was agreed that the revolt should take place on December 1st, 1640; and the conspirators made their wills and received the sacrament.

Two circumstances favoured them. In the first place, the Spaniards were already embarrassed by dangerous discords in Catalonia—a region which, then as now, was always quarrelling with Castile. In the second place, it had been wisely decided to strike the first blow in the capital instead of the country, so as to paralyse resistance by seizing the reins of government after a first success. The plans had been well laid, and the secret had been well kept. Whatever the Spaniards may have suspected, they actually knew very little; and the points selected for sudden attack were practically undefended. Consequently, the "glorious revolution" was also an easy revolution, and very nearly a

THE RESTORATION

bloodless one. Even the gathering of the conspirators in the streets, preparatory to "rushing" the forts and the Palace, was so quiet as hardly to excite remark. For anything that anybody knew, they might have been assembling to attend a levée.

"Where are you going to?" asked a friend of one of the leaders.

"It is nothing," was the reply. "You need not excite yourself. We are only going to the royal audience chamber for a moment, to depose a King and place another on the throne."

And things happened, in fact, almost as simply as his speech indicated. The conspirators drove to the Palace gate in carriages, and, at the appointed signal, jumped out of them, and ran up the steps. The Palace guards were taken by surprise, and the fight hardly amounted to a scuffle. There was an attempt to defend the passages leading to the apartments occupied by the Secretary of State and the Duchess of Mantua, who had lately been appointed Vice-Reine; but the defenders were quickly scattered and disarmed, and Miguel d'Almeida ran out on to a balcony, brandishing a sword and shouting :—

"Liberty! Liberty! Long live King Dom John IV.! The Duke of Braganza is our legitimate King!"

Then the Secretary of State and the Vice-Reine were dealt with. They caught the former hiding in a cupboard, dragged him from it, shot him, and pitched his body out of the window to the mob.

THE ROYAL HOUSE OF PORTUGAL

With the latter, they used no violence, though they threatened it.

The Duchess was a woman of spirit; and she began by throwing open the window, and shouting from it:—

"Come, gentlemen! Come, Portuguese! What is the meaning of this? Where is your loyalty?"

But the Portuguese had thought that matter out; and they forced the Duchess's door, and drew her away from the window. Then, beginning to be frightened, she told them that she would pardon them in the name of the King of Castile if they would go home quietly; but the rejoinder to that was that they recognised no King but the Duke of Braganza, and that she herself had better withdraw lest they should forget their respect for her. She recovered her spirit and demanded haughtily how they proposed to demonstrate their loss of respect, and they demonstrated it on the spot by inviting her to choose between two modes of exit: Would she go quietly by way of the door? Or would she prefer to be propelled through the window? She decided upon the door as the more convenient aperture, and passed in dudgeon to her oratory, where she offered up a sullen prayer.

And that is practically all. The rest is only detail: similar *coups de main* in forts and public buildings, and easy siege operations against such strongholds as made a show of holding out. The whole business was carried through so quickly and smoothly that by mid-day all the shops were open

THE RESTORATION

and all the people were going about their business as usual; the Spaniards having no friends in Portugal, and the disturbances in Catalonia having compelled them to denude the country of troops. The news is said to have been broken to Philip IV. by Olivares in these words:—

"Sire, I have to congratulate you on a most fortunate event. Your Majesty has just obtained a powerful duchy and some magnificent estates. The Duke of Braganza has madly allowed himself to be seduced by the populace, who have proclaimed him King of Portugal. His vast estates are, therefore, forfeited, and become the property of Your Majesty, who, by the annihilation of this family, will in future reign securely and peaceably over that kingdom."

But that was a mistake, for the excellent reason that Portugal had friends wherever Spain had enemies, and Spain had enemies almost everywhere. The new King, therefore, was not only promptly "recognised" by most of the other Courts of Europe, but received promises of help if he should need it, from Sweden, from Holland, and even from France. And that, though Anne of Austria, who sat on the throne of France, was Philip IV.'s sister. "I do not forget," she said to the Portuguese plenipotentiary, "that I am His Catholic Majesty's sister, but I also remember that I am the mother of the Dauphin"; and she put her hand to an offensive and defensive alliance with Portugal which made the little kingdom fairly safe against Spanish designs.

THE ROYAL HOUSE OF PORTUGAL

So that the day which raised the House of Braganza to the throne is as great a day in Portugal as is the date of the destruction of the Bastille in France; but it must be added—or rather repeated—that the Duke of Braganza who became Dom John IV. can in no sense be regarded as the architect of his own fortunes. He took the crown because it was there to be taken, and it was offered to him because there was no one else to whom it could very well be offered—not, that is to say, because he was a great man, but because he was a man in a great position.

Still, though his courage failed him, his manners did not. If he could not play the hero, at least he could play the Grand Seigneur—the man to whom pomp and glory are so much a matter of course that a little additional pomp and glory makes no difference worth considering. It was in that grand style that he received the news that the Revolution had succeeded, and that he was, in very truth, King of Portugal. He had stayed on his estate while the others were bearing the burden and heat of the day; and when the good tidings reached him, he was attending divine service in his private chapel.

It did not flutter him. He kept himself waiting, as he would have kept an inferior waiting, until the ritual of prayer and praise had run its course. Then, when the benediction had been pronounced, he departed, with a proper escort, for Lisbon. It was raining hard when he arrived; but the streets were nevertheless crowded with the loyal subjects who had insisted that a man in so great a position must

THE RESTORATION

at least try to behave like a great man. He braved the elements, though he had braved nothing else, and went out on to the balcony in the wet, in order to bow and be cheered. The populace—persuaded, it may be, that he really was a great man—acclaimed him with enthusiasm; and the bells of all the Lisbon churches rang the new reign in.

CHAPTER VII

Portugal in decadence—John the Mediocre—Affonso the Ill-conditioned—Pedro the Glum—Affonso's insane and violent proceedings—His grotesque appearance—His marriage—Conspiracy of his wife and brother to depose him—His long imprisonment at Cintra—His death in prison—The gleam of reason which came to him on his death-bed.

PORTUGAL, beyond question, had won a glorious victory; but Portugal was, nevertheless, like Spain herself, in decadence; and the two countries, by continuing to fight each other, pushed each other further down the hill, after the manner of two angry men wrestling on a slippery slope.

The audacity which John displayed—under pressure from his supporters—in executing objectionable noblemen, and sending objectionable Bishops and Archbishops to penal servitude, extorted Philip IV.'s admiration. "Now, indeed," he said, when he heard of it, "has the Duke of Braganza made himself a King"; but his admiration did not prevent him from going to war. There ensued a considerable series of wars—desultory wars in which, though the battles were sometimes decisive, the campaigns were not; and Dom John, who died

JOHN THE MEDIOCRE

in 1656, was in his grave before Portugal was definitely at peace and secure.

It must be repeated that, in spite of his triumph, he was not much of a man. His contemporaries called him John the Fortunate; but he might just as well be called John the Mediocre. It is related that, in the year of the Revolution, his courage was only screwed to the sticking-point by the smile of his baby daughter—that Catherine of Braganza who was to be Queen of England. When he was humming and hawing and hesitating, his wife brought the baby to him, and shamed him with the question: "How can you have the heart to refuse this darling the rank of a King's daughter?" That decided him; but now, though the seditious Bishop, Archbishop, and even the Grand Inquisitor were under lock and key, he tired of his responsibilities, and talked of abdication:—

"The King of Portugal" (we find Mazarin writing to the Duc de Longueville) "after giving careful consideration to the state of affairs, is disposed to resign his crown, and retire to the Azores, and to offer the kingdom to any one whom the Queen of France may select, believing that he has influence enough to cause such a one to be recognised as King and obeyed by all the Portuguese."

It rings unheroically, and makes it clearer than ever that this Duke of Braganza was neither born to greatness, nor achieved it, but merely had greatness thrust upon him while he was hankering after the chase and chamber music. We shall presently see another John displaying a similar desire to efface himself at the hour of crisis; and we shall have to note that the contempt which the Portuguese eventually acquired for their reigning House was largely due to these timorous proceedings on the part of the Heads of the House. Meanwhile, confining ourselves to John IV., we need say little more of him than that he did his best in his timorous, conscientious way until he died, leaving three legitimate children of whom we shall have to say something: Affonso, Pedro, and Catherine.

But Catherine may wait. We will first speak of Affonso and Pedro, whom we may call respectively Affonso the Ill-conditioned, and Pedro the Glum.

Affonso was the bad boy of the family—Pedro the good boy and his mother's favourite; and Affonso was the sort of bad boy who would, nowadays, be expelled from any respectable public school as a hulking lout who frequented bad company, exercised a bad influence, and made discipline impossible. Or that, at all events, would have been his fate unless the birch had driven virtue into him—an expedient which his royal birth forbade.

It is said that he was partially paralysed as the result of an illness contracted in infancy; and he seems, at any rate, to have suffered from some such weakness as that which made the feeble Don Francisco d'Assis a most unsuitable husband for the ardent Isabella of Spain. His manner of life, however, suggests not the paralytic, but the insane; for if he was weak in one sense, he was violent in another. One sees what sort of a boy he was from the story of his behaviour when told, as a little child,

AFFONSO THE ILL-CONDITIONED

that his elder brother was dead. He shed no tears at his bereavement, but exclaimed jubilantly: "Hurrah! Now I shall be King of Portugal." And when he became King of Portugal at the age of thirteen he began to amuse himself in various ill-conditioned ways—all of them incompatible with his illustrious station.

Looking out of the Palace window, he saw the common children fighting in the streets. It was as good as a play; and he called to them to come nearer, so that he could see them better. Then he made a particular friend of one of them—a certain Antonio Conti, a hawker of cheap children's toys, who won the heart of his sovereign by offering him a knife and a catapult. After that, he insisted on joining Conti and the others at their games. Their favourite game was boxing, and the participants in that pastime were the lowest of the low. To the horror of the Queen and the courtiers, his Majesty was found one day with a swollen and bleeding nose—the result of the impact of a nigger's fist.

His mother and his preceptors tried to wean him from such pastimes, and forbade him to speak to Conti; but he vowed that he would eat no food if deprived of Conti's society. They gave way to him, and then he engaged in higher jinks than ever. He and his friends arranged dog-fights in the Lion's Court; they knocked up the monks in one of the convents in order to set their mastiffs fighting at the dead of night. They streamed—a ragged and disorderly rabble—through ante-chambers in which courtiers were assembled in preparation for ceremonial reunions; they paid adventurous visits to disorderly houses. Affonso even descended from his bedroom window by a rope in order to join a gang of Mohocks who terrorised the streets; and then, to crown all, he began to bestow honours and emoluments on his boon companions. He invested Conti with the Order of Christ, and he made Conti's brother—a young student at the University—an Archdeacon. Assuredly he was entitled to the style and title of Affonso the Ill-conditioned.

Respectfully scolded, he remained obdurate; so it was decided to kidnap both the uproarious Archdeacon and the pugnacious member of the Order of Christ and send them to Brazil. The thing was done, but still Affonso did not mend his ways. First he cried, fearing lest his own head should be cut off, like the head of Charles of England; but then, with the help of the ambitious Count of Castelmelhor, he took the bold course of declaring his minority at an end and assuming the reins of government; and the next step was to make life in the royal palace so unpleasant for his mother that she was glad to leave it. Some of his loyal supporters used to shout abusive epithets through the lattices of her window; others threw missles at her when she was engaged in prayer. Unable to bear the insults, she withdrew in dudgeon to a convent, where not long afterwards she died; and it is said that when Affonso heard that she was dying, he merely giggled, being as incapable of affecting dignified emotion as of feeling it.

Castelmelhor and the other Ministers did what

AFFONSO THE ILL-CONDITIONED

they could to make a King of him; and he learnt at least to "walk through" his royal *rôle* without making too many blunders. Told what to do, he did it; told what to say, he said it. But the business of the country was conducted by his Cabinet without reference to him; and there was no amendment of his private way of life, of which many people—and the religious in particular—had good reason to complain. His principal offences were as follows:—

1. He fixed a short—a very short—time limit for sermons, as did our own Edward VII.; and he ruthlessly banished from Portugal every preacher who exceeded it by even a fraction of a second.
2. Instead of rising to attend mass in the chapel, he required the chaplain to celebrate it in his bedroom, while he snoozed between the sheets.
3. He paid surprise visits to nunneries, and organised amateur theatrical performances in the convent chapels.
4. He made love to nuns, as well as to ladies of light reputation, and caused his bravos to assassinate men whom he suspected of being his successful rivals in their affections.
5. He continued his activities as a Mohock, enlisting even criminals in his rowdy gang, and going so far as to break up religious processions in the streets.

It occurred to his Ministers that perhaps he would settle down if he married; so they sought a wife for him, without the least regard to the feelings of the lady on whom their choice might fall. It fell, after various negotiations, upon Mademoiselle d'Aumale, the daughter of the Duc de Nemours,

THE ROYAL HOUSE OF PORTUGAL

who duly became Queen Maria Francisca of Portugal in 1666. She had heard vague rumours that her proposed husband was, in various ways, undesirable, but she hoped that her informants were prejudiced by envy of the great station to which her wedding would promote her. She cherished that hope while the waves of the Bay of Biscay did their worst with the ship which carried her from La Rochelle to the Tagus. There, while she was still pallid from sea-sickness, the King rowed out to meet her, and she discovered what sort of an object he was.

Though only three-and-twenty, Affonso was already far too fat. He was the Head of the House of Braganza, High and Mighty King of Portugal and of the Algarves on this side and beyond the sea in Africa, Lord of Guinea, and of the Conquest, Navigation, and Commerce of Ethiopia, Arabia, Persia, and India—and he looked like a jolly little barrel trotting about on two pegs. His corpulence was due to gluttony and indolence—he took most of his meals in bed, and ate and drank so much that he usually was sick afterwards; and his mode of dress, which was more ridiculous than regal, aggravated it. He wore six or seven coats or jerkins one over the other, a hood buttoned under the chin to prevent him from catching cold, and three or four hats perched one on top of the other. And his greeting to his bride was simply a grin—a worthy sequel to the giggle with which he had received the tidings of his mother's death.

AFFONSO THE ILL-CONDITIONED

One can picture her feelings when she reflected that that queer creature was the only man whom it would ever be lawful for her to embrace. One can imagine how she glanced from the grinning King to the Infante Pedro, who stood beside him, admiring her, and looking soulful—glum, it might be, but not grotesque or fat and foolish. One can readily believe those who tell us that she fell in love with her brother-in-law on her wedding day, and that he, in so far as he was capable of emotion, fell in love with her, and that the two of them felt, long before they admitted as much to each other, that the King of Portugal was an obstacle in the path of love and ambition, and must be removed. Their sole object thenceforward was to get him deposed and divorced, and the history of his reign is the history of their plots to end it.

Affonso, being fat and foolish, was not formidable in himself; but his Ministers—and notably Castelmelhor—made him formidable. Castelmelhor was practically the dictator of Portugal, and the first thing needful was to get him out of the way. It was not an easy thing to do, but it was done, without violence, though not without the threat of it, by means impossible to-day, but feasible in an age in which divinity really hedged princes and made it easy for them to acquire personal prestige. Dom Pedro was little more than a boy—about nineteen, in fact—but he was nevertheless able to quarrel with Castelmelhor, not as an equal but as a superior, and to present an ultimatum. Castelmelhor had insulted him, he said—he could not endure the insult. Either Castelmelhor must be dismissed, or he should himself shake the dust of Portugal from off his feet.

His attitude in the matter was rather like that of a Harrow boy who should try to bring his headmaster to his knees by sullenly announcing that unless he got his way in some matter of more importance to himself than to anybody else, he should decline to take part in the cricket match against Eton. The public opinion of the Lower School is apt to be in favour of the boy when such things happen; and the public opinion of Portugal was similarly in favour of the Infante Pedro. It was the more in favour of him because Affonso was known to be fat and foolish and grotesque, and was believed to be unlikely to beget an heir. Whatever happened, people said, Dom Pedro must not leave them—Portugal had need of him to save the dynasty from extinction. What a pity that he, instead of his brother, had not married the comely young Frenchwoman! Perhaps it might be arranged even yet, with the Pope's consent—the Pope would surely be willing to oblige; but, in any case, they must keep Dom Pedro with them. It was impossible to provide the King with another brother, but it would be easy to provide him with another Minister of State.

So Castelmelhor was sacrificed, and Affonso, as usual, manifested his emotions oddly: he attacked the courtier who broke the news to him with a dagger, and chased him round the room. But that did not prevent his favourite from retiring,

AFFONSO THE ILL-CONDITIONED

or from being followed into retirement by all other members of the Cabinet and household who were suspected of loyal sentiments. Their withdrawal left Affonso almost alone in his vast Palace—easy to deal with because he had no one to advise him. The Queen herself left him and took refuge in a convent, whence she issued manifestoes, saying that she was an injured woman, and would be glad if the Portuguese would return her dowry, as she wished to go back to France. But the Portuguese were impecunious, and could not spare the dowry, and Affonso, on his part, had no notion what to do.

He tried to fetch the Queen from the convent; but the Lady Superior slammed the door in his face. It was suggested to him that he should summon the Cortes; but he knew that the Cortes, if it assembled, would depose him; so he said, in his blunt, passionate way, that its members were "a pack of cuckolds," and that he would see them d——d before he sent for them. It was also suggested to him that he had better escape into the country and put himself at the head of his army; but Dom Pedro was corrupting the garrison, intimidating the loyal, and keeping a watch on the roads. It only remained for Pedro to walk into the Palace at the head of his men and exhort Affonso to abdicate.

That was what he did, on November 23rd, 1667, at an hour when Affonso was enjoying his siesta. He kept Affonso locked up long enough to give his temper time to cool, and then he sent two friars in to him to explain what was happening. He was in no immediate danger, he was told; but he must give up two things—his kingdom and his wife. To that end he must be good enough to sign two little papers: the one an act of abdication, assigning all his rights as sovereign to his brother as Prince Regent; the other a testimonial to the effect that Queen Maria Francisca was still a virgin, and therefore entitled to a decree of nullity. It may be that gentle persuasion sufficed; it may be that violence, or the threat of it, had to be employed. Affonso, at any rate, appended his signature to both documents, and his brother—the Pope approving—succeeded to his rights alike as a monarch and as a husband. And once again, it seems, Affonso was inadequate in the presence of a great emotional situation:

"Ah, well!" he is said to have remarked. "I don't doubt that my poor brother will soon regret having been mixed up with this disagreeable Frenchwoman as much as I do."

That was a false prophecy. The marriage was quite a happy one, though it was not until Maria Francisca had died and Dom Pedro had married a second wife that a male heir to the throne was born. No remorse appears to have been felt by either of the partners in guilt; and it is not unlikely that they took a great deal of credit to themselves for having spared their enemy's life. At all events, there were those, even among the ecclesiastics, who considered them entitled to it. "If these things had happened in Spain," said a Jesuit to the Minister of

AFFONSO THE ILL-CONDITIONED

Savoy, "the King of Portugal would not have lasted so long; but here we are good Christians."

He meant, of course, that it would have been very easy to put poison in the King's coffee; and that the resistance of that temptation by Dom Pedro and Maria Francisca was a proof of exceptional gentleness and virtue. Still, though they allowed Affonso to live, it cannot truthfully be said that they showed any tender consideration for his feelings; and Maria Francisca in particular never forgave him for the loathing which he had inspired in her, and made no secret of her wish that he were dead.

"As to the King, Affonso," she wrote to her sister, the Duchess of Savoy, "sometimes he talks as little as if he were of the other world; and he very nearly went there the other day, for, after getting drunk according to his wont, he fell with his head in a basin of water, where he would certainly have been drowned if someone had not promptly pulled him out; but, though he lives as a brute beast, he lives, and that is sufficient to keep us always anxious and exposed to the malice of our enemies."

His first place of detention was the Island of Terceira, in the Azores. He lived there in an isolation like that of Napoleon at St. Helena, with nothing to do but admire the scenery, for a little more than five years. Then, as it was feared, rightly or wrongly, that Terceira might become a rallying-point for malcontents and conspirators, he was brought back to Portugal, and kept, for the last nine years of his life, at Cintra, where, like the Prisoner of Chillon, he trod out a path on the stone floor by pacing up and down his apartment—his relatives and the official people continuing to wish that he would deliver them from their anxiety by dying. He was given every facility for drinking himself to death—a thing which, having developed dropsy, he might very easily have done; and his temporary reversion to sobriety irritated even religious people. The Minister from Savoy gathered as much from a conversation with the Jesuit Father Ville:

"I questioned him," the Minister wrote, "on the subject of the alleged dropsy. Father de Ville replied that at present the King abstained from drink and lived very regularly, and that, thanks to certain remedies, the disease had not gone further; but he spoke with such evident regret, and so full of desire that God would take him from this world, that I am inclined to think the dropsy has gone, and with it the hope that it would free them of this encumbrance."

As Affonso had still another five years to live, the conjecture was presumably correct; but even if his malady was in abeyance, his physical condition was a poor one. He had nothing to do except to grow fat, and so he grew fatter and fatter. His bulk became such that there was hardly room for him in his apartment, while his paralysis got so much worse that it was increasingly difficult for him to leave it. There are stories of his lying down on the floor, when he wanted to be moved, in order that an attendant might roll him out into the passage. It

AFFONSO THE ILL-CONDITIONED

is added that as he grew in girth, he also grew in grace and piety.

That, of course, is a curious evolution. One has been taught so long to associate faith with asceticism that a fat saint inevitably impresses one as a comic figure. None the less, the fact seems well established that Affonso was most devout in the days when he was most bulky; and our last glimpses at him are glimpses at a religious monomaniac with occasional gleams of reason. He had achieved the surname of Affonso the Victorious because of the victories won in his time by Schomberg and other generals while he was living, at Lisbon, the ill-conditioned life which we have described. He remembered the reputation which had come to him through no act of his when his confessor made conversation for him by telling him of the invasion of Hungary by the Heathen Turk in the year in which Vienna and Christendom were saved by John Sobieski. It was as if a flash of lightning had revealed to him the contrast between the things which had been and the things which should and might have been.

"And I," he exclaimed with emphatic gesticulations, "I who am a Christian King! I also must be in that battle!"

But that was not to be—he died of apoplexy almost before he had time to realise that it could not be, and that his globular shape would never be seen charging the heathen hordes at the head of the Christian chivalry.

THE ROYAL HOUSE OF PORTUGAL

"Perhaps," wrote his Confessor to Dom Pedro, "God, who vouchsafed to his Majesty to win so many battles, may have permitted his spirit to have a part in this great victory."

Perhaps; but the sentiment means nothing in particular. It was coin of the base currency in which official religion so often pays tribute to the solemn moments in the lives of inadequate Kings. Dom Pedro, we may be quite sure, accepted it, not at its face value, but at its true value. It mattered little to him what had become of his fat and foolish brother's soul. The essential thing for him was that his brother was now out of the way, and that he himself was now King of Portugal in name as well as in fact.

CHAPTER VIII

Affonso's sister Catherine of Braganza—Her marriage to Charles II.—Her dowry and the haggling about it—Her resentment at the favour shown to Lady Castlemaine—Her reconciliation to Charles—Discomfort of her position after the accession of William of Orange—Her return to Portugal—Her proclamation as Queen Regent of Portugal.

PORTUGAL—known hitherto only by name to the English masses—became real to them when Charles II. announced his betrothal to Catherine of Braganza, the fat and foolish Affonso's only surviving sister, who came to England, to be his bride, in 1662. With her came a Portuguese household —"family" was the word of the period—to show her husband's subjects what the Portuguese were really like; and her dowry consisted of two of the Portuguese oversea possessions—Tangier, which is ours no longer, and the Island of Bombay, which was to be the nucleus of our Indian dominions. It was a dismemberment of the Portuguese Empire for which the House has often been reproached.

There was to have been a heavy money payment too; but finance was then, as always, Portugal's weak point. The Treasury was not in a position

THE ROYAL HOUSE OF PORTUGAL

to honour the draft, and the royal bridegroom was asked to accept "something on account." Lord Sandwich, who had been sent to Lisbon in the matter, agreed to that for fear lest his Sovereign's reputation for gallantry should suffer; but there was yet another surprise in store for him. The dowry was sent down to the quay in bags, to be embarked on an English ship; and when the bags were opened, it was found that they contained sugar and spice instead of coins or ingots. The goods were accepted under protest; but the haggling continued throughout King Charles's reign. As late as 1679, when the Queen was impeached of treason by Titus Oates, and Dom Pedro sent an ambassador to "comfort and assist" her, that emissary was informed that his representations would carry more weight if he brought "evidence of the Prince's intention to pay the residue of the portion more punctually."

Meanwhile, however, England and Portugal had been united in the bonds of political and military, as well as matrimonial, alliance. On the high seas, and in the colonies, England had protected Portugal from the depredations of the Dutch, while, on land, English and Portuguese troops had fought side by side against Spain; and, in these matters also, the weakness of Portuguese finance had been unpleasantly, not to say ludicrously, apparent. At the battle of Ameixial, the conduct of the English contingent under Colonel Hunt evoked from the Portuguese general the admiring exclamation: "These heretics are of more use to us than all our saints!" But when it was suggested to Affonso that the gallant achievement merited a material reward, his response was oddly inadequate. Silver and gold had he none; but he would like, he said, to give to every man a pinch of snuff. It is recorded that, when the snuff was distributed, the soldiers threw it on the ground with gestures of contempt.

That story, of course, takes us a long way from Catherine of Braganza; but her marriage, on its part, takes us a long way from Portugal. The subject has been admirably treated in her Life by Miss Lillias Campbell Davidson; and, in these pages, one need do little more than mention it. It was bound to be an unhappy marriage; but it was by no means such an unhappy marriage as it easily might have been. Catherine was a good girl, but hot-tempered; and she was suddenly introduced into a Court in which morals were loose and manners coarse. Charles, as all the world knows, aspired to be the father of his subjects in the literal sense—was, in fact, the father of about sixteen of them, though his wife was childless—and included in his belief in the divine right of Kings the doctrine that neither maid nor matron lapsed from virtue in becoming a royal mistress.

Naturally, attempts were made to induce Catherine to adapt herself to the new situation while learning the new language. Even the great Lord Clarendon gave her good advice in that sense, and urged her to be polite to Lady Castlemaine—that Lady Castlemaine who was presently to shout insults at him from her window in the day of his disgrace, and to whom he was to reply with a courteous bow, and the stinging words: "Madam, if you live, you will grow old." Naturally Catherine was indignant, lost her temper, and made scenes which were the talk of the town and a nine days' wonder. The scenes were the more violent because Charles was fascinating, and she had fallen in love with him. The Memoirs of the time give abundant details of the demonstrations.

The time came, however—it was not very long in coming—when Catherine tired of demonstrating and gave in. Charles really wished to make things as pleasant for her as he could, consistently with his convenience and the state of his affections; and though there was no Isaac, and the country was full of Ishmaels, his interpretation of the *rôle* of Abraham was sympathetic. If he and his wife were not lovers after the first few days, at least they composed their quarrels sufficiently to become good friends; and he begged her pardon on his death-bed for all the pain which he had caused her. She herself, after his death, was sufficiently forgiving to intercede, though vainly, with James II., for the life of the most famous of the Ishmaels—the Duke of Monmouth, who had raised the banner of revolt. It was not until after another rising had sent James across the water, and William of Orange was on the throne, that she made her arrangements for going back, to die among her own people.

William was not unkind to her. He even, at her request, released Lord Feversham from prison, in order that he might keep the bank at her card-parties. But her position was, nevertheless, un-

Catherine of Braganza.

CATHERINE OF BRAGANZA

comfortable. Queen Mary did not like her, and showed it; and she was a solitary Catholic among a crowd of Protestants so fanatical that they brought in a Bill in the Commons reducing the number of her Catholic servants to eighteen. So she began to write pitiful letters to her brother Pedro, complaining that the Church was "oppressed," and that she herself was submitting to "live outside London in a very small house hardly sufficient for a workman," and protesting that "Portugal is the proper place for me."

Her residence, at that time, was in Islington, though why she should have gone to Islington no one knows. She speaks of it as "a little house which I hire from an apothecary"; her brief description of it is graphic:—

"This palace consists of a small cottage, with two others, one on the right hand, and the other on the left, which could be more properly called closets than houses. These are my apartments; those of my servants are cupboards and alcoves."

Perhaps she exaggerated her discomfort, in order to expedite her recall—women are apt to do such things. She told her brother that she had asked William for ships, but had only been given "compliments which will not carry me to Portugal"; the state of public affairs being such that the ships were wanted for other purposes. Her main desire, she added, was "to be in some religious place where alone I can be happy." She also wanted to go to France, to take the waters; but Louis XIV. would not have her, because the exiled James did not want

THE ROYAL HOUSE OF PORTUGAL

her. Queen Mary, moreover, showed her some petty spite because she neglected to pray for her in her chapel. So the correspondence, and the negotiations, dragged on, not for weeks, or for months, but for years; and it was not until 1692 that Catherine obtained the passport from the King of France, which enabled her at last to start, crossing from Margate to Dieppe, and posting incognito to the Portuguese frontier, where she arrived on January 20th, 1693.

Her troubles were then over. It was open to her to be as religious as she liked in the way that she liked; and it seems that the two things which Catherine of Braganza really cared for were devotional facilities and card-parties. In one of her letters she speaks of "the great comfort of a monastery of Dominicans"—a comfort of which her residence in England had necessarily deprived her. But the path to comfort was also to be the path, if not to glory, at least to a position of unlooked-for dignity—a position to which she was to be called by the sudden failure of her brother's health and intellect.

Dom Pedro was not, as we know, a great man, though some great things happened in his time: the discovery of gold in Brazil, not previously reckoned a valuable colony; the famous Methuen Treaty which made England a port-drinking instead of a claret-drinking country; the capture of Gibraltar by Sir George Rooke, in a war in which England and Portugal co-operated. One might call him Pedro the Glum: a man, at any rate, who

CATHERINE OF BRAGANZA

is chiefly remembered for his melancholy, his sobriety, his great physical strength, and his addiction to long prayers, and low *amours*. Perhaps it was the death of his wife—the partner of his crimes as well as his bed—which developed the less pleasant traits in a character never, at any time, attractive. She only just survived the death of her fat and foolish first husband; and her second husband seemed to have missed her moral support in facing the memory of his evil deeds.

He married again—his second wife being Marie-Sophie of Pfalz Neuburg—in order that Portugal might not lack an heir. She bore him several children, but his infidelities were, nevertheless, numerous and unbecoming. One of his mistresses was one of the Palace housemaids; he selected others among the mulattoes and negresses brought to Lisbon as trophies of Portuguese colonising enterprise. One may, if one likes, discover a proof of the piety of his disposition in the fact that he rewarded the housemaid for her favours by bestowing ecclesiastical benefices upon her brothers. There was, at any rate, nothing jovial about him even when he unbent in the arms of domestic servants. He never pledged his mistresses in the juice of Lusitanian grapes, but made them practise an austere teetotalism. He invited them to no merry supper-parties, but took all his meals alone, squatting on a mat instead of sitting at a table. He dressed in black, and wore a black hat; and his recreations consisted in worrying bulls, to show how brave he was, and twisting horse-shoes

THE ROYAL HOUSE OF PORTUGAL

between his fingers, to show how strong he was. His manner of dealing with the bulls is thus described by one Colbatch, chaplain at an English factory in Lisbon:—

"Nor is he content" (wrote Colbatch) "to deal with that fierce animal on horseback, but he frequently engages him afoot. To this end, he hath a small piece of ground, enclosed with void spaces in the wall on every side, big enough to escape through when the bull proves too hard for him, as he sometimes does, to the endangering of his person; though, upon the least appearance of a discomposure, the company is ready to come unto his rescue; and on such occasions one shall see the main body of the nobility engaged about the bull, every one seizing him by that part he can lay hold on, whether by the neck, the horns, or the tail."[1]

In addition to these activities, Dom Pedro told innumerable beads, and sent out innumerable missionaries to heathen parts. How much credit is due to him for that may be disputed. He certainly cannot be praised for it by those Protestants who denounce his sister for acting as a missionary and trying to "bring in Popery" in England; but the matter is of no great consequence. One's general impression of Pedro, in any case, is an impression of a moonstruck man whom the lunar influences dazed more and more as he grew older. Perhaps remorse and the consciousness of having been a failure also preyed on him. The end, in any case,

[1] It must be remembered that, in Portuguese bull-fights, the horns of the bull were padded.

CATHERINE OF BRAGANZA

was nervous breakdown—a frequent complaint in the House of Braganza—and the need of complete rest, with a Regent to take responsibility off his hands.

That was Catherine's hour. She was proclaimed Queen Regent of Portugal, and proved herself fit for the position. She waged a war, and her armies won victories—a thing of which they had latterly lost the habit. But her reign was brief, lasting, in fact, for less than a year. A sudden colic—presumably appendicitis—seized her; and she died of it on the last day of December, 1705—the only member of her family who had shown any sort of capacity for affairs. The people wept in the streets; the Court wore mourning for a year; and ten thousand masses were ordered to be said for her soul. Pedro resumed his reign after her death, but only survived her for about a year, dying of pleurisy on February 9th, 1706, and leaving his throne to his son John, who was seventeen years of age.

CHAPTER IX

Continued decadence of Portugal—Disastrous reign of John the Dilettante—His passion for building, for endowing monasteries, and for embracing nuns—Voltaire's estimate of his character—Accession of Dom Joseph—The Lisbon earthquake—Success of Pombal in repairing the effects of that disaster—Quarrel of Pombal with the Jesuits.

THE word which might be scrawled at the head of the chronicle of the reign of John V. is "decadence," and if we want to sum John himself up in a phrase, we may call him John the Dilettante. The War of the Spanish Succession was waged in his time; and though England gained glory in that war, Portugal got hard knocks. The Duke of Berwick inflicted a smashing defeat on the Portuguese troops at Almanza, and the French fleet, under Dugay-Trouin, burnt Rio de Janeiro. As for John, he was merely an extravagant dilettante who looked on; and, after the Treaty of Utrecht, he received, though he did not profit by, an interesting lesson in the deceitfulness of riches.

It was assumed that, as gold had been discovered in Brazil, Portugal would henceforth be wealthy; but that was a mistake. Gold, as the Portuguese were

JOHN THE DILETTANTE

now to learn, is of all the constituents of the wealth of nations the most elusive. The more there is of it, the less it is worth, owing to the rapid rise of prices and the temptation to neglect productive industry in order to acquire it. That was the great trouble of the reign of John V. While the colonial gold was squandered, the native resources were neglected. The King could afford to be a spendthrift, but the people got poorer and poorer.

He was not entirely without character—at all events at the beginning of his reign. One begins to have hopes of him when one reads how he brought the Jesuits to heel when they obstructed some of his measures. If they were not more amenable, he announced, he would have them collected, and deported to a desert island, where they would be able to pray without ceasing, but would be unable to interfere with matters which did not concern them—a restricted kind of holy life which was not in their line. That outburst of energy, however, was only an unsustained spasm. The real John V. was, as we have called him, John the Dilettante—a founder of theatres, a collector of books, and, above all, one who squandered his substance on riotous building and spectacular religion. His most notable extravagance was the transformation of the Convent of Mafra, in imitation of the Escorial, to include, as well as a monastery, a Palace, and barracks for soldiers. One may as well give a few facts about it, taken from Murray's Handbook.

The building, we there read, is so large that ten thousand men might be reviewed on the roof. It

THE ROYAL HOUSE OF PORTUGAL

contains 866 rooms, 5,200 doors, 2 towers, 350 feet high, and 9 courts. The number of men ordinarily employed on it during the thirteen years which it took to complete was 14,700; but, towards the end, the services of as many as 45,000 were requisitioned. The mere ceremony of laying the foundation stone cost £40,000; and when the Church was consecrated on the King's birthday, 9,000 banqueters were entertained for a whole week at the King's expense. As a further detail of extravagance we read this:—

"The works of the clocks, chimes, and bells were so exceedingly expensive that the Dutch manufacturers of whom they were ordered declined to undertake them from a fear that the Kingdom of Portugal could not bear the expense. Dom John wrote back that he had made a mistake in the order, as he wished twice the expense to be incurred; and, to obviate all difficulties, he caused the money to be paid before the articles were furnished."

The building might fairly be spoken of as Dom John's Folly; but it was not the only one. The chapel of St. Roque, first built in Rome, and then taken to pieces to be set up again in Lisbon, at a total cost of about £1,000,000, might compete with it for the title; and all the rest of Dom John's expenditure—especially his expenditure on religious objects—was on the same reckless scale.

Whether his religion was true religion is a matter for experts to decide. The essential facts are that he endowed monasteries until there were as many as eight thousand of them established in Portugal, and

JOHN THE DILETTANTE

that nuns took the place in his amorous life which housemaids had taken in that of his glum father. He also lavished the revenues of his kingdom in acquiring those honorific religious privileges which are for sale at Rome. He wanted the Archbishop of Lisbon to be styled a Patriarch; he wanted a Sacred College, with twenty-four prelates attached to it—prelates who should be attired in scarlet, and addressed as "Excellency." As the King of France was called Most Christian, and the King of Spain Most Catholic, he desired a Bull to the effect that the Kings of Portugal should be called Most Faithful.

One after another these requests were preferred at Rome; and the answer to them was always the same. The thing—whatever it might be—could be done; but it would cost money—a great deal of money—as much money, in fact, as the Pope thought it likely that Dom John could be induced to pay. And Dom John was no haggler, but paid whatever he was asked. His Sacred College cost him £98,000 a year; and the total sum which passed from his Treasury to that of the Vatican in the course of his reign is computed at 180,000,000 cruzados. By way of diminishing his assets *pari passu* with the increase of his liabilities, he expelled the few Jews who were still carrying on business in the country; and the upshot of it all was that, when he died, in 1750, there was a national debt of about £3,000,000, and a tenth of the population of Portugal were monks and nuns battening on the labours of the other nine-tenths. Whence Voltaire's epigrammatic summary of his reign :—

THE ROYAL HOUSE OF PORTUGAL

"John V.'s gaieties were religious processions. When he took to building, he built monasteries; and when he wanted a mistress, he chose a nun."

Voltaire was not enthusiastic; but more religious people may be. In their eyes—or in the eyes of some of them—the really disastrous time for Portugal may have been the time when John V.'s successor Joseph sat on the throne, doing nothing in particular, while the illustrious Marquis of Pombal stood beside him, doing a great deal in his name, and, in particular, demonstrating to the Portuguese people that anti-clericalism is the beginning of wisdom. It is, at any rate, of Pombal, far more than of Joseph, that we shall now have to speak.

Pombal was no aristocrat by birth, but merely the son of a country gentleman of moderate means, and at one time a private in the army. He had risen in life by eloping with a lady of higher station, whose family, by way of making the best of a bad job, had got him pitchforked into the office of Ambassador to the Court of St. James's. Dom John, who did not like him, declared that he was only fit to be an assistant in a chandler's shop; but Dom Joseph, when he succeeded Dom John, gave him a portfolio, and presently the terrible Lisbon Earthquake gave him the opportunity of showing Portugal what manner of man he was. Let us pass at once to the striking scene which reveals him.

Lisbon—practically the whole of Lisbon—was in ruins; and various other towns in Portugal had suffered in a less degree. The exact number of the victims is unknown; but there

DOM JOSEPH

were approximately 30,000 of them. The ruins were on fire in several places—the conflagrations kindled, it is said, by the huge candles which were burning in the churches when they fell. The collapse of the walls of the prisons had set the convicts free; and they were prowling about, drunk, looting, and ravishing. The King and the royal family had escaped by accident, being in the Palace of Belem, in the suburbs of Lisbon, at the time. Pombal went out to him, and found Dom Joseph helpless—weeping and wringing his hands, and asking: "What is to be done to meet this infliction of Divine anger?" Prayer and fasting and the appointment of a day of national humiliation were probably the suggestions which he expected; but Pombal was not that sort of man.

"What Your Majesty has to do, Sire," he said, "is to bury the dead and attend to the needs of the living."

It was the *mot de la situation*; and Pombal acted on it, jumping, at once, into his carriage and driving back to Lisbon. For days he lived in his carriage, which was, at once, his place of business and his private residence, hurrying wherever his presence was required, drafting the necessary orders on his knee. He drew a cordon round the city, so as to prevent those who had plundered the churches from getting away with their loot; he summoned troops from the provinces to keep order; he impressed all the able-bodied men who had escaped, and made them work; he established shelters for the homeless,

THE ROYAL HOUSE OF PORTUGAL

hospitals for the sick, and gallows for the felons, whose ghastly heads soon grinned an awful warning in conspicuous places; while, in order to avert the peril of pestilence, he had the bodies of the dead thrown into the sea, with weights attached to them.

Not everyone admired—the Jesuits, in particular, withheld their admiration. These evil men had already had a foretaste of Pombal's anti-clerical activities in the subordination of the Court of the Inquisition to secular tribunals. It seemed to them that, if inquisitors were forbidden to burn and torture whom they would, the foundations of religion were shaken, and the end of all was near; and they tried to persuade the people that the earthquake was God's judgment on Pombal's impiety, and God's vengeance for the suppression of the stake, the thumb-screw, and the rack. On that plea issue was joined; and we must next review the beginnings of that anti-clericalism which was, in the end, to be the salvation of Portugal.

CHAPTER X

Dom Joseph and Pombal—The philosopher King and his
    Minister—Attempt to assassinate Dom Joseph—The
    complicity of the Jesuits—Execution of the conspirators
    —The anti-clerical campaign—The justification for it—
    Pombal's other reforms—His fall on the death of Dom
    Joseph—Dom Joseph's successor—Her incestuous
    marriage and her weak mind—Dom John VI. becomes
    Regent—Approach of the French Revolution and its
    problems.

POMBAL and Dom Joseph were typical figures of the latter half of the eighteenth century: the age of the informal alliance between the philosophers who wrote for encyclopædias and the philosophers who sat on thrones.

It was an interesting alliance; but it is to be noted that the philosophers on the thrones accepted no more of the philosophy than suited them, and quite failed to perceive that it implied the doctrine of Liberty, Equality, and Fraternity and the modern conception of the State. *L'état c'est moi* was the motto of every one of them as surely as it had been the motto of Louis XIV. They approached their problems from the standpoint of men born to a privileged position and

THE ROYAL HOUSE OF PORTUGAL

profoundly convinced of their own immeasurable superiority to the vulgar herd; they regarded their subjects as their little children or their flocks of sheep. Reform, in their opinion, must be produced by pressure from above, not from below; when they struck at the vested interests of the clergy and the nobility, it was in the name, not of democracy, but of benevolent despotism that they did so.

The consequence was that the friends of reform could easily be represented as the enemies of liberty; and they were so represented in this particular instance—not by the common people, to whom the doctrine of the Rights of Man had not yet penetrated, but by the nobles whose noses Pombal put out of joint, and the ecclesiastics whom he would not suffer to regard the commonweal as a carcass to batten on. These hated Pombal, and hated the King as his tool; and the principal result of their hatred was a conspiracy to assassinate Dom Joseph by firing into his carriage on the high road when he was driving to call on his mistress.

One of the leaders of the plot was an ex-Viceroy of India; others were marquises and counts; a Jesuit priest was also implicated. If we could picture Lord Lansdowne, Lord Curzon, Lord Willoughby de Broke, and Father Vaughan potting at his present Majesty from behind a hedge, in the hope of thus obtaining some indirect advantage over Mr. Lloyd George, we should have a modern analogy showing the relative position of the parties; but perhaps the analogy is superfluous.

The idea of the conspirators was to station a

series of firing parties all along the road, in order that, if Dom Joseph escaped the first volley, he might gallop on into a fresh ambuscade, and so fall a victim to the second or the third. What actually happened was that the King, being wounded by the first volley, ordered the coachman to turn back and drive him to the nearest doctor. Thus he escaped; and the next thing to be done was to set spies to work to discover the assassins. It took some months to find them, but when they were caught they were quickly and strenuously dealt with. Some of them were strangled, others broken on the wheel, and others, again, burnt alive, after the barbarous fashion of the time; and, after that, Pombal's position was better established than ever—Dom Joseph having a confidence in him which could not be shaken even by positive proofs that he had exceeded his instructions and abused his powers.

The experiment was tried by the Count of San Lorenço, once a Royal favourite, to whom Dom Joseph admitted that Pombal had done something which placed him technically in the wrong:—

"Well, does your Majesty propose to retain this man in your service?" asked the Count, triumphantly.

"Yes, I do," replied the King, "for where he commits one fault, any of you would commit a hundred."

And then Pombal began his great anti-clerical campaign. An interesting glimpse at one of the reforms in manners due to it may be found in

THE ROYAL HOUSE OF PORTUGAL

Richard Twiss's *Travels through Portugal and Spain in* 1772 *and* 1773:—

"About four leagues from Lisbon," Twiss writes, "is situated the convent of Odivelas, where it is said that three hundred beautiful nuns formed a seraglio for the late King, had each one or more lovers, and were the most attractive mistresses of the Portuguese nobility. At present but a very few of these nuns are living, and they are become old and ugly; so that this convent is no longer a scene of debauchery."

A French author, quoted by Twiss, writes on the same branch of the subject:—

"I was assured that the famous *Portuguese Letters* of which we have a French translation came out of this tender, gallant, and voluptuous convent: that these letters which breathe the most ardent and the most generous love, which paint it with all its shades, in all its details, wherein are found its storms, its inquietudes, its returns, its momentary resolves, the delicacy of its apprehensions, and the heroism of its sacrifices, were really written by an impassioned nun and an unfaithful lover."

The case would certainly seem to be one of those in which, piety having missed the mark at which it originally aimed, the cause of virtue was better served by the anti-clerical new broom than by any of the prelates or other devout believers. It will not be universally admitted, but there is nevertheless good reason for holding, that the cause of civilisation also profited by Pombal's short way with the Jesuits; for though individual Jesuits have sometimes done admirable work in a heroic spirit, the net result of their activities—by which alone it is proper for the historian to judge them—has almost everywhere been to hinder progress.

Indeed, the weak point of all organised religion is this: that, though it may have begun by stimulating progress where civilisation was backward, it seldom fails to end by opposing progress where civilisation advances. In the Dark Ages, though the Church hounded men on to the purposeless slaughter of the Crusades, it also kept the lamp of culture burning in its monasteries; and it was from men who had tended that lamp, and warmed their hands at its flames, that the impetus towards the reform of abuses and the completer illumination of the darkness came. But it came from individuals, not from the organisation or its leaders. To them abuses were dear and reforms odious. They opposed with equal brutality the men who represented that the Pope's Indulgences were not worth the paper they were written on and those who pointed out that the earth went round the sun; and they still claim the right to say, " Thus far and no farther" to all scientific and philosophical inquirers, and to control education in order to prevent the masses from ever being sufficiently well educated to find them out.

It follows—whether it follows or not in logic, it has, at all events, followed as a practical consequence—that the countries in which the influence of the Church of Rome is greatest are, as a rule, the most backward and the worst governed: Spain, Mexico, the extinct Kingdom of Naples, and the old Papal States, for instance. The fact is the chief practical warrant for our aphorism that anti-clericalism is the beginning of wisdom. It shows the reason why the first object of serious reformers in Portugal has always been to break the power of the Church; and it furnishes the particular reason why Pombal was no sooner firmly in the saddle than he set to work to clear out the Jesuits. Seeing that they were implicated in the plot to murder the King, the most ardent Catholic apologist can hardly deny that, far from being pious men, harmless as doves, they were, if not as wise as serpents, at least as poisonous, and much better out of the way.

Still, though the history of the reign is the history of a veiled civil war, in which the nominal combatants were Dom Joseph and his pious relations, while the real combatants were Pombal and the zealots of the monastic orders, it must not be concluded that Pombal was, any more than Dom Joseph, a freethinker. The influences of the French Encyclopædists had not touched him to that extent; he accepted the ministrations of the Church during his life, and received its last rites on his death-bed. But his real interests were elsewhere; and he believed in applying to the clergy the maxim which defines the proper relations of the cobbler to his last. They must preach and pray—there was a real need for sermons and orisons of the proper sort; but they must not set them-

POMBAL

selves above the law of the land, or darken counsel, or pray for the confusion of Liberal ideas, or think that the privileges of the pulpit entitled them to declare, as one of them did, that "it was without doubt an angel from Heaven who fired the shot at Dom Joseph": a most unwarrantable reflection, not only on the character of the King, but also on the marksmanship of angels. The pious men whose piety manifested itself on those lines must either go away or go to prison.

Some of them took the one road, and some the other. Whichever road they took, they continued to intrigue, assured that, whenever Dom Joseph died, his successors would reinstate them in their privileges. As evidence of their attitude, we may quote from a despatch addressed by the British Minister to his Government:—

"The emissaries of the Jesuits endeavour to work upon the minds of the people by persuading them that this kingdom is under the immediate chastisement of Heaven, and may expect some direful calamity. That, as our Saviour's sufferings were for the redemption of mankind in general, so the present sufferings of the Jesuits are for the reclaiming of Portugal from its present errors, and which cannot be safe unless it returns to them (the Jesuits). These and such-like absurdities impose greatly upon an ignorant people who have for their teachers a very ignorant set of clergy; but which the Ministers seem determined to put a stop to as much as possible."

This attitude on the part of the unholy fathers

was the more audacious in view of the fact that their Order had been suppressed, not only by Pombal, but also by the Pope himself; but that is what Jesuits are like. Their suppression, however, was only one of many reforms which marked Pombal's administration. He reformed the army, which had fallen into such a state that the soldiers, not receiving their pay, used to solicit alms while standing in their sentry-boxes. He reformed the finances with a banker's passion for meticulous exactitude, causing a balance-sheet to be made out weekly, and compelling the King to go through it with him, to the end that Dom Joseph "might always retire to rest with the satisfaction of being, at all times, acquainted with the precise condition of his Treasury." Finally, he reformed the University of Coimbra, adding, among other things, a Chair of Mathematics, in spite of the protests of angry clergymen who exclaimed against that branch of learning as heretical.

Nor was that all. Pombal also introduced into Portugal the fashion of using forks as well as knives at the dinner-tables of the polite; and it is hardly too much to say that that was the only one of his reforms which the clerical party neither resisted nor determined to reverse when their hour of opportunity struck, as they knew that it would do on the day of Dom Joseph's death. Most likely they prayed for his death; and some of them certainly acted on the maxim *laborare est orare* by engaging in a second unsuccessful attempt to assassinate him. He lived to be old, however, and died a natural

POMBAL

death in February, 1777; and then there was nothing for it but for Pombal to retire before his clerical enemies drove him out.

He was old enough to retire, being exactly as old as the century; and the clerical faction, though they would doubtless have preferred to burn him alive, could hardly refuse him permission to bow himself out gracefully, leaving them free to fetch the conspirators from their prisons, and revive all the abuses which he had been at such pains to suppress. They drove him from pillar to post; they insulted him by ordering the removal of his medallion portrait which Dom Joseph had caused to be affixed to his own equestrian statue, and the substitution of the City Arms therefor; and when he published a memorandum in defence of his administration, they issued a decree enjoining him to "absent himself from the Court, at a distance of at least twenty leagues, until further orders." And so he died, in more or less honourable exile, at the age of eighty-two, leaving the fortunes of Portugal in the hands of a decadent family, to which we must now return.

Dom Joseph's successor was his only daughter, who had contracted an incestuous marriage with her father's only brother. The purpose of the union was, of course, to keep the crown in the family; but its practical result was to keep the hereditary taints in it. The House of Braganza, indeed, has almost as bad a heredity as the House of Habsburg; but this is a matter which will wait while we go to the British Ambassador, Walpole, for an

THE ROYAL HOUSE OF PORTUGAL

estimate of the new Queen and her husband, who is by courtesy spoken of as the King:—

"The Queen and the King" (Walpole reported) "are very devout. They are of unlimited obedience to the See of Rome and the jurisdiction of the clergy in its most extensive pretensions. The Queen is timid, and consequently easily influenced by the clergy, with whom she has very much conversed. . . . She has a great deference for her husband, and the King has a great admiration for her, and speaks of her as a saint. The King is of a confined understanding, hears three or four masses in the morning in the utmost ecstasy, and attends evening prayers as devoutly. He is liberal in his alms, talks much in precepts of goodness and justice, but as he has no knowledge of mankind or business he is easily governed, right or wrong, by those immediately about him, especially if they belong to the Church. . . . It is not thought that the King, who is allowed to be of a humane disposition, will be prevailed upon to consent to any violent proceedings against the Marquis of Pombal, *unless he should be induced to it to revenge the cause of the Church.*"

It is a pleasant picture of a couple of pious imbeciles forming themselves into a mutual admiration society under clerical direction. The King is described as having been "vicious" on the moral side, but, on the intellectual side, not worse than "silly"—a man who would not trouble to interfere with any Minister who let him sin and pray without ceasing. The Queen, on the other hand, can be described, without qualification, as weak-minded: rather weak-minded at the beginning of her reign,

DOM JOHN

and very weak-minded towards the end of it. Her precise mental condition, at any given moment, appears to have depended upon the character of her confessor. A confessor who made light of the terrors of Hell could keep her comparatively sane; but when she fell into the hands of a confessor who showed less confidence in her salvation, it became necessary to send to London for a specialist in lunacy. She was beyond his help, however, and her son Dom John assumed the reins as Regent—his father, Dom Pedro, being, by that time, dead.

This, it is to be observed, in the years in which the French Revolution was presenting awkward problems to all rulers everywhere. Before, during, and immediately after that great event, with all its manifold international implications, Portugal was, in effect, an absolute monarchy without an absolute monarch, without any constitutional substitute for a sovereign, and without any great man to assume responsibility during the interregnum. It was in 1788 that the decay of the Queen's intellect reached a point at which there could no longer be any mistake about it; but it was not until 1792 that Dom John took over her duties from her, and not until 1799 that he was formally invested with the Regency. And, in the meantime, great things had happened, and the train had been laid for still more momentous explosions.

It was a period, as we know, when Europe seethed with new ideas, which were rapidly being translated into action; and it was important for the rulers of all countries to consider what their atti tude towards those new ideas should be. They might prepare to accept them, or they might prepare to resist them—there was no reasonable middle course; but the rulers of Portugal adopted neither policy. The Queen hardly knew what was going on—her one serious interest in life being the collection of subscriptions for the Latin Convent at Jerusalem. The clerical people who ruled in her name were satisfied to sit on the safety valve, without taking the needful steps to make their seat on it secure.

Their argument appears to have been that, as Liberals had upset the throne in France, Liberals must be persecuted in Portugal before they had time to follow the evil example. To that end they discovered conspirators where there was no conspiracy, and turned the police loose on the "intellectuals" in the spirit in which they might have set dogs at them. They imprisoned their leading poets, historians, and men of science; and they banished the Duke of Lafôes—the Portuguese Mæcenas of his age—for no other reason than because he had offered hospitality to Necker's Secretary, the chemist Broussonet. In that way they set out to purge Portugal; but they purged it without strengthening it—reducing it, on the contrary, to such a state of ineffective weakness that when, in the first year of the Peninsular War, Napoleon ordered Junot to march on Lisbon, no attempt was made to resist the paltry force of two thousand foot-sore men with which he entered the city.

DOM JOHN

So much for the clericals and their management of affairs of which they had the uncontrolled direction; but how about Dom John himself—presently to be Dom John VI.? What was this hereditary representative of the House of Braganza about, and what manner of man was he to let things come to this pass without even putting up a fight, however feeble, to prevent it?

CHAPTER XI

John VI.—Reasons for calling him John the Runaway—His weak mind and his superstitions—Invasion of Portugal by Junot—French scheme for partition of Portugal—Flight of Dom John to Brazil—Southey's description of the Scene—The House of Braganza disgraced.

DOM JOHN VI., whom we may as well call John the Runaway—for he really is famous for nothing except deserting his country in her hour of need—was born in 1761, and married, in 1785, Donna Carlota Joaquina, daughter of Charles IV. of Spain, who disliked and despised him. His elder brother, Dom Joseph, is said to have been a youth of some promise; but little is actually known of him except that he spoke of monks as "the most pernicious vermin by which a country can be infested," and that, after refusing to be inoculated, he caught small-pox, and died of it. The younger brother's most famous recorded saying is to the effect that, as he did not expect to be a King, there was no need for him to cultivate his mind, and no harm in his neglecting the affairs of State in order to go hunting.

He certainly did neglect the affairs of State

JOHN VI

before, during, and after the critical period of the French Revolution; and one finds a vivid picture of the Portugal—and more particularly the Lisbon—which he practically left without a government, in the *Travels in Portugal* of the German, Link:—

"As for the night," writes Link, "the city was formerly lighted, but now this practice has ceased. . . . A host of dogs, without masters, and living on the public, wander about like hungry wolves; and still worse than these an army of banditti. . . . How can a nation among whom are a number of enlightened men bear such an abomination which degrades Lisbon even below Constantinople?"

Link goes into other details. He describes how, at the Carnival, "both high and low delight in throwing all kinds of dirt on the passengers, who, in conforming to custom and to avoid quarrels, must bear it patiently." He speaks of the practice of begging in the streets for the alleged benefit of souls in purgatory: a privilege accorded to the Mendicant Orders, and farmed by them at a profit. He also tells us that the Church forbade work on Fast Days, and that the priests drove a roaring trade in permits for the breach of the regulation. His notes, in short, furnish material in support of all the severest comments which have ever been passed on clerical government; and the strictures are followed by a thumbnail sketch of Dom John himself as a person of no particular importance:—

"No one," he says, "doubts the natural good qualities of the Prince of Brazil, but his talents are questioned, and it is feared he will not escape the

THE ROYAL HOUSE OF PORTUGAL

yoke of the priesthood by whom his mother is so much oppressed. He has no striking passions or inclinations, except perhaps that for the chase. The Princess is a very good-natured woman, of whom it can only be said that she is very prolific and seems therewith to be content."

The Princess did not continue to be content; but the Prince did fall under the yoke of the priesthood. One gets the measure of his intelligence in the matter in a story told by Southey in one of his *Letters during a Short Residence in Spain and Portugal:*—

"When," Southey reports, "the Prince of Brazil married, his confessor, who was a Franciscan himself, told him that he would never have a child unless the Franciscans were reinstated in possession of Mafra. The Prince had faith, the Mendicants had Mafra, St. Francis had pity, and the Princess had a child."

One is left with an impression of a weak-minded fool; and Dom John, in fact, seems to have had no illusions about himself, but to have been well aware that he was weak-minded. The admission comes out in the story of his reply to a remonstrance addressed to him for allowing his clerical friends to persecute one of the most loyal and illustrious servants of the Crown. Why, he was asked, had he shown such a lamentable lack of firmness?

"How could I help it?" he answered. "None of us can change our characters. I have Braganza blood in my veins, and I take after my ancestors."

JOHN VI

It was an explanation of a sort: the Braganzas must make what they can of it. There may be a supplementary explanation in the fact that Dom John fell, for a season, into a sort of melancholy madness—had, in fact, a kind of "nervous breakdown," as the result of which he declared himself "afraid of horses." The clericals, who had not found him quite as amenable as they liked—though the anti-clericals considered that he had been far too amenable—talked of placing him under restraint and declaring a Regency. He recovered before they could carry out their purpose; but he never forgave the Queen, whom he believed to have been at the bottom of the plot, and his estrangement from her dates from that illness. And then came the trouble with France, in which he cut as sorry a figure as any King has ever cut anywhere.

The crisis began to loom in sight in the days when Marshal Lannes was Napoleon's Ambassador at Lisbon. One gathers from Lannes's *Letters*, which have recently been published, that he swaggered about the Portuguese Court as if it belonged to him, preferred his requests to the courtiers in the tone of a man giving orders to his own subordinates, and asserted his claims to precedence by using physical violence towards the diplomatic representatives of other Powers. One further gathers that Dom John bore his bullying like a lamb, and even seemed to like it. He showed that disregard for ancient lineage which Napoleon instilled at the cannon's mouth into so many Heads of ancient Royal Houses, and proposed to marry

THE ROYAL HOUSE OF PORTUGAL

the Prince of Beira to one of Murat's daughters. He also invited Lannes and his wife to act as godfather and godmother to one of his children, and seized the opportunity to present him with three handfuls of uncut diamonds from Brazil.

"Here," he said, lifting the gems from a bowl with as little concern as if they had been grains of corn or lumps of sugar. "Here is a handful for the godfather; here is a handful for the godmother; and here is a handful for the Ambassador."

It seems that Lannes was really moved by this frantic gesture of generosity. It is said, at any rate, that he was offered the command in Portugal which was afterwards accepted by Junot, but refused it, because he did not want to hurt the feelings of his lavish friend; but that refusal did not divert Napoleon from his schemes. Napoleon wanted Portugal to join in his commercial boycott of England; he also wanted the Portuguese fleet to fill the vacancies created in his own navy at Trafalgar; and when Dom John temporised, instead of either defying or obeying him, he laid a deeper scheme, in collaboration with Charles IV. of Spain, and his Minister Godoy.

This scheme was nothing less than a partition of Portugal: a partition arranged, in all its details, at the Secret Treaty of Fontainebleau—a cynical arrangement whereby the paramour of the Queen of Spain was to have become the King of the Algarves. The plan was not carried out—chiefly because Napoleon had designs on Spain as well as Portugal, and was using his designs on Portugal

JOHN VI

to mask his designs on Spain; but the first part of the programme—the invasion of Portugal—was duly executed, though it was ostensibly, in its earlier stages, not an invasion, but a friendly occupation, necessary to save Portugal from the alleged designs of England.

England, of course, had no hostile intentions whatsoever towards Portugal; but that made no difference to Napoleon. He merely wanted an excuse for invading Portugal; and this assumption served. Portugal ought to join his combination against England; Portugal wanted to do so; Portugal only hesitated to do so from fear of England. So he would put heart into the Portuguese by sending them an army: the presence of a French army at Lisbon would counteract the influence of a British fleet in the Tagus. As that army would be occupying their country for their advantage, they must support it; and if the King of Portugal did not see the advantage, he must be frightened away. That, broadly speaking, was the line of argument; and the gist of it was set forth in a notable official communication to the *Moniteur*: the communication which began with the announcement that the House of Braganza had ceased to reign, and ended with the demand that every French soldier sent to Portugal should be provided every day with a bottle of port wine at the cost of the Portuguese people.

The alternative might have seemed a simple one: to welcome the French or to resist them. Policy might have seemed to suggest the former course, and honour the second. A King who was worthy

THE ROYAL HOUSE OF PORTUGAL

to be a King would assuredly, in such a case, have put an army in the field, and taken command of it, arguing with himself that that was what Kings were for. It needed a King of quite exceptionally paltry character to shirk his responsibilities in order to save his skin, and embark in a hurry for a foreign land, leaving his people to their fate. Even passive resistance akin to that of the Roman Senators who gravely kept their seats in the Council Chamber, awaiting the irruption of the Gauls, would have been preferable to that. But John VI. had no courage, no sense of responsibility, no pride—no desire for anything except to hide his shame and keep his comfort.

He remembered—he did not need to be reminded—that he was the sovereign ruler not only of Portugal and the Algarves, but also of Brazil. He could depend upon the British Fleet to escort him to Brazil and see that he was not molested there. So he resolved to go there—covering his retreat with a manifesto to the effect that he believed himself to be the sole object of Napoleon's enmity, and that his subjects would have nothing to fear from the French if only they received them with open arms; and he departed just as Junot was on the point of entering Lisbon, whence he scornfully pointed a gun at the disappearing fleet. That was how John VI. earned the title of John the Runaway.

It is still difficult to realise the public opinion which made such a thing possible. One would have expected a King in such a case to have been shamed into staying by the remonstrances of indignant

FLIGHT OF JOHN VI

noblemen, or pitched into the river by an indignant populace. But nothing of the kind happened. The people, taken by surprise, dazed and bewildered, looked on as if at a spectacle designed for their diversion. The courtiers and the aristocracy, making their loyalty a cloak for their fears, decided, for the most part, to accompany the King and look after him. Almost all the quarterings of Portugal were represented in the emigration; and the fleet of fugitives which Sir Sidney Smith convoyed to Rio de Janeiro comprised eight ships of the line, three frigates, five smaller ships of war, and a number of merchant vessels—a grand total of six-and-thirty sail. One might search the pages of history for a long time before discovering the record of a more shameful scene.

Resistance would have been easy, for Junot only reached Lisbon at the end of a forced march, so exhausting that most of his men fell out by the way, and of the twenty-five thousand who started, only about two thousand arrived. Of their condition on arrival let Southey speak:—

"The troops," he tells us, "arrived without baggage, having only their knapsacks, and a half gourd slung from the girdle as a drinking-cup; their muskets were rusty, and many of them out of repair; the soldiers themselves, mostly barefoot, foundered with their march, and almost fainting with fatigue and hunger. The very women of Lisbon might have knocked them on the head."

And then, in a later passage:—

"They came in, not like an army in collected

THE ROYAL HOUSE OF PORTUGAL

force, with artillery and stores, ready for attack or defence, but like stragglers seeking a place of security after some total rout. Not a regiment, not a battalion, not even a company arrived entire: many of them were beardless boys, and they came in so pitiable a condition as literally to excite compassion and charity; footsore, bemired, and wet, ragged and hungered and diseased. Some dropped in the streets, others leant against the walls, or lay down in the porches, till the Portuguese, with ill-requited humanity, gave them food and conveyed them to those quarters which they had not the strength to find out for themselves."

Against this rabble about fourteen thousand Portuguese soldiers were available; and Sir Sidney Smith, whose fleet lay at the mouth of the Tagus, offered to land a Naval Brigade to help them. But Dom John would not have it so. While his people murmured, but could do nothing because the desertion of their leaders had paralysed their resistance, his one anxiety was to lead the Royal family, the Court, and the Cabinet to a place of safety. We may quote Southey's picture of the scene on the quay :—

"All the ships were crowded with emigrants, for everyone who had the means was eager to fly from the coming ruin. The confusion had been so great that families were separated; wives got on board without their husbands, husbands without their wives; children and parents were divided; many were thus left behind, and many had the joy of meeting in Brazil when each believed that the other was in Portugal."

FLIGHT OF JOHN VI

And meanwhile the walls of Lisbon were placarded with the announcement that the King had "endeavoured by all possible means to preserve the neutrality which his subjects had hitherto enjoyed," and now, to his extreme annoyance, observed that "the troops of the Emperor of the French, to whom he had united himself on the continent in the persuasion that he should be no further disquieted, were marching towards his capital."

And the conclusion was that:—

"To avoid, therefore, the effusion of blood, for these troops came with professions of not committing the slightest hostility, knowing also that his royal person was their particular object, and that if he himself were absent his subjects would be less disturbed, he had resolved, for their sakes, to remove, with the whole royal family, to the City of Rio de Janeiro, and there establish himself until a general peace."

A shameful placard truly; and the shame reaches its climax when we read how Dom John's mad mother, whose face had hardly been seen in Portugal for sixteen years, was shocked into sufficient recovery of her reason to understand, however dimly, that something disgraceful was happening, and to protest:—

"Don't go so fast. People will think that we are running away."

People did think so—they could not think otherwise when they saw John the Runaway thus earning his name. They would have thought so still more emphatically if they had seen the letters in which

THE ROYAL HOUSE OF PORTUGAL

Napoleon instructed Junot as to the proper way of treating the Portuguese :—

"Disarm the inhabitants, send away the Portuguese troops, make severe examples, maintain an attitude of severity which will make you feared. . . . Shoot sixty people or so, and take suitable measures. . . . You are in a conquered country."

Whence it is clear that, though the disgraceful flight of John the Runaway was very much to his personal advantage, it did not confer upon the long-suffering Portuguese people any of those benefits which he had eloquently exhorted them to expect from it. The flight is an episode in the annals of the House of Braganza to which Portuguese patriots still refer with passionate expressions of disgust.

CHAPTER XII

The Peninsular War—Residence of John the Runaway in Brazil—Reforms which he introduced there—The bank which he founded—Its peculiar constitution and methods—The first Brazilian financial crisis—Return of Dom John to Portugal—His farewell speech to his son—Dom Pedro I. crowned Emperor of Brazil.

THE Peninsular War is not our subject. We may sum it up in a sentence by saying that a Regency reigned, but did not govern, during Dom John's absence, and that Wellington chased the French away—first to Spain, and then over the Pyrenees to the place from which they came.

Not, of course, without the help of the Portuguese themselves. Beresford re-organised the Portuguese army; and it could truly be said of it that "the men were splendid." Wellington wanted them at Waterloo, though there was not time to get them there; and the French were so roughly handled by them at Busaco that they accused Wellington of having put English soldiers into Portuguese uniforms, in order to lure them on—a calumnious suggestion for which there was, of course, no warrant.

THE ROYAL HOUSE OF PORTUGAL

But from John the Runaway there came no help whatever. He had not run away in the hope that he would live to fight another day, but in order to avoid fighting altogether. He mustered no fresh forces in Brazil; he did not offer to send either supplies or money. On the contrary, he and his Court had taken with them all the property which they could lay their hands on; and their departure had been like that of the Israelites who spoiled the Egyptians before leaving them.

The Court, in their eyes, was "the thing." It seemed to them that, in saving the Court, with all its extravagance and grandeur, they had gone a long way towards saving the country; and Dom John's attitude, when he heard that the French had committed this, that, or the other outrage on his subjects, reminds one of that of the proud Irish landlord who wrote from comfortable chambers in London to say that, if his tenants imagined that they could intimidate him by shooting his agents, they were very much mistaken. In any case, he took his ease in his Palace while his subjects were dying for him on the stricken field; and it was not until those same subjects, being disgusted with him, showed symptoms of a desire to shake off his authority and that of his Regents, that he bethought himself of returning, to save his throne.

One may admit that he would have been of no use if he had returned before; and one may suspect that he knew it. He was of no particular use in Brazil; and he would have been of no particular use anywhere. He was simply a Man of No Importance, who knew his limitations, and considered that these relieved him of his responsibilities without depriving him of his rights. It was the doctrine of the age, and was probably shared by many of those who despised him. The modern view that a King is a functionary who, like any other functionary, must do his work or go, had not yet gained currency. Napoleon, it is true, was rendering the world a great service by making incompetent kings look ridiculous; but the value of the service was not recognised at the time. The incompetent kings stood shoulder to shoulder; the kings who were not so incompetent backed them up; and the prevalent feeling was that a king's incompetence, however much one might deplore it, had no more bearing on his claim to loyalty than the colour of his hair.

It would seem, too, that John the Runaway had his virtues, though these were mainly negative and did not include courage. He was not an unfaithful husband, though his Queen was a scandalously unfaithful wife. He was not passionately enamoured of clerical influence, though he endured it. He was always eager to reward a personal service from the public purse—lavish in the distribution of sinecures, titles, and decorations. Nor was his presence in Brazil, in spite of the sinecures, entirely disadvantageous to that colony. It gained by some improvement in the forms of justice, and by the introduction of certain useful institutions: a University, a Library, a Learned Society, and a Bank.

Especially a bank; and, in view of all that we have lately heard about Brazilian financial crises,

THE ROYAL HOUSE OF PORTUGAL

we may fairly interrupt discourse on graver matters, in order to tell the story of the first Brazilian financial crisis, and of the part which the bank and the current accounts of the courtiers played in it.

Dom John wanted a bank for the excellent reason that he wanted to borrow money from it. The Brazilians, on the other hand, had only the haziest notion of the nature of a bank, and were very reluctant to subscribe the capital for so unfamiliar an enterprise. That difficulty Dom John got over by promising to confer the honour of knighthood on every applicant for a certain number of shares; and then the fun began. There was a rush of applicants; but very few of the applicants were able, or willing, to put down ready money for the shares allotted to them. Something, it was clear, must be done, and the applicants met and made a pleasant little family arrangement among themselves: an arrangement whereby the shares were registered in their names, and the scrip was deposited in the bank vaults as security for the payment due on it. A further arrangement was made whereby the defaulting shareholders might borrow the scrip when dividends fell due, on condition that they were scrupulously careful to return it after the dividends had been drawn.

That meant, of course, that the bank was started without any assets; but arrangements enabling it to dispense with them were easily and quickly made. Capital was created by a lavish issue of notes. A certain number of the notes were devoted to the purchase of a small metallic reserve; and the others

FINANCIAL CRISIS

were lent, whether with or without security, to the bank's customers, in the ordinary way of business. Dom John, of course, was one of those who were privileged to borrow without security—as the whole country belonged to him, it seemed unnecessary, as well as disloyal, to ask for any. So His Majesty borrowed freely, finding it much more convenient to raise money in this easy way than to provoke unpopularity by increasing the taxes; and the directors readily lent him all that he wanted because they had only to print notes in order to do so.

The money was not wanted for any fantastic purposes, but only for the payment of the stipends of ministers and Court functionaries, and the wages of servants. These willingly accepted payment in notes, and had no difficulty in getting the notes accepted as cash by their tradespeople, and other dependents. Notes were just as convenient as coins, as long as they passed from hand to hand as such. Brazil was not remitting gold to Europe, as it had done in the old days when the Court was at Lisbon, so that there was no premium on it; and, as the Bank of Brazil was a State Bank, it occurred to no one to doubt its solvency. The notes were as good as gold; by means of fresh issues of notes, the rise in wages was enabled to keep pace with the rise in prices. In short, all seemed to be for the best in the best of all possible Brazils; and things went on like that for years, and might have gone on a great deal longer but for the sudden determination of the King to return to Europe, taking the Court with him.

THE ROYAL HOUSE OF PORTUGAL

Then, of course, the fun became fast and furious. The courtiers naturally desired to take their money to Europe with them; and it suddenly occurred to them—first to one or two of them, and then to all of them—that the notes of the Bank of Brazil might not, perhaps, be accepted at their face value in Europe. It seemed, at any rate, the safer plan, to exchange the notes for gold, and draw out their balances in gold, before they started. So the members of the Royal Household—it was an enormous Royal Household, maintained at a cost of £540,000 a year—hearing that a date had been fixed for their departure, set out, with one accord, quite cheerfully, for the bank premises, first filling the streets with a gaily-dressed procession, and then forming a gaily-dressed queue. A certain number of the first arrivals got what they wanted; but then the smash came. The bank vaults contained no ingots, but only the scrip of the shareholders who had not paid for their shares. Its safes contained no coins except the petty cash. Its sole wealth consisted in its own notes—its own promises to pay bearer on demand something which it had not got, and had never had. So the shutters went up, and the creditors were sent empty away.

This is the picturesque story of the first of the financial crises of Brazil—a crisis directly attributable to the King's incapacity to realise the financial world about him. The spread of ideas was, at the same time, combated by a rigid Press censorship—a censorship under which all books were forbidden except those which were specifically permitted,

BRAZILIAN DISSENSIONS

and the newspapers had to confine themselves to the publication of official edicts, communicated Court news, birthday odes, and panegyrics on members of the Royal Family. It was in the midst of these conditions that St. Antony was made a colonel in the Brazilian army, and received his pay regularly—pay which Franciscan Friars were allowed to draw for him on the understanding that they would devote it to the illumination of candles in his honour; and the only rift through which Liberalism had a chance to penetrate was cut by the quarrels between the Portuguese and the Brazilian aristocracies.

The matters at issue between them consisted not of principles, but of perquisites. They quarrelled over commissions in the army, berths in the Civil Service—not to mention sinecures and pickings. When, after the Peninsular War was over, some Portuguese regiments were brought to Brazil, a Portuguese general actually presented a memorandum formally demanding that Brazilian officers should be declared incompetent to hold any higher commission than that of captain. Dom John refused to make any promises, but nevertheless acted on the suggestion. Naturally, the Brazilians were offended; and it was, as the result of their resentment, that Brazilian politics began to take a democratic turn. They took it the more decidedly when the news arrived that there had been a revolution in Portugal—the Revolution of 1820—and that the Cortes proposed to meet and devise a new Constitution. Then there was trouble—riots and risings in

THE ROYAL HOUSE OF PORTUGAL

the provinces; and the dissension in the country was reflected in the Royal Family itself—Dom John taking one side and his son Dom Pedro the other.

Whether Dom Pedro actually conspired against his father is disputed; and it is also not very easy to decide whether he was under the greater obligation to serve Portugal or to serve Brazil. In any case, he preferred the interests of his adopted country to those of his mother country; and the probability is strong that, if he had not done so, Brazil would have subdivided itself, as it has often shown a tendency to do, into a number of independent Republics. Dom John himself seems to have suspected that; or so one infers from his farewell speech when, the anchor being weighed in the Rio harbour, he embraced, for the last time, the son whom he was never to see again:—

"Pedro," he said to him, "Brazil will, I fear, before long separate herself from Portugal. If so, place the crown on your own head rather than allow it to fall into the hands of any adventurer."

It was, indeed, the speech of a King: one who will consent to anything rather than see the crown pass out of the family; and it is a matter of history that Dom Pedro took his father at his word—a decision to which he was brought by the attitude of the Portuguese Cortes towards Brazilians generally and himself in particular. There were considerable negotiations about which we need not trouble ourselves; but the essential facts are these:—

The Cortes was an assemblage of radical doctrinaires: men who meant extremely well, but were

BRAZILIAN DISSENSIONS

novices at the difficult art of colonial government. They understood that peoples had rights as against kings, but they did not understand that colonies had rights as against mother countries. Their dominant idea was that, as Kings had exploited Brazil in the past, so the Cortes must exploit it for the future; and they therefore proposed to deprive it of liberty, in the name of liberty, and proceeded to order Dom Pedro about, much as they might have done if they had been University dons and he an unsatisfactory undergraduate. They told him to come home at once, after first handing over the reins of government to a Regency which they would nominate. They added that he was not to come straight home, but first to take a course of travel in England, France, and Spain, "in order to complete his political education."

That, of course, was more than royal flesh and blood could be expected to stand; and Dom Pedro's not unnatural reply was to announce his intention of staying where he was under the style and title of Emperor of Brazil. Our own Lord Cochrane, entering his service as an Admiral, quickly disposed of such naval forces as Portugal was able to send against him; and that was the end of the matter, though we must not leave the subject without recording the dramatic protest of the young officer who was afterwards to become famous as Field Marshal the Duke of Saldanha. The scene is depicted in the Memoirs of Marshal Saldanha by the Conde Carnota :—

"The Emperor was crowned on the 1st of December. Saldanha was still at Rio. There were great festivities on the occasion of the coronation. At night, the Emperor went in state to the theatre. Saldanha appeared there, dressed in black, and occupied a seat in the box of his sister, the Countess da Ponte. The Minister of Marine, going in, said, 'General, the Emperor wonders why you are in mourning?' 'Can I be otherwise,' replied Saldanha, 'on the day on which the dissolution of the monarchy is effected?'"

An impressive scene truly, and a brave demonstration, though no punishment came of it—but chiefly interesting, perhaps, as an example of the curious mentality which a Court atmosphere sometimes engenders even in intelligent men. Saldanha was quite intelligent enough to know that Dom John was a fool, and that Portugal had treated Brazil very badly, and his subsequent career was to show that he had a genuine sympathy with progress; but he also had, not merely the religion, but also the superstition, of loyalty. He could not think of Brazil otherwise than as an appanage of Portugal, or of Portugal otherwise than as an appanage of the House of Braganza. The unworthiness of the King hindered not, in his opinion, the efficacy of the principle of kingship. The people had no more right to take away the King's crown because he was unworthy than the highway robber has to steal a citizen's purse because he is drunk. Such things were not done in good society—to do them stamped a man; and he therefore thought it necessary to make his gloomy demonstration on the day which Brazil thought the most glorious in its annals.

But that is a digression. We must return to Dom John, and see how he fared in Portugal.

CHAPTER XIII

Personal appearance and character of John VI.—His acceptance of a Portuguese Constitution—Objections of his wife and younger son, Dom Miguel—Dom Miguel's revolt against his father—The intervention of the Ambassadors—Their collective visit to the Palace—Description of the scene by Hyde de Neuville—The Infant cowed for the moment but still rebellious—Dom John takes refuge on the *Windsor Castle.*

IT seems to be well established that John the Runaway was a John who meant no harm. He meant no harm when he fled, leaving his country to the tender mercy of the French; and he meant none when he came back to resume his position in times which he expected to be more comfortable. The worst that can be said of him was that, distrusting both himself and his advisers, he confronted great problems with low cunning. We see him, as it were, on the cinematograph screen in the character sketch of him given in Bollaert's "Wars of Succession in Portugal and Spain":—

"He was of ordinary height, corpulent, of melancholy aspect, large mouth and features, and drooping jaw. . . . His passion was the amassing wealth in diamonds. He was careless in his person. The

THE ROYAL HOUSE OF PORTUGAL

same pair of boots he would not change until patching them was of no utility, and the same nankeen trousers must be washed and ironed every night for the morning's use, so darned and mended that frequently the washerwoman's complaints were loud. His embroidered uniform coat was in constant use, blazoned with thirteen stars. He ate with his fingers. Withal, he was a good man and died beloved, if not respected, by his people."

Perhaps that picture does not make the case for loving Dom John very much clearer than the case for respecting him; but the affection may have had its source in the pity which we are told is akin to love. Dom John, who meant no harm and, indeed, was almost too silly a man to be capable of any, was bullied, under his subjects' eyes, by members of his family who did mean harm: by his wife Doña Joaquina, and his son Dom Miguel—the founder of that party of "Miguelites" concerning which it will soon be necessary to say a good deal. They bullied him on general principles because he was feeble and they were energetic; they bullied him in particular on account of his ready adherence to the new Constitution which the Cortes had drafted while he was in Brazil.

It seemed to Dom John that one Constitution was as good as another, since no Constitution was likely to prevent him from collecting diamonds, and slopping about the Palace in patched and baggy trousers. The Constitution proposed to him—drafted by doctrinaires and providing for a Single Chamber which the Crown could not dismiss—was open to many criticisms; but that particular objection could not be taken to it. So Dom John cheerfully swore to observe it, even before all its articles had been submitted to him, and expected the Queen to do the same. But Doña Carlota Joaquina would not, and gave a woman's reason for her refusal. "She had made a promise," she said, "never to swear to anything, either for good or evil, during the whole course of her life." And Dom Miguel backed his mother up.

Carlota Joaquina was a Spanish Infanta, and a woman of spirit. She had shown her spirit in Brazil by firing a pistol—fortunately with inaccurate aim—at one of the King's friends in the King's presence; and she showed it now by declaring her desire to have every constitution-monger in the country hanged. As for Dom Miguel, who was egged on by her to share that desire, we may, perhaps, best introduce him by quoting the character-sketch of him given by a British officer of Hussars in his account of "The Civil War in Portugal":—

"Dom Miguel," we there read, "was educated as a Portuguese Prince, ignorant of everything he did not wish to learn; therefore it may be well supposed that he was more apt at athletic exercises than literary studies. It is much to be doubted whether the King himself was very anxious on the subject of the education of his sons: perhaps he might have a jealous feeling of their knowing more than himself. Brought up as he was, his own was the only hereditary rank. All others were menials. Virtue and

THE ROYAL HOUSE OF PORTUGAL

worth were only distinguished by him in force and dexterity."

This Dom Miguel was evidently his mother's rather than his father's son; and, indeed, his mother's way of life was such that the actual paternity of any of her son's might always be regarded as dubious. She egged the boy on—he was only a lad of one-and-twenty—in a spirit worthy of a sister of the abominable Ferdinand VII. of Spain, though it might be hard to say whether dislike of her husband or dislike of democracy was her more potent motive. Presumably it was through her influence that the violent youth was appointed, at the age of twenty-two, to be commander-in-chief of the Portuguese army: a position which he promptly used, nominally for his father's deliverance from the revolutionists, but actually for his father's confusion. And so, as we shall see in a moment, there was a counter revolution, which was, at the same time, a Palace revolution.

The story is tangled, and it would take too long to unravel all the threads. Not only were the dissensions in the country complicated by the dissensions in the Royal Family; both these quarrels were further complicated by the desire of the Holy Alliance to interfere and the determination of the British Government that the Holy Alliance should do nothing of the kind. It seemed to the French that, as they had just put down a revolution in Spain, they might as well go on and put down a revolution in Portugal; but the day was to come when Canning, regarding Portugal as a British preserve,

DOM MIGUEL

would send troops, and make a speech which has become famous:—

"We go to plant the standard of England on the well-known heights of Lisbon. Where that standard is planted, foreign dominion shall not come."

British dominion as little as any other. The idea was not to interfere in Portuguese domestic affairs, but only to prevent the French from interfering. The Portuguese were to be left to settle their domestic difficulties as they chose; and the party which at the moment had the upper hand was the party of Dom Miguel and his mother—the party which was more royalist than the King and was prepared to proceed to extreme measures with the King if he did not consent to be as royalist as they thought he ought to be.

Carlota Joaquina had, in fact, been banished by the Cortes on account of her refusal to swear fidelity to the new Constitution; but she had declined to go on the ground that her health did not permit her to travel, and now her position was so strong that there was no longer any question of her going. She had beaten the Cortes, and could aim at higher game: at the King's friends, and even at the King himself. So the extreme measures began; and the first extreme measure was the assassination of the Marquis of Loulé, who was actually knocked on the head in the throne-room. The purpose of the crime was obvious—to intimidate the King by murdering his agents. He might be indifferent to the fate of his agents as long as they were in Portugal and he was

THE ROYAL HOUSE OF PORTUGAL

in Brazil. In Lisbon the thought was bound to occur to him that he himself would probably be murdered next; and then he might offer to abdicate in favour of his son.

A few more murders of the kind, indeed, would probably have induced him to do so; and other murders of the kind were, in fact, feared by him and planned by his enemies. A letter written by Mme. Hyde de Neuville, the wife of the French Ambassador, tells us how the plot was brought to her knowledge, and how she checkmated it.

It was at a ball given at the British Legation in honour of George IV.'s birthday; and the Countess of Subserra came up to Mme. Hyde de Neuville with a frightened face and a terrible story. She had heard, she said, from a sure, confidential source, that an ambush had been arranged, and that her carriage was to be fired into as she was driving home from the dance. What was she to do to escape? Could Mme.—could the Ambassador—suggest anything? "Come home in our carriage instead of your own," was the obvious reply to that; and the risk which it involved for the French Ambassador and his wife was taken cheerfully. The coachman was told to drive slowly, so that there might be no mistake about the French arms on the panels; the assassins saw the arms and respected them. But the Absolutists, nevertheless, broke out into open revolution immediately afterwards; and it is from Hyde Neuville's recently published Memoirs that we get our most graphic account of the events.

PALACE REVOLUTION

The wicked Queen had egged on the impudent Infant; the impudent Infant had egged on the silly soldiers. On the one hand, the Infant had spread reports of a plot to murder the King and, on the strength of those reports, was ordering the arrest of his most devoted adherents; on the other hand, in his capacity as commander-in-chief of the army, he kept the King in the Palace, to all intents and purposes a prisoner, declaring that the country and the dynasty were in danger, and that Dom John was too feeble a fool to save them. The streets were full of soldiers, shouting: "Death to the Freemasons! Long live the Queen! Long live the Infant!" A White Terror appeared imminent, if it had not yet begun; and it seemed to Hyde de Neuville that, as there was no one else to take charge of the situation, the *corps diplomatique* must do so; so he gathered up its members, one by one, and led them to the Palace of Bemposta.

Little persuasion was required to induce them to go; international rivalries were struck dumb by the need for instant action. "Wherever you lead, Mr. Ambassador, I will follow," said the Papal Nuncio, whom Hyde de Neuville describes as "pious but timid." "Let us start at once," cried the representatives of Spain, Russia, and Denmark, in chorus. General Dearborn, of the United States, had his scruples about meddling in the domestic broils of the Portuguese, but allowed these to yield to the necessity of rescuing "a king, the father of a family, and a really respectable old gentleman." Sir Edward Thornton, on behalf of

THE ROYAL HOUSE OF PORTUGAL

Great Britain, said : "There is nothing better to be done. I'm with you"; and he dismissed his hired carriage, and took a seat in the French Ambassador's coach. The Austrian and Dutch Ministers fell into line as the procession was forming.

"It was," Hyde de Neuville writes, "like a thunderbolt for the leaders of the conspiracy to see the whole of Europe passing through the midst of their serried bayonets to bring succour to the royal prisoner. All Lisbon knows how, in the presence of the spectacle, they exchanged silent glances, and turned ghastly pale. From that moment, as they have since confessed, they knew that they were lost. So little had they thought out their plans that they had forgotten all about the diplomatic representatives of the Powers."

But they did not yield at once—they were as little prepared to give way as to resist. Certain orders had been given; certain barriers had to be forced. The carriages were stopped at the Palace gate, and the diplomats had to enter the courtyard on foot. A second attempt was made to stop them at the foot of the grand staircase, where a dusky minion with savage moustaches demanded their tickets of admission. The Infant, he said, had given instructions that no one should be admitted without a ticket. It was necessary to speak to him in a severe tone of voice—to remind him that the Infant was not a sovereign, but a subject, and could give no orders in the King's Palace, and even to conclude with a threat :—

"Remember, my man! A rebellious Infant may

PALACE REVOLUTION

perhaps be pardoned; but his mutinous supporters will infallibly be hanged by the neck till they are dead."

Then there was hesitation, and talk of sending to the Infant for further instructions; but Hyde de Neuville would not be put off. He caught sight of the Viscount de la Villa nova da Rainha, and addressed himself to him:—

"It is you, Sir, who ordinarily usher Ambassadors into His Majesty's presence. Be so good as to walk before us, and announce us now. If these mutineers try to prevent you, tell them in their own language, that their heads will answer for their insult to collective Europe."

He objected; the Ambassadors insisted; he gave way. The party were conducted through three empty ante-chambers to the throne-room, where Dom John was sitting with Marshal Beresford. It is said that he received them with the exclamation: "Thank God, it is you! I thought it was the rebels coming to sentence me to execution." Hyde de Neuville does not tell that story, but he describes Dom John as dazed, bewildered, and terrified. Marshal Beresford tried to answer the questions addressed to him on his behalf; but once more Hyde de Neuville was peremptory. He would be delighted, he said, to converse with Marshal Beresford at any other time, but, at the moment, it was with the King himself that he had business. And then the King spoke timorously whispering his confidence in Hyde de Neuville's ear:—

THE ROYAL HOUSE OF PORTUGAL

"The Queen is here. She came to the Palace an hour after the revolt of the troops. It is she who is egging my son on. What had I better do?"

Hyde de Neuville was ready with his reply:—

"Send for the Infant; and if he comes, as I feel certain that he will, receive him in the presence of the *Corps Diplomatique*."

The plan was adopted, and the impudent Infant came. He made vague promises with a jaunty air; and Dom John, instead of roughly calling him to order, depriving him of his military command, and placing him under arrest, wept hysterically while listening to his protestations, and once more whispered to Hyde de Neuville: "I wish you would speak to him for me." But that Hyde de Neuville would not do; it was one thing to give the King advice, and quite another to usurp his authority. He even stopped the pious Nuncio, who began to lecture the Infant in broken Portuguese; and the upshot of the matter was that Dom John, being still in a state of terror, implored the Ambassadors to stay to dinner, in order that their presence might protect him.

They stayed; and the party must have been a queer one, for most of the other guests were known to belong to the party of the conspirators, and were, in fact, conspiring at table, all through the banquet, from the soup to the dessert. Their great desire was to induce the King to name a new Ministry, the members of which should be selected from among the impudent Infant's friends; but Dom John, reassured by the presence of Ambassadors, had at least backbone enough to withstand that proposition.

"No," he said. "That would not do. The Ambassadors, as you see, have made up their minds to have no relations with any new Ministry, as long as they know that I am not a free agent in nominating it."

So the dinner ended, and the Ambassadors went home, declining Dom John's pressing invitation to spend the night with him, but promising to return, and make sure that he was still safe, at noon on the following day.

It was quite clear to them, when they returned, that he was very far from safe, and that the impudent Infant had no intention of keeping any of his promises. If he released one prisoner in compliance with the demands of the Ambassadors, he made up for that by ordering the arrest of others. A procession of no fewer than forty-seven cart-loads of prisoners, escorted by a squadron of cavalry, destined, it was said, for the penal settlements in Africa, was seen passing through the streets of Lisbon. There was beginning, in short, a real White Terror, such as absolutists love. Anything might happen—especially as the impudent Infant had had the impudence to fire on the mail packet which carried the ambassadorial despatches concerned with his impudent doings; and something serious was sure to happen unless Dom John could be made to recover his nerve.

But how was he to be made to recover it? The

THE ROYAL HOUSE OF PORTUGAL

only practical course was to get him to a place of safety, even if he had to run away for the second time in order to reach it. On board one of the foreign ships lying in the Tagus, he would at least be out of danger; and, being out of danger, he might be persuaded, if not to be energetic, at least to give others a free hand to be energetic on his behalf. With that object in view, they hustled him on to a boat and rowed him out to the *Windsor Castle*.

CHAPTER XIV

Dom Miguel summoned to the *Windsor Castle*—Reproaches and penitence—The Ambassadors assert themselves—Proposal to banish the Queen—Her refusal to go—Dom Miguel sent on his travels—His reception in Paris and Vienna—Proposal to marry him to his niece, Maria da Gloria—Death of Dom John—Metternich's opinion of Dom Miguel—The Duke of Wellington's opinion—Dom Miguel, instead of marrying Maria da Gloria, usurps her throne.

NOT until he was on board the *Windsor Castle* could Dom John give his orders without trembling for his life; but there, braced to his task by British tars, he dismissed the impudent Infant from his command, and summoned him to his presence.

The Infant humbled himself, and obeyed the summons. He too, it seems, had his nerves, his capacity for shame, and his doubts whether he had not gone too far. His father, though a silly old man, was popular; if he had hurt his father, his boon companions might have failed to protect him from the vengeance of the mob. That thought had flashed upon him, and his courage had, temporarily at least, oozed out of the soles of his boots. So he came to apologise in the awe-inspiring state-

THE ROYAL HOUSE OF PORTUGAL

room of a British man-of-war; and he did not apologise by halves, but threw himself, like a prodigal in melodrama, at his father's feet, sobbing convulsively:

"My father, I should have followed you, even if I had to go to the end of the world to find you."

To which speech Dom John, with equally melodramatic propriety, returned no answer, but stalked out of the state-room without a word. His daughters, whose indignation had also left them speechless, followed him; and the impudent Infant was left crying like a baby under the eyes of the British Marines who stood on sentry duty at the state-room door. Not until he had thus done penance for half an hour did Dom John, who had been attending to his own emotions, deign to return and reproach him for having let himself be made the tool of conspirators who would not have hesitated to deprive him of his life as well as his throne. Whereupon there followed this brief dialogue:—

"My father," sobbed the Infant, "if they had done anything so wicked, I would have plunged a dagger into my own heart."
"My son," replied Dom John, "you can withdraw. My further orders shall be communicated to you at the proper time and in the proper way."

So magically bracing was the atmosphere of H.M.S. *Windsor Castle*. It was practically by that change of air that the attempt at revolution was quelled; and after that remarkable interview everything went, as it were, on wheels.

DOM MIGUEL

The impudent Infant could no longer pose as a great revolutionary leader after the marines had seen him sobbing at his father's feet; and, as there was nothing at the back of the revolution except his impudence, it ceased as suddenly as it had broken out. The prison doors were opened, and the prisoners were released. The command was issued that no one should any longer obey the Infant's orders; and the Infant—so recently commander-in-chief—uttered no word of protest. The public were notified that the Infant had received permission to travel for the benefit of his health; and the Infant set out obediently for Paris. The King came ashore, and gave a dinner-party. There were tears and cheers—congratulations and illuminations; and then came the problem which we may speak of as that of clearing up the mess.

It is characteristic of Dom John that, instead of clearing it up himself, he asked the Ambassadors to clear it up for him; and it is characteristic of the state of Portugal at the time that his Ministers deemed that a reasonable course. There can, indeed, have been few more remarkable conferences in modern history than that at which the King of Portugal asked the diplomatic representatives of France, England, Spain, and Russia what they thought he had better do with the Queen; and those counsellors, one after the other, exhorted Dom John and those about him to try to quit themselves like men.

"Like Richelieu," said one.
"Like Pitt," said another.

"Like Pombal," said a third, feeling that perhaps, after all, a Portuguese precedent would make the most potent appeal to the pride of Portuguese statesmen.

But that was a hopeless exhortation, though the Ministers were, in fact, braced to the point of proposing the banishment of the Queen who, on her part, was equally determined not to be banished. The King's letter, requiring her to leave the country, was handed to her by the Archbishop, and her brother, Ferdinand of Spain, was inclined to advise her to do as she was told. Madeira was suggested as a suitable place of residence—she was promised that she should be made quite comfortable there; but she replied emphatically that she intended to stay where she was, in her Palace at Queluz.

"I reply," she wrote, "first that I am very ill, as everybody knows, and that, at this moment, I am suffering from an attack of rheumatism, with great pains and fever, which has deprived me of the use of my legs, and I am still but little better, and consequently not in a condition to undertake a journey. Secondly, I insist upon being tried judicially, as the laws direct that no one can be punished without being heard. . . . Would that I were as pure before God as I am before the King!"

Etc.; and she kept up the pretence of illness before Hyde de Neuville, whom she invited to visit her, receiving him stretched on a couch, in the midst of pillows and cushions, and calling him to witness that she was much too ill to be moved. He saw through the comedy, which was no doubt transparent, and advised her to make an effort; but her only answer to that was to tell him—or rather to tell her lady-in-waiting in his presence—that "he was really very handsome, and it was a pity he had got mixed up in a bad set." Whereat he bowed, and retired, feeling that, after all, the business was the King's, not his; and the King refrained from violence. It sufficed to publish the order of banishment and hold the Queen up to opprobrium as a cantankerous woman who insisted upon staying where she was not wanted. He probably felt that she was powerless for evil now that Dom Miguel was out of the way.

And Dom Miguel, meanwhile, was enjoying himself in Paris, where much was made of him: how much we are enabled to gather from one of Villèle's letters to Hyde de Neuville:—

"We have received the Infant Dom Miguel very well," Villèle wrote, "and we are treating him very well. To-morrow he is to dine with me. I have asked all the members of the Cabinet, the Presidents of the two Chambers, and the principal functionaries of the Court to meet him; and we shall drink to His Most Faithful Majesty's good health."

A striking compliment truly to an obnoxious youth who had tried to kick his father off the throne for granting the country a Constitution, and to dispatch the constitutionalists themselves to penal servitude! It doubtless persuaded the Infant that, as Kings were above the law, so Princes were above morality, sure of being treated as superior beings, however badly they behaved; and the impression must have been confirmed when he went on to Vienna and found himself regarded as an eligible *parti* for a Princess in whom Metternich was interested. It is not surprising, in the circumstances, that he continued to cherish the ambitions which he had sworn to abandon; and it is said that the fear of his returning to Portugal, to pursue them, frightened his father into his grave. In any case, Dom John wrote many letters, imploring the Austrian police to keep his terrible son under careful observation.

And yet, even to his relatives, he was not so terrible that they could not entertain the idea of a friendly family arrangement. He was at least a Braganza; and the family pride of the Braganzas was like that of the Habsburgs. If a Braganza fell from grace, he was at least a fallen angel, and could not conceivably fall so far as to cover the distance which separated the Braganzas from the common people. So why not kiss and be friends? Why not patch up the family quarrel by means of a consanguineous marriage? That was the next question to be raised. That Dom Miguel would make a bad husband was likely enough; and it was still more likely that he would make a bad King. Still, he was a Braganza—and the interests of the House of Braganza were far more important than the interests of the Kingdom of Portugal—and therefore——

The legitimate heir, of course, was Dom Pedro, now Emperor of Brazil—a colony whose inde-

MARIA DA GLORIA

pendence Portugal had, at last, consented to recognise; but Portugal had as little desire to be ruled by the Emperor of Brazil as Brazil had to be ruled by the King of Portugal. Dom Pedro, it was tolerably clear, might sit on whichever of the two thrones he preferred, but would lose his balance if he tried to sit on both of them at once. He would have to choose between them, and there was little doubt that he would choose Brazil. In that case, of course, his eldest son would also stay in Brazil as heir-apparent. But Dom Pedro also had a daughter—Maria da Gloria. Suppose he abdicated the throne of Portugal in Maria da Gloria's favour—suppose they married Maria da Gloria to Dom Miguel: then, it was thought, the peace would be made, and all would end happily.

Dom Miguel, it will be observed, was Maria da Gloria's uncle. The projected union, that is to say, was one from which ordinary human nature instinctively revolts; and it transgressed the list of forbidden degrees drawn up by the Church to which both the proposed bride and the proposed bridegroom belonged. But those considerations did not matter. It seemed reasonable to assume that an Infant who had come within an ace of parricide would be able to surmount any objections which he might entertain to incest, and that the Pope, when consulted, would approve of his doing so. The assumption that the visible Head of the Church has too little faith in its laws, even when these coincide with the accepted precepts of morality, to insist upon them if they conflict with the con-

THE ROYAL HOUSE OF PORTUGAL

venience of his influential friends, has always been common in royal circles in Catholic countries; and Catholics defend it on the ground, so far as one can make out, that just as Kings are above human laws, so Popes are above divine laws, and incest ceases to be incestuous if they sanction it.

That, at all events, was the assumption of Dom John, Dom Miguel, and Dom Pedro; and it would doubtless also have been the assumption of Doña Maria da Gloria if she had been old enough to give the matter a thought. After all, Dom John's own father and mother had been nephew and aunt; and it may well have seemed to him, and the other members of his family, that even if a Prince of the House of Braganza wanted to marry his grandmother, it would only be necessary to lay the Pope under a pecuniary obligation in order to procure his acquiescence.

But the scheme fell through: not because the Pope refused to be complacent, but because his complacency was not put to the test, as we shall see when we return from comment to narrative; the events which immediately concern us being these:—

1. Dom John died in March, 1826—his daughter Maria Isabel being then made Regent.
2. Dom Pedro, who succeeded Dom John, abdicated the throne of Portugal, in May, 1826, in favour of his daughter, Maria da Gloria, aged seven, after first granting Portugal another Constitution.
3. Maria Isabel ignored the grant of a Constitution until General Saldanha, then Governor of

Queen Maria Gloria.

DOM MIGUEL

Oporto, announced his intention of marching on Lisbon unless it were promptly sworn to.

4. Rebellions organised by the Absolutist party were promptly put down by Saldanha.

5. Spain, alone among the Powers, refused to recognise the Constitution, but was warned by Canning that any attempt to interfere with it would bring England into the field on the side of her old ally.

6. Dom Pedro appointed Dom Miguel Regent, on the understanding that he should marry Maria da Gloria as soon as she was of age—the Pope's approval of the incestuous union being regarded as a matter of course—and should govern "conformably with the Constitution."

7. Dom Miguel swore the necessary oath, and left for Lisbon, in December, 1827, in order to take up his duties.

And now we may pause to take note of the lofty hypocrisy of high politics, and the solemn way in which illustrious statesmen credit princes with noble qualities, when it suits their purpose to do so, without reference to the facts.

The facts have already shown us what manner of youth the impudent Infant was. We have seen him bullying his father, and practically frightening the poor old man into his grave. We have seen him prepared to commit parricide if he could not deprive the Portuguese people of their liberties in any other way. We have seen him breaking promises which he had made in the presence of the

THE ROYAL HOUSE OF PORTUGAL

entire *Corps Diplomatique*. We have seen him losing nerve, and breaking down, and crying like a baby in the presence of the Royal Marines. And now for the testimonials.

Metternich wrote, in a circular letter addressed to the Austrian Envoys at the various Courts:—

"A young Prince who, by the precious qualities of his heart and mind, has acquired the strongest possible claims on the friendship of our august sovereign."

And also:—

"I consider it no less than a duty to do this young Prince the justice of saying that his ideas are as correct as they are noble and sagacious."

And the Portuguese Ambassador at Vienna wrote:—

"The leave-taking between H.S.H. the Infant and H.I.M. the Emperor was, on the part of both, painful in the extreme; this monarch equally with Her Majesty the Empress having regarded and treated His Highness as if he were their son. Their Majesties, as well as the Archdukes and Archduchesses, testified their sincere grief and regret at the departure; and I can assure Your Excellency that the same feeling prevails in the entire Court, as well as among the people, by whom His Highness is much loved, he having, during his three years' residence here, conducted himself with such propriety, dignity, affability, politeness, and kindness that he became the admiration of the Court, and obtained the respect, love, and esteem of all. I, more than anyone, by the confidence with

DOM MIGUEL

which His Highness was pleased to honour me, was placed in a position to observe closely his high and noble character."

The writers of those testimonials could hardly have said more if they had been praising Marcus Aurelius, or Henry of Navarre, or Alexander I. of Russia. It is therefore piquant to set side by side with the testimonials a certain passage in the Greville *Memoirs* which gives us the unprejudiced opinion of the Duke of Wellington:—

"Talking of Miguel, the Duke related that he was at Strathfieldsaye with Palmella, where, in the library, they were settling the oath that Miguel should take. Miguel would pay no attention, and instead of going into the business and saying what oath he would consent to take (the question was whether he should swear fidelity to Pedro or to Maria) he sat flirting with the Princess Thérèse Esterhazy. The Duke said to Palmella, 'This will never do; he must settle the terms of the oath, and if he is so careless in an affair of such moment, he will never do his duty.' Palmella said, 'Oh, leave him to us; we will manage him.'"

Here we have, of course, the voice of tittle-tattle passing its sly comments on the utterances of history; and it is a commonplace with critics with a certain habit of mind that tittle-tattle, being devoid of authority, is unworthy of the serious attention of the historian. A mere Diary, a mere *chronique scandaleuse*—what is that to set beside documentary evidence emanating from such a pen as Metternich's? For Metternich really knew, and wrote with a sense of responsibility; whereas Charles Greville, that inveterate gossip with the evil tongue —a mere reporter of anecdote——

And yet there are cases in which the casual and malicious innuendos of tittle-tattle do, after all, inspire more confidences than the deliberate statements of the well-informed; and perhaps the case of the character of the impudent Infant is one of them. The facts to which we are coming will help us to decide.

CHAPTER XV

Dom Miguel burns the Charter which he has sworn to observe—Doubts as to his parentage—Anecdotes illustrative of his character—Victor Hugo's hopes for him—That he would be hanged upside down—Dom Miguel's reign of terror—Anecdote illustrative of the state of the prisons—Dom Pedro's decision to come to his daughter's help—The rally in the Azores and the swoop on Oporto.

DOM MIGUEL had not been back in Portugal very long before the constitutional charter to which he had sworn fidelity in London was burnt, with his full approval, in a public square; and he was equally unscrupulous towards his affianced bride. It can hardly have been scruples of conscience which decided him not to marry her; for these, if he had entertained them, would have prevented the betrothal as well as the wedding. What he really objected to was the humble position which would be his as merely the husband of the Queen; so he decided to break off his engagement and usurp the throne. Before considering how he did it, we may pause once again to see what manner of man he was, and how his contemporaries regarded him. And that at the risk of being charged with retailing scandalous reports.

THE ROYAL HOUSE OF PORTUGAL

It has been stated already that he was far more his mother's than his putative father's son; and it must be added that the question whether his putative father was his real father was raised at the time of his birth. It has been stated in print—in a work entitled *Dom Miguel: Ses aventures scandaleuses, ses crimes, et son usurpations. Par un Portugais de distinction*—that he was the offspring of Queen Carlota Joaquina's *amours* with the gardener at Cintra, where "it was her custom, every evening, to quit the society of her ladies and retire to her bedroom with her bucolic lover."

The rumour cannot very well be checked; but Dom Miguel's character and behaviour assuredly warrant the most serious historian in calling attention to it. Dom Miguel inherited none of Dom John's qualities: neither his virtues nor his flabbiness. He had not even—in his youth, at all events —the outward semblance of a gentleman. His manners, no less than his morals, were those of a child of the gutter: such manners, in short, as might have been expected from the issue of a low-born favourite, brought up as a spoiled child.

Portuguese etiquette seems to have required that all the royal Infants should be brought up as spoiled children. There was no discipline for them—none whatever. It was prescribed that their tutors, as soon as they were old enough to have tutors, must kneel and kiss their hands whenever they entered their presence, and that every order must be given in the form of a humble entreaty. That being so, it is not surprising to hear that Dom Miguel reached

DOM MIGUEL

the age of nineteen without learning to read or write—that he spelt his own name incorrectly when he subscribed the Constitution—and that, when he began to choose his own companions, his preference fell upon a groom. Dom John, being a flabby man, had nothing effective to say in the matter; and the things which Dom Miguel is alleged to have done, alike in Brazil and in Portugal, make a truly appalling list of effronteries and horrors.

They will be most impressive if set forth in the form of a catalogue. Thus:—

1. Dom Miguel, desiring to practise marksmanship, shot all the ducks belonging to an aged widow who lived by keeping ducks, and refused to compensate her for her loss.
2. Dom Miguel drove a bull into one of the Palace courtyards, at a time when a number of courtiers were assembled there, with the result that several people were injured, and one lady died of fright.
3. Dom Miguel was seen walking in the streets of Rio de Janeiro with notorious prostitutes of the lowest class, and kissing them good-bye in public places.
4. Dom Miguel made his barber a baron, to the great disgust of the existing aristocracy, as a reward for services rendered in the capacity of quack doctor, at a time when he was suffering from a malady due to his debauched way of life.
5. One of Dom Miguel's favourite recreations was to "make hay" in the houses of private citizens

THE ROYAL HOUSE OF PORTUGAL

—bursting in upon them with a band of boon companions, smashing up their furniture and crockery, and then requiring them, under penalty of instant death, to kneel and do him homage.

6. Another of Dom Miguel's favourite recreations was to gallop about the streets of Lisbon, knocking off the hats of all the pedestrians with his stick.

7. A third of Dom Miguel's favourite recreations was to toss sucking-pigs into the air and catch them on the point of his sword.

8. It was a further favourite recreation of Dom Miguel to require all wayfarers to get out of their carriages and kneel on the ground while he passed them in the street: a recreation which was only abandoned when the American Minister, whom he thus tried to humiliate, drew a pistol and threatened to blow off the head of anyone, whether Prince or commoner, who molested him.

9. Dom Miguel liked to pluck fowls alive, in order to watch their agony.

10. While he was lodging in Paris, Dom Miguel killed his landlady's Angora cat, and then summoned her to his presence, and told her to jug it for her dinner.

11. In Vienna, by way of celebrating his betrothal to Maria da Gloria, Dom Miguel executed a naked dance, together with a number of naked companions of both sexes, round a blazing dish of snapdragon.

12. Dom Miguel sent, one day, for a street singer, whose voice had pleased him, made her go through her repertory in the presence of the Court, and then —still in the presence of the Court—gave her his

DOM MIGUEL

arm and ostentatiously conducted her to his bed-chamber.

13. At the time when he was boy commander-in-chief of the Portuguese army, Dom Miguel sent for a septuagenarian lieutenant-general who had expressed approval of the Constitution which Dom Miguel had himself sworn to observe, and kicked him round the room as an intimation that such sentiments were out of date.

14. At the time of his abortive revolution against his father, he not only caused Baron de Renduffe, the lieutenant-general of police, to be arrested, but had him turned into the dog-kennels, and there, with his own hands, pelted him with mud.

Those are the charges preferred by Dom Miguel's enemies; and it is, of course, at this time of day, no more possible to guarantee their exactitude than it is possible to warrant the literal accuracy of all the anecdotes contained in Pepys's *Diary* or Saint-Simon's *Memoirs*. But the historian can no more ignore the indictment than he can ignore Saint-Simon and Pepys. The mere fact that such stories were told in such profusion about Dom Miguel is at least an indication that Dom Miguel was the sort of man about whom such stories could be told with some degree of plausibility: a point of which the force will be realised by anyone who tries to picture himself building such an edifice of odious legend around, let us say, the present King of Italy or the present German Emperor. The bitterest enemies of those sovereigns would obviously feel that that line of attack would be unprofitable because it would be unconvincing.

Dom Miguel's enemies, as obviously, felt nothing of the kind. They saw him—and they knew that people in general saw him—as an unlicked cub, with the cruel instincts of a bully: a sort of Portuguese Flashman, with more than Flashman's power, and therefore sure of the support of toadies. Assuredly we may trust their denunciations for colour and atmosphere, if not for detail, far more confidently than we can trust Metternich's testimonial; and we may further feel—as they would certainly have felt—that, even if there be exaggeration or error in some of the particulars, the calumny does not matter because the picture is still artistically faithful. The proved facts, as we shall see, are so bad that the unproved gossip adds nothing to them except a picturesque garment. When we know that a man was a perjurer and a murderer, it is impossible to clear his reputation by calling for better evidence of the statement that he smashed a citizen's crockery or shot a widow's ducks.

He had, of course, if not friends, at least allies: men whose political ideal it really was to turn an unlicked cub into an absolute king, and who clothed that aim with magniloquent phrases. The aristocracy, the clergy, and the beggars—those, roughly speaking, were the groups which joined forces in support of his claims; the strength of the constitutional party residing mainly in the middle-classes. The methods adopted—the methods of the nobles and the clergy as well as of the usurper himself—

DOM MIGUEL

combined low cunning with unmeasured brutality. Before we come to the details, we may quote a cursory view of the Pretender's personality from a speech delivered in our own House of Commons at the time when there was some question of his "recognition":—

"It was astonishing" (said the speaker) "that so young a man could have accomplished so much wickedness in so short a time; for, at the early age of six-and-twenty, this man, this Dom Miguel, had perpetrated every crime, and displayed every vice which historical truth or historical fiction had attributed to the most sanguinary monsters that ever waded through the blood of innocent people in the pursuit of their ambitious objects. It was to be hoped that he would finish a life of infamy by a death of violence."

That is what we may call the Palmerstonian view of Dom Miguel; and we may supplement it with Victor Hugo's eager anticipation of a good time coming when Dom Miguel's subjects would hang him, upside-down:—

> Quand Lisbonne, jadis belle et toujours en fête,
> Pend au gibet les pieds de Miguel sur sa tête.

These character-sketches—confirming, as they do, all that is essential in the fourteen counts of the pamphleteer's indictment—are quite as respectable in their origin as Metternich's testimonial; and they fit in better with the facts which we discover when we examine Dom Miguel's public acts. We may as well set his proceedings forth in a second numbered catalogue, so that readers may judge whether they

THE ROYAL HOUSE OF PORTUGAL

are such as to make the miscellaneous charges of the pamphleteer incredible:—

1. Dom Miguel arranged, by means of military terrorism, to receive petitions from Municipal Chambers begging him to usurp his niece's throne.

2. Dom Miguel ordered the election of a new Cortes which should offer him the throne, issuing instructions that "the votes of those electors who, by their known sentiments and political opinions, had declared themselves enemies of the true principles of legitimacy and followers of the new institutions, should be considered factious, and not be allowed to be enrolled": a long-winded way of saying that no one who was not likely to vote for him should be permitted to vote at all.

3. Having accepted the crown from the Cortes thus constituted, Dom Miguel obtained what was called a "national vote" in support of his accession: a vote in which respectable people took no part, but which received the adherence of all the inmates of all the houses of ill-fame in Lisbon.

4. As soon as there was any sign of resistance of these proceedings, or even of resentment at them, Dom Miguel inaugurated a Reign of Terror.

The Reign of Terror was also a reign of anarchy: how anarchical may be shown by a story of an atrocity committed by turbulent students of the University of Coimbra. A gang of these ill-conditioned youths, taking a leaf out of the book of their royal master, waylaid a number of their professors in a wood, court-martialled them on a charge of exacting too high a standard of proficiency in examinations, sentenced them to be shot—and actually shot them. It is not, of course, a crime for which Dom Miguel was directly responsible—only a crime due to the state of social order which prevailed during, and in consequence of, his savage rule; but the list of crimes for which he can be held personally responsible is quite as black and longer.

Records were not carefully kept, so that only approximate statistics can be given; but approximate statistics will suffice. Ringleaders, or persons regarded as such, were hanged or garrotted or shot— colonels, captains, judges, and other functionaries among the number. If the lives of any were spared, they were transported to the penal settlements— some of them being publicly flogged before they started. Not hundreds, but thousands, of prominent men fled from the country, threatened with similar treatment if they stayed in it. Of those who did remain it is said that 40,000 were imprisoned, and 50,000 had their property confiscated.

Moreover, the state of the prisons then, as at a later date, was scandalous. "The cells are full," an Oporto gaoler is said to have reported to the Governor—the notorious Telles Jordâo. "Are they full to the ceiling?" he asked. "No, not quite that," was the reply. "Then how dare you tell me that they are full? Put more men into them."

It is no wonder, in the circumstances, that Dom Miguel had a difficulty in obtaining "recognition" from the more civilised Courts: the wonder is rather that he so nearly got it. It was only, in fact, his

THE ROYAL HOUSE OF PORTUGAL

refusal to grant an amnesty which blocked the way. At all events, that was the only condition imposed by the Duke of Wellington, who had now succeeded Canning as Prime Minister of England; though the Duke added the wish that Dom Miguel would make haste and marry his niece and settle down. One can imagine the Duke's indignant horror if it had been proposed that King William should, for political reasons, marry his niece, the little girl who was presently to succeed him as Queen Victoria; but he probably held that incestuous unions, though grossly improper for Britons, were all right for foreigners. He certainly had the kind of mind which is capable of arguing in that way.

Even to please the Duke of Wellington, however, Dom Miguel would neither commit incest nor forgive his enemies. The motive for the two refusals was, no doubt, the same—a determination to do what he chose, and not what he was told to do; but that does not and did not matter. A more important fact was that Dom Miguel, in spite of his Reign of Terror, failed to keep order, or to protect foreigners from outrage; so that foreign fleets, both French and English, had to enter the Tagus and demand satisfaction at the cannon's mouth. Recognition consequently hung fire; and while it was hanging fire, the voice of Dom Pedro, Emperor of Brazil, made itself heard across the sea.

What was that? he asked. Dom Miguel had refused to marry his niece? Dom Miguel had torn

ARRIVAL OF DOM PEDRO

up his Charter—the Charter which he, the rightful heir to the throne of Portugal, had drafted? Dom Miguel had usurped the throne? It could not be; and if it had been, why then, it must cease to be. The tree of liberty should take root and grow in Portugal, however copious the flow of blood required to water it. He would shed his own blood for it, if necessary—for it and his little daughter's rights. Let the constitutionalists hold out how and where they could; he would himself come to Portugal and help them.

The Constitutionalists, in fact, beaten in Portugal, were holding out in the Azores; and so it was arranged that the Azores should be the rallying-point of the great expedition. Dom Pedro repaired thither by a circuitous route, taking London by the way. In London he borrowed money, bought and fitted ships, and recruited soldiers and sailors of fortune in a little eating-house in Threadneedle Street. Captain Sartorius, Captain Napier, Captain Hodges, Captain Shaw, Sir J. M. Doyle, Mr. Bollaert, the mining engineer—most of whom have written their recollections of their experiences—were the most notable of his English allies. He had French and Belgian allies, too; and he assembled them all in the Azores, together with the Portuguese troops which had remained faithful to him—an army, all told, of about 7,500 men—and prepared to make his swoop.

He swooped upon Oporto, which he carried by a *coup-de-main*; and then the Miguelites closed round him and besieged him there.

CHAPTER XVI

Dom Pedro's "cause"—Constitutional government and consanguineous marriage—English view of the rivals—The siege of Oporto by Dom Miguel—Dom Pedro's neglect to pay his troops—Precarious position of Dom Pedro—Saldanha to the rescue—Lisbon seized and defended against Dom Miguel—Final triumph of Dom Pedro—His early death.

Dom Pedro's "cause" comprised two causes rolled into one: consanguineous marriage and constitutional government.

One mentions the ideals in that order deliberately, because that seems to have been the order of their importance in Dom Pedro's eyes. Or such, at all events, was the popular interpretation of his heart and mind when his followers, seeing him hard pressed, speculated as to the terms of peace which he would accept. Whatever points he might waive, he would certainly, they agreed, insist that the uncle should fulfil his promise of marriage to the niece. The Constitution might be sacrificed under the stress of *force majeure*; but the consanguineous union was a *sine quâ non*. And that though Dom Pedro was, for a Braganza, emancipated—a freemason, and an anti-clerical!

That estimate of his character may be found in

SIEGE OF OPORTO

the writings of more than one of his English allies, from whom we may also derive an account of the beginning of his anti-clerical campaign in the Azores. Among other measures, he closed convents there; and there are indications in the narratives that it was high time that those convents were closed. The nuns, we are informed by Colonel Hodges, not only entertained the officers of the constitutional host at garden-parties, enlivened by the merry regimental bands, but invited them, without being pressed, to step upstairs and visit them in their cells. It is added that, when the nunnery doors were opened, the young and beautiful nuns gladly quitted their retreats for positions of greater freedom, and that the old and ugly nuns who elected to remain were loud in their complaints of the impiety of confessors who no longer troubled to visit the nunnery.

In Portugal, too, Dom Pedro continued to be the enemy, if not of all the priests, at least of all the "religious." But not without reason, for the religious were also the unscrupulous. They had spread the report that the constitutional army was a band of brigands who would rob the peasants of all that they possessed and return to the Islands with the booty. In the towns, too, they served Dom Miguel as spies; while, in the country, they potted at Dom Pedro's reconnoitring-parties in the character of sharp-shooters. They were, in short, disciples of Fra Diavolo, without that friar's excuse of patriotism; and it is not surprising that Dom Pedro dealt with them severely.

THE ROYAL HOUSE OF PORTUGAL

What manner of man he was, apart from his anti-clericalism, one has a certain difficulty in making out. Jealousies were rampant in his army; and men's estimate of him seems to have varied with his own estimate of the value of their several services. Some found his manners of an affable simplicity, and his greetings more cordial than those of kings in general; others resented his apparent disdain for the services of the foreign allies, without whose help he probably would never have taken Oporto, and certainly would never have held it. What people thought of him in England may be judged from a note in the Greville Memoirs: " Nobody joins them, and it seems pretty clear that, one *coquin* for another, the Portuguese think they may as well have Miguel."

People in England, however, derived most of their information from dissatisfied officers who had quitted Dom Pedro's service—he was, in truth, as different from Dom Miguel as chalk from cheese. For one thing, he cared so little for pomp that he fell asleep during gala performances at the Opera —with the result that the curtain was respectfully lowered and the house respectfully emptied in the middle of the piece. A great point in his favour was that he was a sticker who took hardship as it came. Even when the garrison of Oporto was reduced to its last barrel of powder, and people suggested that he might surrender the Constitution if only he could get his daughter married to her uncle, he refused to listen to talk about surrender.

As for the siege itself, it has no place in any list

SIEGE OF OPORTO

of the great sieges of history; and any attempt to record its operations would be tedious and bewildering. There were the usual horrors—shells bursting in the houses and killing and mutilating the non-combatants—an epidemic of cholera, made more hideous by the fact that the parrots (and Oporto was full of parrots until they were killed for food) took to imitating the shrieks and groans of the dying. There were the usual pleasantries between the outposts which sometimes bartered tobacco for food, and sometimes exchanged repartees.

"Bah!" shouted the Miguelites. "Your King has so small a kingdom that he can see it all at once when he sits on his throne."

"Bah!" shouted back the Pedroites. "Your King has so large a kingdom that, though he has been marching for nine months, he hasn't yet got inside his capital."

There were also the usual atrocities—usual, at all events, in the civil wars of the Peninsula. One hears of prisoners being bayonetted, hanged, burnt alive, and tortured to death in various ways; one hears that the prisoners got specially short shrifts, and specially painful deaths, when they fell into the hands of the Miguelite monks. It is impossible, however, to check the truth of more than a few of these stories, and equally impossible to get any exact information about the casualties. "No account," Badcock writes, "was kept, and unless some person of distinction was killed, nothing was said."

At the same time, both jealousy and mutiny were

rife among both commanding officers and soldiers. The Portuguese said that their English allies were always drunk; the English retorted that the Portuguese were too fond of taking up sheltered positions in the rear. A grievance, however, shared by the soldiers of all nations was the irregularity with which they received their pay. An English contingent marched on one occasion to the Palace, to demand something on account from Dom Pedro in person. On another occasion, Admiral Sartorius himself made a similar request, threatening to withdraw his forces if it were not granted. Dom Pedro sent Sir J. M. Doyle to arrest him; but the Admiral ordered the messenger below, amid the approving grins of the sailors, and announced his intention of keeping him locked up in a cabin until the money was forthcoming. Dom Pedro paid; but he soon afterwards dismissed Sartorius, and gave his post to Captain Napier, who afterwards, as Admiral Napier, commanded the Baltic Fleet in the Crimean war.

Sartorius, however, had, at any rate, achieved some successes; whereas on land the operations were conducted with gross incompetence until the sudden arrival of Saldanha, some six months after the commencement of the siege. The French General Solignac was then in command; and his appointment had been signalised by the publication in the Oporto *Cronica* of a eulogistic biography in which it was set forth that as a misunderstanding with Napoleon had prevented his services in the French army from being rewarded by any higher

SIEGE OF OPORTO

post than that of General of Division, he had retired in dudgeon to his ancestral estate in order to devote himself to the cultivation of potatoes. It was an honourable, though not a martial, pursuit; but the idea tickled the soldiers' sense of humour. Instead of recalling the glorious example of Cincinnatus, they nicknamed Solignac "General Potatoes"; and they gave him the alternative nickname of "Doña Anna"—meaning pretty much what we should mean if we called a General Mary Anne or Betsy Jane.

Solignac was, in fact, a fussy, incompetent warrior, whereas Saldanha was a thoroughly practical fire-eater. Jealousies—one cannot stop to go into all the reasons for all the Portuguese jealousies—had prevented him from being called in at first; but when the Miguelist nut proved too hard for Solignac to crack, he was sent for. He came at once, and made no secret of his opinion of Solignac's capacity. "Well! What do you think?" Dom Pedro asked him, after his first tour of inspection of the defences. "What I think," replied Saldanha, "is that, if I were outside with one of my old regiments, we should be through these lines in next to no time"; and he pointed out what needed to be done in order to make the place secure.

Solignac agreed, and it was done; but, after that, Solignac ceased to count. Out-voted at a Council of War, he offered his resignation in a huff; and it was accepted in a hurry. Then Saldanha became Chief of Dom Pedro's staff—in effect, that is to say, commander-in-chief; and the Miguelite fortunes

THE ROYAL HOUSE OF PORTUGAL

gradually declined. Their leader was Marshal Bourmont—the Marshal who had deserted Napoleon on the eve of Waterloo, and had afterwards espoused the cause of the Duchesse de Berry in La Vendée. With him were various ferocious Vendeans with famous names—a Cathelineau, and a Larochejacquelain, for instance; but their gallantry, though undeniable, was ineffective. Saldanha not only held out at Oporto, but spared a force to operate elsewhere. Napier, having first taken security for the payment of his men, swept the Miguelite fleet from the seas; and the Duke of Terceira, landed with a small army in the Algarves, brushed the Miguelites aside, and established himself in Lisbon. Bourmont came down from Oporto and tried to take Lisbon; but was held up at Torres Vedras, just as, years before, Massena had been held up by Wellington.

Even that was not the end; but the rest is only the story of the gradual wearing down of the Miguelites by attrition. Baffled at Lisbon and Oporto, Dom Miguel transferred his headquarters to Santarem; and when Bourmont tired of him, and left him, he gave the command of his army to Macdonell. Hunted out of Santarem in such a hurry that he left the royal dinner service behind him, he took refuge in Evora; and there, at last, he surrendered, with sixteen thousand men, and signed an undertaking that he would "never directly or indirectly interfere in the political affairs of Portugal and its dominions." He was promised a pension of £15,000; but he was also warned that, if he ever

FALL OF DOM MIGUEL

again crossed the Portuguese frontier, he would be brought before a court martial, and shot as soon as his identity had been established.

So he went—to Rome, where the Pope promptly recognised him as the lawful sovereign of Portugal[1]: a circumstance which need not affect our opinion of Dom Miguel one way or the other, but may, perhaps, influence our opinion of the Pope. For the facts appear to justify one in saying this: that the barbarities of Dom Miguel's Reign of Terror—of which the Pope could not conceivably have been ignorant—seemed to the visible Head of the Church a mere straw in the scales when weighed against the probability that Dom Miguel would, like a good clerical, take money away from laymen and give it to clergymen.

Such, in outline, is the story of the Civil War in which an army at first consisting of no more than 15,000 men overcame an army which, at first, numbered no less than 80,000. It sounds like a great feat of arms, and, no doubt, some great feats of arms were performed in the course of the conflict. Whether Dom Pedro, in virtue of his great triumph, is entitled to be classed with great men is another

---

[1] His son, the Duke of Braganza, who lives in Vienna, still claims the throne; but his grandson, Prince Miguel of Braganza, waived all his royal rights on the occasion of his marriage to Miss Anita Stewart, daughter of the widow of James Henry Smith, the Chicago millionaire, by her first husband, William Rhinelander Stewart, of New York. Prince Miguel undertook, on that occasion, never to assume or claim any title which his wife could not share with him; and it was announced that he and she desired to be known as Duke and Duchess of Viseau.

question, and one which it would probably be necessary to answer in the negative if any high standard of genius were to be applied. Some of the qualities of greatness—strong nerves and untiring tenacity—he did, no doubt, display; but one's final impression of him does not go beyond that of a well-meaning man, conscientiously doing his best. There were greater men about him; and he seems to stand among them as an amateur among professionals, or a clever boy among adults.

He chiefly interests one, however, as a Braganza of a new type. His predecessors had, in the main, been fools, but proud fools, convinced of the innate superiority of royal people to other people, but dominated by clerical superstitions. Dom Pedro descended from the Olympian heights on which they had dwelt, and rubbed shoulders cordially with what they would have regarded as the vulgar herd. He took men's hands and shook them, instead of offering his own hand to be kissed; from time to time, he himself kissed an officer or a Minister on the cheek. Moreover, he was an amateur of the arts, even in the midst of clash of arms—fond of playing the piano, and of composing patriotic songs for the use of soldiers and constitutionalists: a thing which one does not readily picture Napoleon, or Wellington, or even Saldanha, doing. It was a simultaneous advance towards simplicity, affability, and culture, which almost marks an epoch.

Very possibly the atmosphere which he escaped from was an atmosphere which he needed; very possibly he would have inspired hero-worshippers to a more exalted enthusiasm if he had contented himself with directing the constitutional movement from behind a mysterious cloud of glory, and shown less anxiety to set his loyal supporters at their ease. His personality might have been less conspicuously overshadowed by those of his subordinates, and might have encouraged them to think, as Louis XVIII. expected his subordinates to think, that, when they had done all, they had done nothing; for the best chance of mediocrity in a high station is always to seek a safe cover behind the rigid prescriptions of etiquette.

But that was not Dom Pedro's way. He was too artless; and precisely because he was so artless, the people who had their doubts about him were able, or thought that they were able, to put those doubts to the test. The result is that his contemporaries' eulogies of him have the air, sometimes of apology, and sometimes of patronage. Still, though we must not over-rate him, we must be equally careful not to under-rate him, and must give him full credit alike for his originality and for his fixed ideas. He often deplored the fact that he was a self-educated Prince; but that was not altogether disadvantageous, for it meant that he had thought things out for himself on anti-clerical and democratic lines. His Constitution may not have been all that a Constitution ought to be; but his enthusiasm for it reminds one of the enthusiasm of an inventor for his patents.

It is, indeed, hardly an exaggeration to say that

THE ROYAL HOUSE OF PORTUGAL

he gave his life for his Constitution. He might easily have made himself comfortable while others fought for him; the inglorious example of his father, John the Runaway, might easily have encouraged him to do so. It seemed better to him, however, to share the hardships of his armies; and he did not spare himself even when he found his health suffering. Throughout the later period of the war he was spitting blood; but he was too busy to go to bed and be nursed. He simply spat and went on with his work; and though he lived to finish it, he did not live much longer. At one and the same time, he was wasted with consumption and bloated with dropsy; so that the end was obviously near. The doctor's advice to him to take the waters at some health resort was only a counsel of despair. He took them, and got worse, and died in his thirty-seventh year.

In Portugal he was succeeded by Maria da Gloria, who was still a little girl; in Brazil his throne had for some years been occupied by his son, Dom Pedro II., who was still a little boy. Our theme requires us to follow the fortunes of both of them; and we will take the career of Dom Pedro first.

CHAPTER XVII

Dom Pedro II. Emperor of Brazil—A scholar—A poet—Specimen of his poetry—Descriptions of his Court by various visitors—By Prince Adalbert of Prussia—By Agassiz—By Messrs. Fletcher and Kidder—Dom Pedro as patron of literature—His great admiration for Longfellow.

IF Dom Pedro I. was a Braganza of a new type, Dom Pedro II. may be saluted as a Braganza of the same type, with all the modern improvements added. For Dom Pedro I., with all his virtues, had some regrettable limitations.

In the first place, he drew the line at the domestic virtues, ostentatiously preferring the Marchioness of Santos—a light woman whom he had made a Marchioness—to his lawful wife, the Archduchess Leopoldina; and the preference offended the Brazilians. In the second place, though a Constitutionalist, he was rather an arbitrary Constitutionalist. If he adopted " Independence or death " as his motto, he also said, when popular pressure was put upon him: " I will do everything for the people, but nothing by the people." In the third place, his endeavours to comport himself as a great man were, as he himself was painfully aware, hampered by a defective education.

In all these various respects his son had the advantage of him. In his domestic relations, Dom Pedro II. lived as the best of good bourgeois. Brought up from childhood in a constitutional atmosphere, he felt no temptation either to limit liberty or to patronise it. Having for his tutor, Don Jose Bonifacio da Andrada, who has been styled "the Brazilian Benjamin Franklin," he took to study as a duck to water, became, probably, the most learned man in his dominions, and one who might, at any rate, challenge comparison with the Duke who declared his library to be Dukedom large enough. "Emperor and Man of Science" was Pasteur's description of him; and his interest in science was equalled by his interest in education. Two of his utterances on that subject are worth quoting:—

"If I were not an Emperor," he once said at a public meeting at Cannes, "I should like to be a schoolmaster. I know of no mission which is greater or more noble than that of directing young intelligences and forming the men of the future."

That is one manifesto. The other was called forth by a proposal made by his Ministers to build him a new Palace, on the ground that the one which he occupied—the former residence of the Portuguese Viceroys—was not grand enough for him:—

"What!" he exclaimed. "Before we have enough schools in the country, either secondary or even elementary, you begin to talk about Palaces! There will be time enough for that, later. Roads, emigration, school—those are the things we must first attend to."

It is really a fine picture—an Emperor receiving a proposal for a Palace in the same spirit in which such a proposal might have been received by Arnold of Rugby, or Thring of Uppingham. There is a touch of the autocrat in the rebuke, but it is the autocracy of the pedagogue rather than of the Lord's anointed; and deeds confirmed the words. When the sum of £120,000 was subscribed for the erection of a statue to Dom Pedro, he refused the monument and insisted that the money should be applied to educational purposes.

He was a poet, too, and—what is rarer—a modest poet, indifferent to the attractions of publicity. When he came to Paris, where publicity is, to most men, the very breath of life, a French journalist contrived to buttonhole him in the *foyer* of the Opera, paid insidious compliments to his literary gifts, and begged for a few lines of verse from his pen, in order that he might reproduce them in facsimile; but that snare was set for the Emperor in vain:—

"No, no," said Dom Pedro. "I am no poet. It is true that I scribble verses from time to time—but only for my amusement—only when I have nothing better to do. I don't mind showing them to my intimate friends; but nothing on earth would induce me to publish them."

Not all the lines, however, have been altogether

THE ROYAL HOUSE OF PORTUGAL

lost; for one of the intimate friends to whom Dom Pedro consented to show his compositions was a charming Maid of Honour, who wheedled His Majesty into writing a poem in her album. An American traveller persuaded the Maid of Honour to let him copy the poem from the album, and took it to Mr. D. Bates, of Philadelphia—known as the author of "Speak Gently"—and Mr. Bates translated it. Imperial poetry is so scarce a flower of imperial genius—and the probability that any reader of this work has ever seen the lines is so remote—that one need offer no excuse for quoting the whole of it:—

> If I am pious, clement, just,
>   I'm only what I ought to be;
> The sceptre is a weighty trust,
>   A great responsibility;
> And he who rules, with faithful hand,
>   With depth of thought and breadth of range,
> The sacred laws should understand,
>   And must not, at his pleasure, change.
>
> The chair of justice is the throne;
>   Who takes it bows to higher laws;
> The public good, and not his own,
>   Demands his care in every cause.
> Neglect of duty—always wrong—
>   Desirable in young or old—
> By him whose place is high and strong,
>   Is magnified a thousandfold.
>
> When in the East the glorious sun
>   Spreads o'er the earth the light of day,
> All know the course that he will run,
>   Nor wonder at his light or way:
> But if, perchance, the light that blazed
>   Is dimm'd by shadows lying near,
> The startled world looks on amazed,
>   And each one watches it with fear.

PEDRO II

> I likewise, if I always give
>   To vice and virtue their rewards,
> But do my duty thus to live;
>   No one his thanks to me accords.
> But should I fail to act my part,
>   Or wrongly do, or leave undone,
> Surprised the people then would start
>   With fear, as at the shadow'd sun.

The lines, it may be conceded, stop short of the sublimity to which some poets have attained. As it is not the privilege of every man to go to Corinth, so it is not given to every man to climb Parnassus; and those who try to travel across country from Olympus to Parnassus seem particularly liable to lose their way. Perhaps Hadrian discovered it, by a happy accident, when he wrote *Animula, vagula, blandula*; but Dom Pedro, it is evident, found Parnassus a Hill of Difficulty. He never got beyond the lower slopes, though he doubtless enjoyed the exercise which he took on them; and the intention was assuredly admirable, though the achievement fell short of it. Not even the Meditations of Marcus Aurelius are better meant; and no one can contradict the enthusiast who affirms that the lines are worthy of the Emperor who said that, if he were not an Emperor, he would like to be a schoolmaster. They should have an honoured place in the Brazilian School Readers; and the compilers of the Brazilian copy-books would find them a mine worth quarrying in.

But that is a digression, and rather an unfair one. Dom Pedro is not the only great man who has, for his amusement, written poetry which has revealed

THE ROYAL HOUSE OF PORTUGAL

the limitations of his greatness. They are, in this case, limitations which do not matter—perhaps even limitations which were positively advantageous. The nation over which Dom Pedro ruled was in its childhood, if not in its infancy; and a ruler who was, at once, simple, studious, and practical was the best sort of ruler it could have. A great poet—a Byron or a Shelley, for example—was no more wanted on the Brazilian throne than in a kindergarten. It was the pedagogue who was there the right man in the right place: a pedagogue whose wisdom had a gentle, paternal tone about it—a pedagogue who thought Longfellow and Whittier the greatest poets in all literature, and was as accessible to his subjects as a father to his children.

Dom Pedro was all that; and we will consider presently how it came about that, being all that, he was, nevertheless, gently but firmly invited to descend from the throne which he adorned and seek another sphere of usefulness in the Old World. For the moment we are only concerned with the patriarchal period in which he enjoyed unbounded popularity, and was likened to Saint Louis, administering justice under the oak at Vincennes—"receiving," as he said, "his Brazilian family,"—extending an equal affability to the officer in his uniform, the savant in his sober suit of customary black, and the unwashed workman in the garb of toil. The picture is the easier to draw because he always regarded himself, not merely as one of the institutions, but also as one of the "exhibits" of Brazil. An interview with him was always easy to

PEDRO II

obtain—much easier than, let us say, an interview with the editor of the *Times*, or with a popular actor-manager. To all who could present even the most modest credentials, the doors were thrown wide open by a friendly negro butler, who grinned a genial welcome, saying: "Want the Emperor? He'll be glad to see you. Walk right up."

That being the case, we have a rich choice of sketches of his personality from a variety of observers, ranging from Prince Adalbert of Prussia to sundry American journalists, missionaries, and commercial travellers. This is how Prince Adalbert spoke of Dom Pedro in 1849:—

"Dom Pedro has a mental vigour and development most remarkable for his age. He is not very tall, and is inclined to be stout. His head is large, his hair is fair, and his features are well chiselled; his expressive blue eyes are full of vivacity and benevolence. Though he is only seventeen, he has the gravity and bearing of a full-grown man. . . .

". . . . The Emperor always gets up at six o'clock in the morning. He devotes to reading all the time which he can spare from the affairs of state, and his excellent memory makes his studies very profitable to him.

"How happy is this country in possessing a ruler who so clearly perceives the duties of his position, and is keenly anxious to make his people happy!

"May Heaven bless his efforts!"

This is how Louis Agassiz spoke of him in 1865:—

"Dom Pedro is still a young man. Though only just forty years of age, he has already been for twenty years the sovereign of Brazil. He looks a little aged and anxious; but the expression of his face is masculine and noble. A little stern when in repose, his looks are animated and softened when he converses; and his courteous manners are of a seductive affability."

The portrait drawn by the Hohenzollern is, we see, substantially identical with that outlined by the Swiss man of science who became an American citizen; and their joint verdict is confirmed, with an ampler provision of detail, in the interesting work on "Brazil and the Brazilians," written by two American divines, the Rev. James C. Fletcher and the Rev. Dr. Kidder. Their account is too long to be cited in full; but we may quote a few selected sentences from which it appears that Dom Pedro was indeed an Emperor who had taken all knowledge for his province. In the first place he was a chemist:—

"He has devoted much time to the science of chemistry, and his laboratory at San Christovao is always the scene of new experiments."

He sent for the naturalist, Dr. Reinhardt, to assist him in his experiments; and Dr. Reinhardt related that:—

"The young monarch, in his enthusiasm, paid no attention to the time that flew by as they, in a tropic climate and a close room, were cooped up for hours over fumigating chemicals."

Dom Pedro, further, was a painter—he presented Prince Adalbert with one of his paintings—a

PEDRO II

linguist, a student of literature and history, and a generous patron of men of letters:—

"He has a great *penchant* for philological studies. I have heard him speak three different languages, and know, by report, that he converses in three more; and, so far as translating is concerned, he is acquainted with every principal European tongue. His library abounds in the best histories, biographies, and encyclopædias. Some one has remarked that a stranger can scarcely start a subject in regard to his own country that would be foreign to Dom Pedro II. There is not a session of the Brazilian Historical Society from which he is absent; and he is familiar with the modern literature of England, Germany, and the United States to a degree of minuteness absolutely surprising. When Lamartine's appeal for assistance was wafted over the waters, it was the Emperor of Brazil who rendered him greater material aid than any other, by subscribing for five thousand copies of his work, for which he remitted to the sensitive *littérateur* one hundred thousand francs. His favourite modern poet is Mr. Longfellow."

In his inspection of an American passenger steamer, attended by one of the authors of "Brazil and the Brazilians," he was equally curious, and equally thorough:—

"He was not content with beholding the mere upper-works of the machinery, but descended into the hot and oily quarters of the lower part of the ship, where the most intricate portion of the engine was situated: a half-hour was afterwards devoted to studying the engraved plan of the machinery."

THE ROYAL HOUSE OF PORTUGAL

Similarly, when the same gentleman guided him round an Educational Exhibition at Rio:—

"Being himself a thorough student of physical science, and a good engineer, he examined with minuteness the splendid edition of the United States Coast Survey.... For half an hour he pored over Youman's Atlas of Chemistry, and praised its thorough excellence and simplicity. While examining a work on physiology, I heard him remarking upon the superiority of the Craniology of the late Dr. Morton; and he informed me that he possessed the writings of that eminent student of the human frame. He was also well-read in the immense tomes of the pains-taking, erudite, and conscientious Schoolcraft, whose works on the aborigines of North America were sent out by the Chief of the Bureau of Indian Affairs at Washington."

Nor must one omit Mr. Fletcher's account of his reception by Dom Pedro, when he came to present him with an American Dictionary, and some volumes of American poetry:—

"Presently Dom Pedro appeared, his fine, manly form towering above every other. He was dressed in black; and, with the exception of a star which sparkled on his left breast, his costume was simple, and its good taste was most apparent when contrasted with the brilliant uniforms of the Court."

Mr. Fletcher expected to be kept waiting while His Majesty conversed with his more gorgeously decorated visitors. But not at all. Dom Pedro walked straight up to the plain man with the books, talked to him about the books, and made it clear that he was familiar with them. He had heard of Hawthorne, and was eager to read "Mosses from an old Manse"; but it was upon Longfellow that he harped. He had read all Longfellow's poetry, and was about to begin upon his prose, making a start with "Hyperion"; and he concluded with a special message to Longfellow :—

"Mr. Fletcher, when you return to your country, have the kindness to say to Mr. Longfellow how much pleasure he has given me, and be pleased to tell him *combien je l'estime, combien je l'aime*—how much I esteem him, how much I love him."

It is a trivial story, perhaps; but Dom Pedro stands out in it, as he would not stand out in any conventional eulogy. Other Emperors have patronised the arts. Napoleon did so—the present German Emperor does so; but there is no other Emperor of whom we can say, as confidently as we can of Dom Pedro, that he loved them. When other Emperors have praised poets, they have always seemed, somehow or other, to be patting them on the back, and saying, with lofty condescension : "Well done, thou good and faithful servant!" It has been as if they were appraising a school-boy's theme, and adjudging it worthy of a prize; not as if emotion mastered them, and constrained them to bow the knee to art.

That, without a doubt, is the distinction of Dom Pedro of Brazil. His feeling for literature was that, not of a patron of letters, but of a man of letters. He was one of them at heart, and would have liked to be one of them in fact; and he had

THE ROYAL HOUSE OF PORTUGAL

even more respect for their work in the world than for his own. He thanked them, not because they supported him, or agreed with him, but because they inspired him, and lifted him to a higher plane. He would not have hesitated to say that they were his superiors, and had done far more for him than he could ever hope to do for them: an appreciation of the realities which must be very hard to come by in the atmosphere of incense which surrounds a throne.

Very similar, too, was Dom Pedro's attitude towards science and the *savants*. If he was the Poets' Emperor, he was also the Scholars' Emperor. We shall see him in both characters when we follow him on his travels through Europe.

CHAPTER XVIII

A day in Dom Pedro's life—Testimonials to his merits—By Mme. Ristori—By Gladstone—By Darwin—His visits to France—Interview with Mistral—Conversation with Arsène Houssaye—Flattery from Lamartine—Exchange of civilities with Victor Hugo.

THE story of a day in Dom Pedro's life at Rio would be sure, though one picked it at random, to be the story of a day well spent.

He went to bed late; but he was always up again at six. The reading of the newspapers, the writing of his letters, the informal reception of all and sundry, filled the early hours of the morning. The next thing to be done was always to go and inspect something: a school, a hospital, a fortress, a man-of-war, a charitable institution, or what not. Then, perhaps, there might be a quiet interlude devoted to pottering about the garden, unless it happened to be the day for presiding over the Cabinet or receiving the *Corps Diplomatique*. In the evening, the Emperor either went to the theatre, or devoured a book; and he might have said, like his favourite singer's Village Blacksmith:—

> Each morning sees some task begun;
> Each evening sees it close.

THE ROYAL HOUSE OF PORTUGAL

His treatment of dramatic artists, it is to be noted, was widely different from that of the average European potentate. They were not merely part of the show, to be complimented with condescension, paid their fees, presented with scarf-pins, and dismissed. They were men and brothers—or women and sisters—with whom to hold rational conversation, as one gathers from Mme. Ristori's Memoirs :—

"How kind was the Emperor's heart, and how cultivated his mind! He honoured me with his friendship, and I am proud of it. Neither time nor distance have effaced the recollection. I was received at Court with my husband and my son, and I am at a loss to describe the cordiality and affability of this angelic family. How often have I been given the opportunity of admiring His Majesty's culture and genius. All the literatures are familiar to him."

Mme. Ristori, assuredly, would not have been able to say as much as that for any other Emperor, even if all the Emperors had been paraded in a row for her inspection. The others, one feels sure, would either have tried to make love to her—a courageous undertaking, for she was not quite that sort of actress—or else have flattered her with that excessive politeness which keeps people at a distance as effectively as a quick-set hedge. And as it was with Ristori, so it was with the men of science and the men of letters, who were Dom Pedro's favourite associates when he came to Europe. It is they who, in the end, make reputations; and no other Emperor has ever had Dom Pedro's success with them. There was not a man among them all who would not gladly have given him a testimonial; and many of them did so.

There was Gladstone's testimonial, for example, delivered at a banquet at which he proposed the Emperor's health :—

"He is a man—being absent I can say it more freely than if I spoke it in his presence—who is a model to all the sovereigns of the world in his anxiety for the faithful and effective discharge of his high duties. . . . That it is what I call, ladies and gentlemen, a great and good sovereign, who, by his conduct, is enabled to make the high station which he holds a pattern and a blessing to his race."

And then there is Darwin's testimonial, contained in a letter to Sir Joseph Hooker :—

"The Emperor has done so much for science that every man of science owes him the greatest respect; and I hope you will express to him in the most heartfelt fashion, as you may with entire sincerity, the honour which I feel at his desire to see me, and my regret that I am away from home."

Excellent testimonials these—infinitely more valuable than the testimonial which Metternich wrote for Dom Miguel; and they are only two among many. In France, in particular, Dom Pedro made friends in a way in which Emperors rarely make friends, by demonstrating his preference for classes of society in which Emperors, as a rule, are bored. "He stripped himself," wrote Arsène Houssaye, "with perfect grace of the imperial

THE ROYAL HOUSE OF PORTUGAL

purple; and this man who rules over a larger Empire than any other sovereign except the Emperors of Russia and China, behaved as a simple traveller, witty and well-informed." And not only witty and well-informed, but also tactful, with the kind of sympathetic tact which never fails to win the hearts of Frenchmen.

He came to France, for the first time, just after the Franco-German War, and visited Rouen while the Germans were still in occupation of that town. The German general, not only called to present his homage, as was right and proper, but also proposed to send one of the regimental bands, to serenade the Emperor. Dom Pedro would not have it.

"If I were in Germany," he said, "I should be delighted. But I am in France; and I cannot accept the salute of the Victors on the soil of the vanquished."

Whereupon his biographer, M. Mosse, comments:—

"The Prussian general had no choice but to defer to his wishes. He had done his duty towards the Emperor of Brazil; the Emperor of Brazil had done his duty to France."

After that, Dom Pedro's success with all classes of Frenchmen was secure; and it may be added that he was an Emperor born to succeed with Republicans—especially with French Republicans—because his estimate of the relative value of different

PEDRO II

men coincided with theirs. In France, more than in any other country—and among French Republicans more than among other Frenchmen—it is realised that, as the greatest events happen in the intellect, the really interesting men are the artists, the men of letters, and the men of science. Their place in French esteem is far above that of the captains of industry, the millionaires, and the sportsmen; and it was precisely because Dom Pedro sought them out, eager to learn what they could teach him, and yet able to hold his own with them, that French opinion singled him out as the one Emperor thoroughly worthy of Republican respect.

One hears from the younger Dumas of his attendance at some of the sessions of the Academy of Letters. He did not go to the Academy as he might have gone to a raree show, but begged that the Forty would do him the honour of treating him as one of themselves and allow him to bear his share of the labour when they toiled at the compilation of the Dictionary. He attended lectures at the Institut, took notes, like any other member of the audience, and declined to be placed in any seat of honour. "No, no," he said. "Let me sit next to my friend, M. Franck. That is what I should like best." At the receptions which he gave, it was the scholars and the poets who were his favourite guests; and many stories are told of the simple cordiality with which he sought them out.

He went to see Frédéric Mistral in his home in Provence, taking the Empress with him, complimented him on *Mireio*, and assured him that South

THE ROYAL HOUSE OF PORTUGAL

America watched the Provençal renaissance with enthusiasm, and that *Magali* had been sung in his own Palace at Rio. "Be sure you send me everything you write—you may depend upon me to read it," were his parting words, as he shook hands; and Mistral promised, and, no doubt, kept his promise. And then Dom Pedro went to see Arsène Houssaye, in circumstances described, long ago, in the *Revue de Paris et de Saint Pétersbourg* :—

"M. Gaston Calmette had written in the *Figaro* that Dom Pedro might easily be mistaken for Arsène Houssaye. A few days later, Dom Pedro, meeting Arsène Houssaye, led him in front of a looking-glass, and said :—

"'Here we are! Now let us see whether we are really like each other.'

"'Yes, I think we are,' replied Arsène Houssaye; 'but there is this difference between us. I feel, sometimes, that I should like to be Dom Pedro; but you never feel that you would like to be Arsène Houssaye.'

"'Who knows?' replied the Emperor. 'Every man has his crown of thorns to wear. So it would be of no use for us to change places : neither of us would be wearing the crown of perfect happiness.'

"'But has Your Majesty ever known a perfectly happy man?'

"'I have.'

"'He is . . . .?'

"'Myself, when I see that my people are satisfied.'"

Perhaps there is just a touch of the copy-book about that story—a touch which we have already detected in the poem which Dom Pedro contributed to the album of the Maid of Honour. There is, indeed, nearly always a touch of the copy-book in the utterances of those of the good and great who have invented goodness and greatness out of their own heads in conditions in which courtiers hung upon their words, and flattery, from some source or other, was equally sure to be their portion, whatever their qualities and their way of life. To such it is not often given to be quite at ease in Zion, or to get rid of the feeling that they are expected to do the honours of the Celestial City with the air of a Dean in his Cathedral; and it would seem that it was not given to Dom Pedro.

But we must not insist. Dom Pedro had not the copy-book manner badly, though he had a touch of it. The shyness natural to every man who moves, whether from choice or from necessity, in an unaccustomed medium, was one of the causes of it; the flattery which helped to provoke it had been unconscionable. Lamartine, in particular, was of Disraeli's opinion that, when flattering a crowned head, one should "lay it on with a trowel"; and the letter in which he thanked Dom Pedro for purchasing five thousand copies of his collected works had all the fulsome rotundity of an illuminated address. Brazil, he wrote, enjoyed, under the Emperor, the liberty of Republics without their instability, and the permanence of Monarchies without their despotism; and he went on to liken himself to Voltaire, and Dom Pedro to Frederick the Great:—

THE ROYAL HOUSE OF PORTUGAL

"Voltaire was encouraged by him who is styled the Great Frederick; but Voltaire was young and happy. It is in old age and adversity that I am comforted by Your Majesty's munificence.

"Voltaire could bestow the gift of glory, whereas I have nothing to offer but my gratitude.

"The benefits conferred by his royal friend were invited, whereas those of Your Majesty are spontaneous.

"The royal philosopher surpasses in merit the crowned poet of Potsdam."

It was the strong wine of eulogy, and might easily have turned a weak man's head. One suspects that it may have been a stronger wine than Dom Pedro liked; but it was not a stronger wine than he could carry. How little it affected his essential simplicity of character and manner is shown by the story of his visit to Victor Hugo.

It is an interview of which many accounts have been given—some of them most obviously embroidered if not fabricated. It may or may not be true that Victor Hugo consulted Jules Simon as to the mode in which it would be correct for him to address the Emperor, and that Jules Simon replied:—

"Call him Sire or Your Majesty, as other people do. It is an opportunity of condescension which you should not miss."

It may or may not be true that Victor Hugo welcomed his imperial guest with the words: "Enter, Sire! We poets also are kings." Be that as it may, here is the poet's own account of the incident,

PEDRO II

taken from an unpublished note-book, and read the other day by M. Barthou at a luncheon party given by a member of the Brazilian diplomatic service. The date of the first entry is May 22nd, 1877:—

"A call from the Emperor of Brazil, who saw *L'art d'être grand-père* lying on the table. I asked him to accept it, and picked up my pen. 'What are you going to write?' he asked. 'Two names— yours and my own,' I answered. 'Write nothing than that, I beg of you,' he said; so I wrote:—

"'To Dom Pedro of Alcantara,
"'Victor Hugo.'

"'And the date?' he said.
"I added: 'May 22nd, 1877.'
"'I should like one of your drawings,' he next said.
"I happened to have a sketch which I had made of the Château of Vianden, so I gave it to him. 'At what hour do you dine?' he inquired. 'At eight,' I answered. 'One of these days,' he said, 'I shall ask you to let me dine with you.' 'Name your own day,' I replied. 'You will always be welcome.' Then he kissed Georges and Jeanne.

"His words when he entered were: 'Please put me at my ease. I am rather shy.'

"In speaking of Kings and Emperors, he called them 'my colleagues.' Once he spoke of 'my rights'; but then he corrected himself, saying: 'I have no rights—only a certain power which I owe to accident. I must use it for good—for progress and liberty.'"

Once more we note the copy-book touch; but no

THE ROYAL HOUSE OF PORTUGAL

matter. It is soon effaced, and does not reappear. Victor Hugo's Diary continues:—

"When Jeanne came in, he said to me: 'I have one ambition. Pray gratify it by presenting me to Mlle. Jeanne.' So I said to Jeanne: 'Jeanne, I present to you the Emperor of Brazil.' Jeanne said, in a low voice: 'He isn't dressed up'; but the Emperor said to her: 'Kiss me, young lady'; and then, when she put up her cheek: 'Put your arms round my neck, my dear.' Jeanne clasped him in her tiny arms.

"He asked for her photograph, and mine, and promised me his own; and he left me at eleven. His conversation was so serious and so intelligent, that, when we parted, I said to him: 'Sire, you are *a great citizen.*'

"Another detail. Leading up Georges, I said: 'Sire, I present my grandson to Your Majesty.' He said to Georges: 'My boy, there is only one Majesty here, and that is Victor Hugo.'"

It was as if he wished to return to Victor Hugo the compliments which he had received from Lamartine; and it might even be said that he went so far in modesty as to allow Victor Hugo to patronise him—an art in which Victor Hugo indubitably excelled. A few days later he came, as he had promised to take pot luck with the poet; and this is Victor Hugo's note on the banquet:—

"When I got home, I found the Emperor of Brazil, who had invited himself to dinner. He had brought with him the Viscount of Bom Retiro, whom he introduced with the words: 'I have brought my

PEDRO II

friend M. de Bom Retiro to see you.' M. de Bom Retiro is a very distinguished gentleman.

"The Emperor gave me his portrait, signed: Pedro d'Alcantara,' and dated ' May 29th, 1877.'

"We had Vacquerie and our other Tuesday guests to dinner. At the dessert, I proposed the health of my distinguished guest. He replied by proposing mine. We went on talking until midnight, and then we had supper. He went home about one in the morning."

That is another pleasant picture; and it seems a strange thing that, whereas the decorative and haughty Emperors, who are never seen out of their uniform, and never tire of insisting that they have a divine right to rule, have had no difficulty in keeping their thrones, this gentle and modest Emperor, who would not dazzle people for fear lest he should hurt their feelings, but went about doing good and making himself agreeable in a frock coat and a silk hat, was rudely expelled by his subjects.

CHAPTER XIX

Causes of the revolution in Brazil—The Cave of Adullam—Unpopularity of Princess Isabel and her husband, the Comte d'Eu—Story of the marriage of Princess Isabel and her sister—Character of the Comte d'Eu—Sudden decision of the Brazilians to have a Republic—The provisional government—It deports Dom Pedro, giving him twenty-four hours to pack.

PERHAPS the historian who seeks to assign a cause for a South American revolution is superfluously conscientious. The wind bloweth where it listeth, and the South American is like the maid-servant in his perennial desire for "a change." Why trouble to go behind that elementary passion? Still, if one must, one can, even in the case of the Brazilian Revolution, which broke out at five minutes' notice and took the civilised world by surprise.

There were, of course, certain general causes. Dom Pedro's monarchy was the only one in the New World; and that fact alone made its position difficult. In America a citizen despises a subject, much as big boys in a school-room despise small boys in a nursery. The subjects resent the contempt of the citizens, fear that it is deserved, and resolve to remove the occasion for it. They are not grown up? They cannot be trusted to walk

REVOLUTION IN BRAZIL

alone? The people who think that must be shown that they are mistaken; and the monarch—though the gentlest and most genial of men, and the most discreet of constitutional rulers—must be immolated on the altar of their self-esteem.

That may not, of course, be everybody's view; but it does tend to be the view of political adventurers and professional politicians. One of the results of Dom Pedro's zeal for education was to educate such a class in Brazil. They were called "the bachelors"; and they may be said to have corresponded to the "failed B.A.'s" and other gifted Babus who make political trouble in Bengal. They hung on the words of a certain Benjamin Constant—a disciple of Auguste Comte, and a professor at the military college. He and they got it into their heads that they could not celebrate the centenary of the French Revolution more appropriately than by declaring a Republic in Brazil; and they sent to Paris for some suitable flags— the ordinary Brazilian flag with a Phrygian cap of liberty substituted for the imperial crown.

That was all that there was in the movement to begin with, and there was not much more than that in it at the end; but there were also, as always happens, certain concrete discontents for which the abstract Republican idea served as a cloak. The emancipation of the slaves by the Emperor had caused the slave-holders to lose their interest in the imperial principle; the favour shown to the Jesuits by the Emperor's daughter had disgusted the anti-clericals. There were also certain individuals who had grievances, not so much against the Emperor as against his Ministers: the grievance —to take one instance among many—of the highly placed civil servant whom the Minister of the Interior sent to a military prison because he had found him asleep and snoring in his office instead of attending to his work There were others who had been similarly affronted; and of such was the Cave of Adullam.

Even so, however, most of the malcontents were in favour of leaving well alone during Dom Pedro's lifetime. It was admitted that he had deserved well of the country, though there were those who derided him as a bookworm, or declared that he had neglected his duties for the sake of his pleasure trips to Europe. He had no personal enemies; and as he was old, and suffering from diabetes, his throne was likely, in the course of nature, to fall vacant very soon. Better wait, a good many Brazilians said, till he was dead, and the Republic could be established without hurting his feelings. Unfortunately, however, the rumour spread that Dom Pedro, weary of the weight of his crown, proposed to abdicate in favour of his daughter, Princess Isabel; and then it was, indeed, as if fat had been thrown into a fire. The malcontents did not wait to ascertain whether the rumour was true or false, but decided to act at once. They did not like Princess Isabel. Still less did they like her husband, the Comte d'Eu; and it is not too much to say that the Brazilian Revolution was an indirect outcome of the Brazilian marriages.

REVOLUTION IN BRAZIL

The story of those marriages is itself sufficiently interesting to detain us for a moment, though it would be superfluous to enter into all the match-making intrigues which preceded them. Enough to say that Dom Pedro had two marriageable daughters—Doña Isabel and Doña Leopoldina—and that two eligible Princes were brought to Brazil to marry them. Augustus of Saxe-Coburg, the brother of the present Tsar of Bulgaria, was to marry Doña Isabel; and his cousin, the Comte d'Eu, son of the Duc de Nemours, was to marry Doña Leopoldina. But though that was what was arranged, that was not what happened, the trouble being that, though the cousins were equal in rank, they were not equal in personal charm.

Augustus of Saxe-Coburg, according to his candid friends, had a face like a Dutch cheese, lighted up with an intelligent leer. The Comte d'Eu, on the other hand, was exceedingly handsome—albeit in a somewhat insipid style—and what the French call *beau garçon*. It came about, therefore, that both the Princesses fell in love with him, and that neither of them fell in love with his cousin. Doña Isabel insisted that, as she was the elder, she had a right to the first choice of a bridegroom. Doña Leopoldina replied that, however that might be, she was not going to put up with her sister's leavings. There was both heated argument and diplomatic correspondence on the subject; but the decision was ultimately allowed to rest with the Comte d'Eu. Not being in love with either of the two sisters, though both of them were in love with him, he announced his preference for the heiress; and the matter was settled on that basis —Doña Leopoldina being induced to overcome her feelings and marry Prince Augustus, who, by all accounts, made her an excellent husband.

So far, so good; but the Brazilians, as we have seen, did not like either the Comte d'Eu or Doña Isabel.

The objection to Doña Isabel was threefold: she was too haughty; she was too devout; and she took herself too seriously when Dom Pedro appointed her his Regent. Her pride impelled her to keep the Brazilian ladies at a distance, protesting that their proximity was only tolerable when they were perfumed. Her piety constrained her not only to ridiculous acts of religious humility, such as the scrubbing of the floors of chapels, but also to the seeking of the society of obnoxious Jesuits. As a Regent, she took sides in controversies which, in the opinion of the Ministers, did not concern her— and always in a manner which showed that her heart was with the clericals. She also pushed her husband forward in a way which the Brazilians considered unconstitutional; and he, on his part, was quite willing to be pushed forward.

Naturally, seeing that he had, on his mother's side, Saxe-Coburg blood in his veins. The Saxe-Coburgs, as we all know, are the *arrivistes* of the royal houses—always lucky, always self-confident, and not infrequently successful. They like to be the powers behind the thrones on which they do not actually sit; and they have the valuable

REVOLUTION IN BRAZIL

faculty of persuading their wives that they are great and good. No man, one feels, can ever have been quite so great and good as Queen Victoria believed Prince Albert of Saxe-Coburg to be; and Doña Isabel took a very similar view of the qualities and talents of Prince Albert's cousin, the Comte d'Eu. She wanted him to be to Brazil all that Queen Victoria wanted Prince Albert to be to England, and more. She even wanted him to be commander-in-chief of the Brazilian army.

He was a good enough soldier. The Spanish Marshal O'Donnell had decorated him for gallantry on a battlefield in Morocco; and he had acquitted himself creditably in the Brazilian war against Paraguay. The Brazilians, however, objected to him as a foreigner, and—more particularly—a foreigner who was feathering his nest at their expense. He had bought up a good deal of house property in Rio, and his reputation as a landlord was not a good one. Some people compared him to the worst kind of Irish landlord; others to the worst rack-renters of the London slums. Very likely there are two sides to that story; but it does not matter. The Brazilians, in any case, did not want the Comte d'Eu, and did not mean to have him, as the power behind the throne. They saw that he would infallibly be the power behind the throne if Doña Isabel became Empress; and so they made their revolution.

It has been written of that revolution that a dynasty was dissolved in it "as quietly as a pearl in vinegar"; and the metaphor may justly stand.

THE ROYAL HOUSE OF PORTUGAL

Dom Pedro himself does not seem to have had the faintest inkling that anything serious was about to happen until he saw what serious things were actually happening. He was at his country seat at Petropolis when a message reached him that urgent business required his immediate presence in the capital. He hurried back, like the slave of duty that he was; and the gentlemen who then came to see him introduced themselves to him as the members of a provisional government. They had no personal animosity to him, they said—on the contrary, they had the deepest respect for him; but they felt that the time had come for a change in the form of government, and therefore they had proclaimed a Republic. Every arrangement had been made for his comfortable journey to Europe; they relied upon him to fall in with those arrangements, and start within twenty-four hours. He would, unfortunately, have no time to pack; but he could throw a few toilet requisites into a bag, and the rest of his luggage should be sent after him. In order to avoid demonstrations which might conceivably cause bloodshed, it had been thought better that his departure should take place after nightfall.

That is practically the whole story, though it remains to be said that the Republicans suggested abdication. It would, they pointed out, save trouble. It would be tactful. It would be a noble act of self-denial, setting a worthy coping-stone upon a glorious career. But they would not press the point if the Emperor did not see his way

REVOLUTION IN BRAZIL

—it was a mere matter of form. Facts were more than signatures; and the fact was that the House of Braganza had ceased to reign in Brazil, as it had once before ceased to reign in Portugal; and the deportation of all members of the House was necessary. It would be to their own interest as well as to the interest of the country. The details had been planned with every consideration for their comfort; but the programme must be carried out. What did the Emperor think?

The Emperor, in truth, did not know exactly what to think. He was an old man, and a sufferer from diabetes—a complaint which makes men irritable without making them energetic. Moreover, he had always supposed that he ruled over Brazil with the consent of the Brazilians, had no desire to rule on any other terms, had always, to the best of his knowledge and belief, done his duty to his subjects, and regarded himself as the father of his people. He had no improper pride, and no desire to press his services if they were no longer wanted. On the other hand, he doubted whether the voice of the provisional government was really the voice of the people—it might be only the voice of a military camarilla; in which case abdication would look like desertion of the post of duty. So he took a middle course.

"No," he said, "I shall not abdicate; but I shall not resist. If you are in a position to use force, I shall submit."

They were in a position to use force; so there

was no more to be said. The only point which Dom Pedro argued related to the hour of his departure. He did not like the idea of being smuggled out of the country in the dark; he wished to embark in broad daylight, as one who, having nothing to be ashamed of, bade his subjects a dignified farewell. But the will of the Republicans was adamant.

"There might be a demonstration," they protested.

"It is not impossible," replied the Emperor. "My people love me. It is not unnatural that they should wish to give me a sign of their love when I am leaving them."

"Assuredly the people love Your Majesty; but they do not love Your Majesty's son-in-law, the Comte d'Eu. The difficulty of affording protection to the Comte d'Eu——"

Dom Pedro himself, it is said, was not bound to the Comte d'Eu by any passionate attachment. He doubtless was quite aware that his own unpopularity was the reflection of the unpopularity of his son-in-law. But he did not want an unseemly scuffle in which the Comte d'Eu would probably be hurt; and there had already been a little shooting—just enough to wound the unpopular Minister of Marine. That was one consideration which weighed with him; and another may well have been the tired invalid's desire to avoid fuss and excitement, get the disagreeable business over quickly, and rearrange his life to suit the altered circumstances. So he yielded without more ado, kicked his heels in his Palace, at every door of which sentries were

DEPORTATION OF PEDRO II

posted, until the appointed hour, and then let himself be conducted to his cabin.

It was a sorry end truly to a reign which had really demonstrated that "even in a Palace life may be lived well." Dom Pedro had, indeed, been the Father of his People. He had refused to have a Palace while his country was without schools at the beginning of his reign; and he had given up a Palace, to be used as a hospital, towards the end of it. He had never presumed on his position, and had neither squandered money nor amassed it, but when there was a surplus in his domestic budget, as there generally was, he had given the balance to a charity or paid it back into the Treasury. In many other ways, too, he had shown himself worthy of Victor Hugo's description of him as "the grandson of Marcus Aurelius." All that; and yet at the end of all that we see him expelled as summarily as a maid-servant who has been caught stealing the spoons or making love to the son of the house.

And yet—strangest fact of all, perhaps—he bore no malice. His first act, when the vessel which deported him was well out at sea, was to release a white dove which he had brought on board with him—a carrier pigeon charged with a last message of regret and farewell to the beloved Brazilians who had turned him out. The sense of tears in human things touches one when one reads of that; and then one chokes the emotion back and turns to see what Dom Pedro was able to make of his life, now that he was doomed to live the latter part of it as Emperor in exile.

CHAPTER XX

Departure of Dom Pedro from Brazil—Incidents of the voyage—Arrival at Lisbon—The initiation into private life—Dom Pedro in Paris—Visit to M. Flammarion's Observatory—Last years and death—Wrangle at the funeral.

THE dispatch of the dove, charged with the olive-branch, was, as it were, a symbolic act, dividing Dom Pedro's life in two, and setting him free to begin a new career.

Most likely the Empress felt more bitter than he did. She was sea-sick; and sea-sickness in the course of a compulsory voyage may well be trying to the sweetest temper. It was a nuisance, too, that, packing hurriedly in the heat of the tropics, they had all quite forgotten to take the warm clothes which they would be sure to need when the ship struck colder weather; as one of the Princes was ill, this might even have been a serious matter. The ship's resources, however, supplied their needs, though not perhaps as decoratively as the imperial passengers would have liked. The invalid boy and the sea-sick Empress both recovered; while Dom Pedro, who was a good sailor, plunged at once into

PEDRO II. IN EXILE

that simple artistic and intellectual life which, when all was said and done, was the life which pleased him best.

The Republicans had, at all events, remembered his tastes and provided for them. In his daughter's cabin there was a piano; while, for his own delectation, all the booksellers' shops in Rio had been ransacked for the latest numbers of the scientific periodicals. They had forgotten, indeed, to have the piano tuned—an omission which gave Doña Isabel an unimpeachable excuse for looking that gift-horse in the mouth; but there was no fault to be found with the quarterlies, monthlies, and fortnightlies. They were current, uncut numbers, full of the latest learning. The exiled Emperor was soon at his ease in his deck-chair, slashing the leaves apart with his paper-knife, and drowning his sense of injustice in a welcome bath of erudition. Now, at last, he was free to improve his mind without being accused of neglecting his duties.

He was bound for Lisbon, and preparations were already in progress for making much of him on his arrival there. Royalists and Republicans alike seem to have assumed that he would find in pomp the best consolation for the loss of power. The latter instructed their diplomatic agents that, though he had been sent to Europe like an empty bale of goods, he had not forfeited respect, and was still to be offered the homage due to Emperors on all ceremonial occasions; while his Portuguese relatives sent a messenger to meet him at Madeira, offering him a lodging at the Necessidades Palace

THE ROYAL HOUSE OF PORTUGAL

—the Palace wherein another sovereign was, only a few years later, to entertain the dancing-girl and present her with the costly diamond-studded garters which she was to show to her friends in theatrical dressing-rooms as trophies of her artistic triumph and proof of her power to please.

But Dom Pedro cared for none of these things. Having lost the substance of imperial dignity, he was quite indifferent to the shadow of it. Having proved that life could be lived well in a Palace, he proposed to show that it could be lived just as creditably in a hotel. The Braganza Hotel was his choice. He announced that he would spend about three weeks there, and would then proceed to Cannes, in order to read the scientific periodicals in a more genial climate. If his subjects recalled him to Brazil, as seemed, at the moment, not impossible, he would, he said, strain a point and go. But he did not really want to go, and he would do nothing to foment a counter-revolution: not only because he hated the idea that blood should be shed for his sake, but also because he was a tired old man who would really prefer to devote the evening of his days to the feast of reason in the society of students. He would be glad, he said, of the opportunity of taking up the study of astronomy, and of visiting M. Camille Flammarion in his Observatory.

So the ship, in due course, steamed up the Tagus; and an immense number of friends and journalists came on board to greet the Emperor. He looked a noble, though not perhaps precisely an imperial, figure, in a flowing mantle, a spreading wideawake hat, and a light blue tie; and he talked cheerfully, and without any trace of indignation, of his experiences and his plans. He shouted greetings in Portuguese to his relatives as soon as he caught sight of them, and he assured an English journalist, in English, that "they no treat us badly." After that he spoke of the matters which really interested him, asking what would be on that night at the Opera, and expressing his desire to take part in the proceedings at the next meeting of the Portuguese Academy.

One may see in that scene the ceremony of initiation, as it were, into private life: the final transformation of the best of the Emperors into an admirable citizen of the world. To say more would be superfluous, because it would be little more than a repetition of what has been said already. There was a little talk, at the time, of a movement to confer the crown of Brazil on his younger daughter's son, Peter of Saxe-Coburg; but it was the talk of people with whom the decision did not rest, and it never even began to be translated into action. The Brazilians, if consulted, would probably have replied that, though they knew nothing to Peter's discredit, they knew nothing in his favour, and that the fact that nothing is known to a young man's discredit is no more, in itself, a sufficient reason for making him an Emperor than it is a sufficient reason for making him an Admiral of the Fleet or an Archbishop. Their attitude, however, was not tested, and need not be discussed. Our business

THE ROYAL HOUSE OF PORTUGAL

is still with Dom Pedro, though even about him there is little more to be related.

One further sorrow awaited him—the death of his wife, who seems to have possessed all the *bourgeois* virtues of the Bourbons, without any of their intolerable arrogance. He wept for her, and did not survive her very long—an invalid, though still able to go about. He had refused the pension which the Brazilians offered him, taking the proud view that, if his services as Emperor were not required, there was no reason why they should be paid for. Consequently he was a poor man; but his poverty was only comparative, and he was not the sort of man that that sort of poverty could trouble. His younger daughter was dead; and his elder daughter settled at Versailles, where she lived on an allowance of £4,000 a year, made to her by her father-in-law. He knew, therefore, that his family did not suffer; and he had enough for his own simple needs.

He often went to Versailles to visit Doña Isabel —now a dingy blonde of massive dignity—but his own headquarters were at Paris, where he was near the artists and the men of science whose society he loved. His promise to visit M. Flammarion in his Observatory was fulfilled; and it is also said, perhaps untruly, that he took up astrology as well as astronomy in his later years. In any case, he continued his demonstration that life could be lived well even in a hotel; and it was, in fact, in a hotel that he, like his wife before him, died.

It was not much of a hotel—not one of those

DEATH OF PEDRO II

magnificent modern hotels which can almost be mistaken for palaces. On the contrary, Dom Pedro's last earthly resting-place, according to a contemporary journalist, was "a commonplace and rather poky bedroom, furnished in dark blue rep and *palissandre* rosewood, with a narrow mirror, wardrobe, bed, two armchairs, two armless ones, and a small table." In that shabby-genteel apartment he lay in state for four days, to be viewed by a procession of 17,000 people. Though he had always lived as a civilian, and was, in reality, nothing if not a savant, his relatives thought to add to his glory by dressing up his dead body in the uniform of a general of division.

Then came the funeral, which, of course, was great and grand—an occasion for the gathering together of all the crowned and discrowned Bourbons in Europe. There were assembled the Bourbons of Naples, the Bourbons of Parma, the Bourbons of the reigning House of Spain, and the Bourbons of the Carlist branch—Bourbons nicknamed respectively by the French the Tapiocas, the Macaronis, the Olla Podridas, and the Blancs d'Espagne. The ceremonial was magnificent and imposing, and yet it did not pass without its stroke of irony. There was a quarrel—a brawl even—as to the precedence to be accorded to General Brugère as the representative of the President of the French Republic whose hospitality the royal exiles were enjoying; and when that stimulating wrangle was over, Doña Isabel is said to have fallen asleep in church. *Sic transit gloria mundi.*

THE ROYAL HOUSE OF PORTUGAL

It seems strange, in all the circumstances, that any member of the family should have thought it worth while either to assert or to renounce his shadowy claims to the overtoppled throne; but the pretence was nevertheless kept up that one or other of them must be the rightful heir to a dignity which had disappeared, and that that right could be forfeited by marriage with a social inferior. So, in October, 1908, we find Pedro d'Alcantara, the eldest son of the Comte d'Eu, solemnly renouncing his imaginary claims because he was about to marry Countess Dobrzensky de Dobrzencz, and his brother Louis as solemnly taking them over from him because he was about to make a more distinguished match with Princess Maria Pia of the extinct kingdom of Sicily.

A pretty example truly of the game of make-believe which kings in exile love to play! A case, one feels sure, in the eyes of the majority of the Brazilians, of Tweedledum asserting his immeasurable superiority to Tweedledee!

CHAPTER XXI

Reign of Maria da Gloria—Her visit to England as a child—Impressions then formed of her—Her first marriage to the Duc de Leuchtenberg—His death—Her second marriage to Ferdinand of Saxe-Coburg—General characteristics of the Coburgs—Belgian Minister's impression of the situation in Portugal.

WE left Portugal at the end of a civil war: Dom Miguel in flight, but still intriguing; Dom Pedro dying of an illness brought on by the hardships of the campaign; Doña Maria da Gloria called to the throne while still a child. She was only fifteen; but the Cortes declared her of full age, so as to avoid the embarrassment of choosing a Regent. It also decided to find her a husband as soon as possible, so as to remove all awkward questions as to the succession.

Her reign consisted mainly of revolutions. Fourteen revolutions in fifteen years—that is the history of the reign in a nutshell. No doubt they were among the revolutions which Tennyson was thinking of when he spoke of continental revolutions as being, for the more part, "no graver than a school-boy's barring-out." Certainly they are no more interesting to read about, and not of much more conse-

THE ROYAL HOUSE OF PORTUGAL

quence to the world; so we will take them for granted instead of studying them in detail, considering only their effect upon the fortunes of the Queen herself, and the light which an incident here and there may throw upon her character.

We first hear of her as a child of tender years taken to London because she could not go to Lisbon, and made much of by George IV. This is what Greville says:—

"Yesterday the King gave a dinner to the Dukes of Orleans and Chartres, and in the evening there was a child's ball. It was pretty enough, and I saw for the first time the Queen of Portugal and our little Victoria. The Queen was finely dressed, with a ribband and order over her shoulder, and she sat by the King. She is good-looking, and has a sensible Austrian countenance. In dancing she fell down and hurt her face, was frightened and bruised, and went away. The King was very kind to her. Our little Princess is a short, plain-looking child, and not near so good-looking as the Queen. However, if nature has not done so much, fortune is likely to do a good deal more for her."

The two royal children became friends—sufficiently so to address each other by their Christian names when they corresponded in after life; but Maria da Gloria was not wanted in England. Though the King was kind, the Duke of Wellington made himself unpleasant. He was in favour of Dom Miguel; and it was complained that he treated Dom Pedro's wife and daughter as if they had been the female relatives of a brigand chief. It was largely in consequence of his discouraging attitude

MARIA DA GLORIA

that Doña Maria was taken across the Channel, to be educated in France; and it is permissible to think that an English education would have been better for her. She might, at least, have learnt with us what Constitutions were, and why people wanted them; and that—in view of the storms which were to rage in Portugal—would have been useful knowledge.

Having drifted, however, out of the range of English vision, she came in sight again when her father, realising that he had not long to live, made haste to get her married. That was in 1833, in the reign of William IV.; and we may once more quote Greville:—

"The young Queen of Portugal goes to Windsor to-day. The King was at first very angry at her coming to England, but when he found that Louis-Philippe had treated her with incivility, he changed his mind and resolved to receive her with great honours."

It was not only that William IV. hated Louis-Philippe and all the French "with a sort of Jack Tar animosity." The King of the French had also been putting forward candidates for the young Queen's hand :—

"He wanted the young Queen of Portugal to marry the Duc de Nemours, and when he found that impossible (for we should have opposed it) he proposed Prince Charles of Naples, his nephew. This was likewise rejected. The Emperor Dom Pedro wants the Duke of Leuchtenberg, his wife's brother, to marry her."

THE ROYAL HOUSE OF PORTUGAL

That was the marriage which was eventually arranged; the Duc de Leuchtenberg being the son of Napoleon's stepson, Eugène de Beauharnais, and the grandson of the Empress Josephine. His sister, it must be added, was not Doña Maria's mother, but only her stepmother, so that the alliance was, at any rate, an improvement upon that projected with her uncle Miguel. He was a young man of some promise; but his death, about two months after his marriage, prevented promise from maturing as performance. He caught a fever while the Portuguese were discussing the propriety of his appointment to be commander-in-chief of their army. It was round his death-bed that the storm raged; and the Ministers then urged his widow to stifle her grief and marry again as soon as possible.

She was still quite a child, and she consented; and once more the various Chancelleries engaged in the congenial task of match-making, and watching and checkmating each other's schemes. The Duc de Nemours was once more proposed and once more rejected; the brother of the Duc de Leuchtenberg was proposed and rejected; and so was the King of Sardinia's cousin, the Prince of Carignan. And then the question—the almost inevitable question—was raised: Why not a Saxe-Coburg? No one was prepared with any conclusive objection; and so it was on Ferdinand of Saxe-Coburg that the choice fell. He was persuaded to propose, and was accepted. His uncle, Leopold I., King of the Belgians, tried to cram him, in a few lessons, in the duties of constitutional government. He went to

FERDINAND OF SAXE-COBURG

England and Paris, to receive the benedictions of the English and French Governments; and then he proceeded to Lisbon—a boy of nineteen, about to marry a girl of sixteen, and try to carry out his uncle's maxims of statecraft in the country in which, as we have casually mentioned, there were to be fourteen revolutions in fifteen years.

The marriage indubitably marks an epoch—perhaps the most important of all the epochs—in the annals of the Braganza family. The House had, so far, depended too much—and, indeed, had depended almost entirely—upon consanguineous marriages. Infusions of fresh blood had been too rare—and the fresh blood had been too much like the old blood—for the family characteristics to be much affected by it. The Coburg marriage was, therefore, a new departure which might be expected to have far-reaching results; for the Coburgs were not only unrelated to the Braganzas, but unlike them. The Braganzas had, for some time, been slack, and prone to fail in their tasks; whereas the Coburgs had the new northern conceptions of efficiency, and had got a name for succeeding. There is a recent work on the Coburgs by Mr. Edmund B. d'Auvergne, in which their average qualities are well summed up :—

"It is the Coburgs who have made monarchy respectable. Before their time the King's trade seemed fit only for gilded libertines and gloomy tyrants. Leopold of Belgium and Albert of England changed all that. They introduced middle-class standards into the Palace. They were excel-

THE ROYAL HOUSE OF PORTUGAL

lent husbands and fathers, and showed the bourgeois that a king could be a respectable married man as well as he. And the bourgeois has loved them for their likeness to himself. Only one of the Coburgs ever married an actress, and he taught her to make her own tea-cakes."

No doubt these generalisations, like most generalisations, need to be qualified in order to fit all the facts. One could certainly, as Mr. d'Auvergne knows quite well, smite a good many joints in the armour of it by citing stories from the career of that other Leopold of Belgium who, if he did not marry an actress, was at any rate very fond of deviating from the paths of respectability in order to consort with such ladies. Perhaps, too, one could pierce other joints by referring to the case of the Prince of Saxe-Coburg who shut up his sane wife in a lunatic asylum from which she was rescued by a gallant Croatian officer whom she not unnaturally loved better than her husband. A Saxe-Coburg, in short, who wants precedents for levity can find them in his own family as easily as in any other.

That, since it cannot be contradicted, may be granted; but, at the same time, there is not much to be made of it. What is more important is that the touches of modernity and professionalism which the world expects from Saxe-Coburgs are generally supplied by them. Their influence, on the whole, is a steadying influence. They enter riotous countries in the spirit in which a Rugby prefect enters a fourth-form room; and the riot dies away. They enter disorderly countries with something of the bed-

THE HOUSE OF COBURG

side manner of the consulting physician entering the sick-room; and the patient takes heart, and begins to be convalescent. It has been so, at all events, in Belgium, and in Bulgaria; and it remains for us to consider whether it was so in Portugal—and if not, why not.

The answer will be that it was so to some extent —but not sufficiently—and not immediately; and the answer will be found to hold good whether we study the question in the Palace or in the political arena. Indeed, the two investigations are hardly separable.

That the House of Braganza needed an infusion of fresh blood badly is a proposition beyond dispute. It needed it as the consumptive need cod liver oil, and as the anæmic are said to need pink pills. It was currently believed, as we have seen, that there had, in fact, been an infusion of fresh blood at the time when Dom Miguel's mother preferred the gardener to the King; but that experiment had not saved the situation. It was—to revert to the metaphor—as if the patient had taken the wrong medicine: calomel, we will say, instead of cod liver oil, or opium instead of iron. The result had not been to enhance, but to lower, the moral vitality of the House. In this Coburg alliance, on the other hand, it did seem as if the right step had, at last, been taken to stabilise the moral constitution of the family. We shall be able to test the expectation when we come to the cases of the succeeding Kings: Dom Pedro V., Dom Luis, Dom Carlos, and Dom Manoel. The fact that the bridegroom was only

THE ROYAL HOUSE OF PORTUGAL

nineteen years of age had, of course, no bearing upon it. He was old enough to transmit his natural qualities; and the evolutionists tell us that acquired qualities cannot be transmitted.

Prince Ferdinand, however, was called in, not only as the doctor of the House of Braganza, but also as the doctor of the Portuguese body politic. Though he did not need experience for the former half of his task, he did need it for the latter; and his youth handicapped him. It was all to the good that Doña Maria fell in love with him at once, and soon began to bear him a large family; but they were, nevertheless, not a man and a woman, but a boy and a girl—too young to realise the conditions of the world about them.

What those conditions were we may gather from a report of a conversation of a member of the Portuguese Cabinet, with the Belgian Minister, Sylvain Van der Weyer:—

"I ought to warn you," the Portuguese said, "that we are on the surface of a volcano, and that the eruption may break out at any moment. Looking at royalty, as you see it here, surrounded with honour and receiving homage from ministers, officers of high rank, soldiers, and Palace guards, you would imagine, no doubt, that it was firmly established and secure from every risk. The fact is that the crown is lying on the ground. There is not a man among all those whom you see bowing low before the Queen who could not upset her throne if he chose. They all do obeisance within the precincts of the Palace; but they all begin to conspire as soon as they get outside."

PORTUGUESE PARTIES

What it meant, when we come to details, was that there were three parties in Portugal, and not what could, strictly speaking, be called a loyal party among them. Such loyalty as existed was loyalty, not to an individual, but to a cause, or an idea. There were Constitutionalists who would have nothing to do with the Queen unless she governed in accordance with the democratic Constitution of 1822. There were Chartists who would have nothing to do with her unless she ignored that Constitution and adopted the more Conservative Charta of 1826. There were Legitimists who wanted to restore Dom Miguel, in the hope that he would take money away from laymen and give it to clergymen. And each of these factions was prepared to fight, if it saw a chance of winning—for or against the Queen, accordingly as she sided for or against them.

Truly it was a perplexing situation for a boy and a girl to cope with. It was not even open to them to solve it by backing the winning side—for there were no obvious means of guessing which side was likely to win; and they had no personal authority which could help them to solve it in any other way. How little personal authority he himself possessed, or was likely to acquire, Prince Ferdinand must have realised on the day on which he landed and was received in stony silence by a populace which did not "hold with" foreigners; and Doña Maria, at sixteen or seventeen, could not be expected to have any more authority than a school-girl who stamps her foot, and says "Shan't." It remained

THE ROYAL HOUSE OF PORTUGAL

for them, therefore, to improvise solutions from time to time, without understanding the true nature of the problem, and, when in doubt, to suffer their feelings to be their truant guides.

That is what we are about to see them doing. The promise to forgo all attempts to give a connected account of the fourteen revolutions which enlivened fifteen years shall be kept; but a few salient scenes and episodes may be picked out, in the hope that they will give a better impression of the period than could be derived from the most minute and conscientious narrative of unimportant events.

CHAPTER XXII

Scenes in the life of Maria da Gloria—Fourteen revolutions in fifteen years—Battle for Court influence between Herr Dietz and Father Marcos—Visit to Lisbon by Duke Ernest of Saxe-Coburg—His description of Palace life there—Dumplings for dinner—Marshal Saldanha's revolution—The Queen's reconciliation to him—Her domestic virtues and her death.

NOT as a chronicle, but as a series of *tableaux vivants* shall the reign of Maria da Gloria and her husband, Ferdinand of Saxe-Coburg, appear before us.

Tableau I. shows us the sympathetic young couple shedding warm tears because they had to subscribe the Radical Constitution of 1822—a most distressing blow to dignity. Maria would have said of the Radical who extorted her signature that he

> Robs me of that which not enriches him,
> And makes me poor indeed.

So the tears streamed from her eyes as she dipped her pen in the ink; and when she afterwards went for her usual afternoon drive with Ferdinand, it was observed that his eyes were also red. Their public lamentations gave heart of hope to the reactionaries, who inferred, quite correctly, that Maria would dish the Radicals when she saw her way to do so. Mean-

THE ROYAL HOUSE OF PORTUGAL

while, they may remind the historian of the helpless griefs of the Babes in the Wood.

Tableau II. shows us Doña Maria taking refuge at Belem under the guns of a British fleet, and there recovering confidence sufficiently not only to dismiss her Ministers, but to be rude to them. It seemed to her that, as the British Government had protected her from violence, it regarded her caprices as her rights, and would support them; but that was a mistaken inference. The old doctrine of the freemasonry of crowned heads was dying—killed by the higher criticism of the Palmerstonian School; and though Doña Maria stamped her foot, saying that she could not possibly retain in office "men who had reduced the country to such a miserable condition," her petulance produced no impression on them, and they retained the upper hand.

In Tableau III. we observe a battle for influence at Court (and, indirectly, for influence over the Cabinet) between Ferdinand's tutor, Herr Dietz, and his Confessor, Father Marcos: an episode more interesting because the *rôles* which one might have expected the two men to adopt were reversed.

The tutor, in this case, was a prig of the German variety, with all the German lack of elasticity, and all the German feeling that, when constitutions encroach upon the authority of Kings, the ark of the covenant is profaned. The priest, on the contrary, having been Dom Pedro's Confessor, was one of the few priests who favoured constitutionalism; and he was also a jovial ecclesiastic of the Rabelaisian variety—one who kept the Court in roars of laughter by an endless stock of indecorous anecdotes. So we have to picture King and Queen torn this way and that by their simultaneous desire to profit by the tutor's good advice and enjoy the Confessor's good stories; while Confessor and tutor alike insisted that a choice must be made, and that one or other of these advantages must be sacrificed. The Tableau shows us how young and inexperienced the royal couple were.

The changing picture further shows us the prig, though he was wrong, prevailing, and the Rabelaisian, though he was right, constrained to take a lower place. The prig, indeed, was an unscrupulous mischief-maker, and tried to make even more mischief than he actually made. It was under his influence that Doña Maria presently appealed for the help of foreign bayonets in overthrowing the Constitution which she had just sworn to observe. The proposal, elaborated in concert by Dietz and the Belgian Minister, was that Belgium should supply troops, that English transports should convey them to Portugal, and that the Portuguese people should be taxed to pay for their services— to pay, that is to say, for the suppression of their own liberties. But the project fell through because, though Belgium was willing, England was not; and the principal result of it was to confirm Ferdinand's unpopularity. He was so unpopular, for a season, that people shouted offensive nick-names at him in the streets, and a Portuguese lady made a democratic demonstration by emptying a basin of slops on to him from an upper chamber.

THE ROYAL HOUSE OF PORTUGAL

So the time passed; and, on the whole, as he grew older, Ferdinand may be said to have justified himself, and to have sustained the reputation of the Coburgs. When Palmerston, some years later, at the time of the dispute about the Spanish marriages, declined to press a Coburg candidature for Queen Isabella's hand, on the ground that, as he told Sir Henry Bulwer, all the Coburgs seemed to him to be "below par," he expressly excepted the King of Portugal from his generalisation. He certainly was not below par on the occasion on which the revolutionists, believing that they had overcome him, scrawled on the wall of his Palace the lampoon:—

> Dom Fernando goes away,
> The Queen begins to cry;
> The Infanta starts to pray,
> And Dom Miguel draws nigh.

The Queen may have cried on that occasion; but Ferdinand assuredly did not show fear. The lampoon frightened him as little as the slops; and when the Palace Guards deserted him, he is said to have pursued them sword in hand. Moreover, as the revolutions, frequent though they were, did not, like Dom Miguel's civil war, entirely interrupt social life, he found time to reform a good many matters which needed reformation. His cousin Ernest, who visited him in 1839, drew quite a pleasant picture of the Portuguese scene in a letter to the English Prince Consort. He found that Ferdinand was growing up rapidly and was "already ashamed of his former faults and want of education and knowledge of the world." He reported Doña

FERDINAND

Maria to be "stout" but "a psychological conundrum," though fat people are usually simple, and also "an exemplary wife and mother." As for the reforms:—

"Lisbon may thank Ferdinand for two things of the greatest importance. Firstly, the cleaning of the City and the improvement of the police. Secondly, the improvement and support of agriculture."

As for the routine of Court life:—

"The arrangements in the castle itself, such as table, cellar, service, are in good order, and are on exactly the same scale as at the Saxon Court. The cooking is particularly good, as it bears a great resemblance to our own beloved household fare; I have already been surprised to see dumplings."

There we get the domestic touch which seems inseparable from the Coburgs: as a Coburg introduced dumplings into Portugal, so, we all know, did a Coburg introduce Christmas trees into England. Having dealt with the dumplings, Duke Ernest goes on to describe the "order of the day":—

"At ten o'clock we sit down to breakfast; those who are present are the Grand Almoner, the Chief Minister of Ceremonies with the Court ladies, the Chamberlain, the Adjutant on service, and the Officers of the Watch. It is a kind of luncheon at which rice constitutes the principal dish. . . .

". . . . I generally spend the morning with Ferdinand and Doña Maria; the Ministers often come to hand in some document, as do the Chamberlains

THE ROYAL HOUSE OF PORTUGAL

and Generals. The Queen receives no one alone, but every one comes to Ferdinand, who listens to them, arranges their affairs for them, and then only admits them to kiss the Queen's hand. When the person enters the drawing-room, Ferdinand always precedes him, and usually kisses her hand first. This struck me particularly. At two o'clock we generally ride out with the Queen, to examine anything worthy of notice in the City, or beautiful views and landscapes; we rarely return home before half-past five o'clock. Dinner is at seven, at which meal it is the exception for more persons to be present than are at breakfast. After dinner, people come to pay their respects, as they do at Grandmamma's at Gotha. In the evening one is quite free to go or stay as one likes, which I look upon as a very pleasant arrangement for those who live at Court. I play billiards almost daily with Ferdinand and several gentlemen."

It is not a disagreeable picture, that of a royal party encamped on the edge of a volcano, eating freely of rice and dumplings, in an interval between the eruptions—the Queen bearing children, and the King playing billiards, as calmly as if cataclysms were unheard-of things. The Coburg touch pervades it; and one finds other Coburg touches in Ferdinand's continual interest in the Theatre, the Opera, the Academies, and the arts and sciences generally. But the cataclysms were equally continuous; and it is these which make the history of the reign for the more serious historians.

Doña Maria, in spite of her unceasing maternal duties, generally faced those cataclysms with spirit;

and that whether the upheavals were domestic or due to foreign complications. She made a spirited retort when Queen Victoria, shocked by the language used concerning her royal cousin in the British Parliament, wrote to apologise. "I replied," she told Saldanha, "that I paid no attention to what was said concerning myself by an English Deputy, because I know that their House always had its sittings after dinner." Nor was she less spirited when her people's resentment against foreign influence displayed itself in manifestations against the tutor, Dietz. "Who," one of the papers asked concerning him, "is this boor who keeps his hat on in the royal presence?" And threatenings were breathed :—

"If Councillor Dietz," a journalist wrote, "does not at once quit the Palace of the Queen, the people themselves will go themselves and drag him from the abode which is sullied by the presence of so vile and shameless a parasite."

Whereupon Dietz offered to retire at once, and Doña Maria turned on him contemptuously, saying :—

"Go to a nunnery! Sooner will I lose the crown than continue to submit to these insults and this calumny. If you like, I will myself mount my horse and ride with you to the nearest barracks."

But Dietz, nevertheless, had to depart, though the jolly Father Marcos remained, and continued to divert the Court with Rabelaisian stories over the rice and dumplings. In a general way, indeed, one may sum the matter up by saying that Doña Maria's spirited attitude always enabled her to keep her throne, but never—or hardly ever—enabled her to get her way. The revolutions continued—those fourteen revolutions in fifteen years—and she had to accept the results of the revolutions, whatever they might be. Sometimes she liked those results; sometimes she did not. All the Ministers seem, at one time or another, to have taken the field against her as rebels; all the rebels seem, at one time or another, to have held Cabinet office. Sometimes, it would appear, her heart was really with the rebels; and there certainly were those among the rebels who loved her while they chastened her. Saldanha was one of these.

Dom Pedro had, in a sense, bequeathed Doña Maria to Saldanha—the effective fire-eater who had recovered her kingdom for her while she was a child. "Regard her as your own daughter," he had said to him; and Saldanha had obeyed the injunction, albeit placing his own interpretation on it. He may be said to have treated Doña Maria, not merely as a daughter, but as a child—a girl who never grew up—a girl who was apt to be naughty, and whom it was necessary to subject to discipline from time to time; and she, on her part, may be said to have accepted the relationship in the proper spirit. Saldanha's voice, it has been recorded, "was music in her ears"; and she trusted him, knowing that no great harm would come to her, even when he was marching on Lisbon at the head of an insurgent army.

MARIA DA GLORIA

Nor did any harm come to her. Doña Maria might have preferred—she doubtless would have preferred—the reactionary administration which Saldanha overthrew to the progressive administration which he introduced. But she had confidence in Saldanha, all the same, was sure that he would not hurt her, and that he meant well; and she wrote to him to say so:—

"I render justice," she wrote, "to the sentiments of Marshal Saldanha, because I believe him to be incapable of wishing to abuse the situation in which he is. I have faith in his honour as a soldier, and in his chivalry. I confide, in all safety, to the General and friend of my father the future of this country and crown. I request that he may come at once to Lisbon. He will find me firmly resolved to give him all my help, for I know it is necessary to root out all abuses, so that the constitutional system may not be a fallacy, and my name may never be used to cover injustice."

It is distinctly the cry of a naughty girl promising to behave better for the future. Saldanha accepted it in the spirit in which a father might accept such a pledge from a revolting daughter. He kissed the Queen's hand, and expressed his confidence that she would take a proper view of a rebellion which the circumstances had imperatively required. It was solely for Her Majesty's sake, he said, that he had risked his reputation in a hazardous enterprise; and, by so doing, he had done more for Her Majesty than he would have been willing to do for his own wife and family. For them, he would have been willing to risk his life and fortune—but not his honoured name.

After that, it was comparatively easy for them to kiss and be friends; and they did so. On the whole, Doña Maria probably felt relieved at having been beaten; for the man who had beaten her was a strong man, and the last years of her life were comparatively tranquil in consequence of his victory. Of the manner in which those years were spent we have an agreeable picture in Bollaert's *Wars of Succession in Portugal and Spain:*—

"It was the desire of the Queen that Saldanha should pay her a visit every evening at nine, remaining until eleven. After tea the Queen did her embroidery; the King occupied himself in works of art, such as sculpture of ivory, engraving, and drawing; conversation being of a friendly and familiar nature. . . .

". . . In the Queen's room there were only three chairs, of different patterns, but most commodious; they were called the Queen's chair, the King's chair, and the Marshal's chair. One evening, when the Marshal was seated, the Queen thus addressed him: 'We are going to put your sincerity to the test; after tea you will tell me of all my faults, and then you will tell the King of his.'"

A request with which Saldanha promised to comply on one condition: that his remarks should be received in the spirit in which Mme. de Maintenon listened to the strictures of Fénelon. Doña Maria agreed to the condition, with the result that, at the end of a stormy scene, the curtain can be

MARIA DA GLORIA

dropped upon a final tableau of a domestic order: the tableau which shows the sympathetic fire-eater on the hearth—half paternal in his manner and half deferential—telling the Queen and her consort of their faults, every evening from nine until eleven. When, by any accident, he failed to come, the Queen wrote him a pretty, intimate note—such a missive as the following:—

"My dear Duke,

"As you did not come last night, I beg you will appear to-day about 12 o'clock, and that you wil persuade the King to go to-morrow to the bull-fight. When you come I will tell you why I am so anxious about going to the bull-fight. We shall be to-night at the French theatre. Do not fail to come to us. "Maria."

So that the end of Doña Maria's life was tranquil, though she only enjoyed the tranquillity for about two years. In 1853 she died, worn out with child-bearing, having been the mother of eleven children, three of whom had died in infancy. Her enemies, at the end, had forgiven her faults in consideration of her exemplary domestic virtues. She was the first Queen of Portugal who compelled her children to beg the pardon of inferiors to whom they had been rude—a circumstance in which we may perhaps find yet another proof of the value of the Coburg influence; and Saldanha said that he had never, in any circle, seen a husband and wife more devoted to each other.

"Doña Maria," writes a contemporary Portuguese chronicler, "was of moderate stature, robust, had dark eyes, and was fair—a pattern of domestic virtues, and an enlightened woman."

"Enlightened," one fears, is an exaggeration due to flattery—spoiled children are hardly to be called "enlightened"; but Doña Maria was at least teachable—though she was not taught easily—and one cannot help coming to like her, as her subjects did, as one approaches the end of her career.

CHAPTER XXIII

Ferdinand of Saxe-Coburg as Regent—His son, Dom Pedro—Queen Victoria's attempt to marry Pedro to Princess Charlotte of Belgium—His marriage to Princess Stéphanie of Hohenzollern-Sigmaringen—Death of Stéphanie—Death of Pedro—Uncertainty as to his abilities.

THE eldest of Doña Maria's children was still a minor. A Regent was necessary, and Ferdinand took the office. Nobody minded—some people were even glad—and, for once in a way, there was no trouble. After enduring fourteen revolutions in fifteen years, the Portuguese people were temporarily tired of trouble; and they were not yet tired of the respite from it which they had gained when the fire-eater subsided on to the hearth and murmured criticism from his arm-chair in the Queen's boudoir instead of blazing it violently abroad in pronunciamientos. The Regency, therefore, has no history; and when it terminated, in September, 1855, Ferdinand was able to relapse into private life and enjoy himself.

As he had been a good husband, so also he was a good father, as one would expect a Coburg to

THE ROYAL HOUSE OF PORTUGAL

be; and we find yet another unmistakable Coburg touch in the attention which he gave to the education of his sons. For the first time in Portuguese history kingship was treated as a profession for which Princes must be prepared as carefully as are physicians or lawyers or any other professional men for their respective callings. The Portuguese Democrats, as we have seen, had already demanded reform in the education of their Princes, and had brusquely proposed that the heir of John the Runaway should prepare himself for his duties by a course of travel which they were good enough to map out for him.

It was a sound proposition, albeit presented with something of the arrogance of a don warning an undergraduate that his ignorance is a disgrace to his college; and Kings, of course, do not like to be talked to in that tone. The King of Portugal did not, nor did his son, the Emperor of Brazil; but Ferdinand, on his part, stood in no need of the admonition. His own boys were first taught by his own old tutor, the solemn Dietz, and then, in 1854 and 1855, sent round the Courts of Europe to pick up useful information. They seem to have been liked and admired. Pedro, the elder, in particular was liked and admired by Queen Victoria, who tried to find him a wife, and thought that he would be the very husband for Princess Charlotte, the daughter of the King of the Belgians:—

"You may rely," she wrote to Leopold, "on our divulging nothing. We are, however, both very

PEDRO V

anxious that dear Pedro should be preferred. He is out and out *the* most distinguished young Prince there is, and, besides that, good, excellent, and steady, according to one's heart's desire, and as one could wish for an *only and beloved daughter*. For Portugal, too, an *amiable*, well-educated Queen would be an immense blessing, for there *never* has been one. I am sure you would be more likely to secure Charlotte's happiness if you gave her to Pedro than to one of those innumerable Archdukes, or to Prince George of Saxony."

But Charlotte had her own point of view. Perhaps she saw—what Queen Victoria perhaps did not see—that Pedro, with all his virtues, was rather a gloomy young prig. Those who knew him best said that they never saw him laugh, except on one single occasion—when he heard the Duke of Saldanha, then quite an elderly fire-eater, say that he thought of proposing marriage to a certain lady, but wished first to ascertain whether she wore a wig. On that occasion, it is said, he laughed as if he would never stop; but he was then still in the school-room. On attaining manhood, he ceased to laugh; and Charlotte thought that she would prefer a jollier lover. So we next find Queen Victoria writing:—

"My object is and was that Charlotte should decide as *she* likes it, and uninfluenced by what I might prefer. *I* should *prefer* Pedro, that I confess, but that Archduke has made a favourable impression on Charlotte; I saw that long before any question of engagement had taken place."

And yet Queen Victoria *did* want to influence

Charlotte, as the next letter, in which she tries to do so, shows:—

"I *still hope* by your letter that Charlotte has not finally made up her mind—as we both feel so strongly convinced of the immense superiority of Pedro over any other young Prince even *dans les relations journalistes*, besides which the position is so infinitely preferable. The Austrian society is *médisante* and profligate and worthless—and the Italian possessions very shaky. Pedro is full of resource—fond of music, fond of drawing, of languages, of natural history, and literature, in all of which Charlotte would suit him, and would be a *real* benefit to the country. If Charlotte asked *me*, I should not hesitate a moment."

But Charlotte did not ask Queen Victoria, for she had made up her mind. A Sailor Prince attracted her more than a Scholar Prince; and, in the Archduke Maximilian, she had found such a one. He was the brother of the Emperor Francis Joseph, presently to be called the Emperor Maximilian, and to be shot, in the Square of Queretaro, by the Mexicans whose Emperor he claimed to be; and Charlotte was that Empress Charlotte who still lives on, dead to the world, under restraint, in the Château de Bouchout. Queen Victoria, it may be added, got over her disappointment at the failure of her matchmaking when she met Maximilian, and sat between him and the subsequent German Emperor Frederick at a luncheon-party. She found him "so *English* in his feelings and likings"; and she exclaimed—

DEATH OF PEDRO V

the exclamation in view of the event is very pathetic:—

"I wish you really joy, dearest Uncle, at having got *such* a husband for dear Charlotte, as I am sure he will make her happy, and is quite worthy of her."

So Pedro had to seek a wife at another Court; and he found one in Princess Stéphanie of Hohenzollern-Sigmaringen. Duke Ernest supplied the Coburg touch, on that occasion, by expressing the hope that the bride would confirm the bridegroom in his "German habit of thought"; but that expectation was never put to the test. The new Queen died almost as soon as she was married; and Dom Pedro only survived her a few months. People said, as people are apt to say in such cases, that he died of grief; but he died, in fact, of typhus fever—a disease which grief does not cause, and from which joy gives no immunity. Practically the whole of the royal family was down with it; and only one of the four brothers who took it recovered. The people in their sorrow—for they did really love the boy King in whose brief time there had been peace—declared that he must have been poisoned, and, not knowing by whom, went about the streets of Lisbon smashing all the windows of all the chemists' shops, in the hope that thus they could not fail to smash the windows of the right one; but the result of an autopsy reassured them.

There remained Dom Luiz, Duke of Oporto, who was at sea, and knew nothing of his bereavement

THE ROYAL HOUSE OF PORTUGAL

until his ship entered the Tagus on the morning of November 14th, 1861, and the Prime Minister came on board to break the news to him. "I have lost at one stroke," he said, "the two things which I most prized in this world—my brother and my liberty." And Queen Victoria, writing yet again to the King of the Belgians, poured out her soul thus:—

"How the hand of death seems bent on pursuing that poor, dear family! once so prosperous. Poor Ferdinand, so proud of his children—of his five sons—now the eldest and *most* distinguished, the head of the family, *gone*, and the youngest *still* ill! The two others at sea, and will land to-morrow in utter ignorance of everything, and poor, dear, good Louis (whom I thought dreadfully low when we saw him and Jean for an hour on Friday) King! It is an almost incredible event! a terrible calamity for Portugal, and a *real* European loss! Dear Pedro was so good, so clever, so distinguished! He was so attached to my beloved Albert, and the characters and tastes suited so well, and he had such confidence in Albert! *All are gone! He* is happy now, united again to dear Stéphanie, whose loss he never recovered."

Perhaps Pedro died too young for the historian to judge him. Certainly it is idle to speculate as to what he might have succeeded in doing for his country and his dynasty if he had lived. Perhaps, too, the value of Queen Victoria's judgment is a little impaired by her known reluctance to see anything but good in any Coburg anywhere. Still, the impression which he made, not only on her, but also on the Portuguese people, was entirely favourable;

Stéphanie of Hohenzollern-Sigmaringen.

and it is impossible not to deplore that he died too soon to have a chance of showing whether his capacity was on a level with his character, and whether the qualities of the Coburgs, at their best, were such that Portugal could be saved by them.

Assuredly it must have been clear to everyone—if anything in politics is ever clear to anyone—that Portugal needed a vast deal of saving. The position of the King of Portugal had begun to be—and was to continue to be—pretty much like that of a headmaster, obliged to govern his school through his prefects, but not allowed to choose his prefects, and not at all sure that he can trust them. That is to say, that the professional politicians had begun to be—and were to continue to be—the curse of the country. They were men—not all of them, of course, but a great many of them—who were in politics for what they could get out of them; and we shall see their methods of procedure passing through two distinct stages: a stage in which they contended jealously for the privilege of plundering the country; a stage in which they came to a friendly arrangement whereby they took it in turns to plunder the country.

A King, it is obvious, cannot fairly be blamed for everything which happens under such conditions. On the other hand, a King who contents himself with presiding in dignified magnificence over such a family party of political bandits cannot be praised. If he does so, a third party is likely to arise and sweep both him and them away; while, if he tries to create such a party, and place himself at the head of it, there remains the chance that the existing parties may repudiate their allegiance to him before he has had time to create it. That, in a nutshell, has been the problem; and one would have liked to see it faced by Dom Pedro, the flower of the House of Coburg, of whom so much was expected. As it is, we must content ourselves with seeing how Dom Luiz, and Dom Carlos, and Dom Manoel failed to solve it.

But not immediately. First we must turn back and follow Ferdinand as he subsides into domesticity, and finds happiness in the society of a morganatic wife.

CHAPTER XXIV

Later life of Ferdinand—His refusal of Kingly Crowns—An Opera artiste consoles him for the loss of his wife—His marriage to her—Rudeness of the Portuguese Court to her—Domestic life at Cintra—The gardens and the parrot—A visit from General and Mrs. Grant.

IT was not because he had to, but because he preferred to, that Ferdinand, for the remainder of his days, did nothing but, as the æsthetes used to say, "exist beautifully." He was the most eligible of the unemployed members of the family which, having invented professional Kings, was expected to supply them; and many onerous appointments of the kind were offered to him. He might, if he had liked, have been Emperor of Mexico, or King of Greece, or King of Spain; but he had had adventures enough, and turned a deaf ear to all applications for his services.

The Greek adventure was proposed to him after the bloodless revolution which had expelled Otho of Bavaria—a Prince who, be it remarked, had made himself unpopular with the Greeks, just as Ferdinand had made himself unpopular with the Portuguese, by introducing German counsellors into

THE ROYAL HOUSE OF PORTUGAL

his kingdom, and treating their advice as the last word of wisdom. Ferdinand, with his extensive experience of revolutions—fourteen revolutions, be it repeated, in fifteen years—seemed the very man for the delicate office. The King of the Belgians, feeling that the honour of the Coburgs was at stake, pressed him to undertake it, holding out various inducements :—

"Since they urged it in England," he wrote to Duke Ernest, "I sent J. Devaux, van Pradt's nephew, to Lisbon. I intended by arguments to make an impression. I even went so far as to say that the beauty of the Levantine women was known to be very great."

To those to whom the late Prince Consort is the typical Coburg the last sentence may not seem characteristically Coburgian; but it fits in well enough with what we know of the son and successor of the monarch who threw out the hint. His career, at any rate, proves that the Coburgs—some Coburgs, at all events—are susceptible to the charms of miscellaneous ladies; and Leopold I. may have had his reasons for supposing that the temptation would appeal to Ferdinand. What he did not know, apparently, was that Ferdinand had already yielded to a temptation of the kind, and had no desire to let his fancy stray further.

The lady who had so successfully tempted him was Mlle. Elise Frederica Hensler, the daughter of the pianist who accompanied the artistes at the Coburg Theatre. It had seemed to the accompanist that his daughter's morals were not safe in that

FERDINAND'S SECOND MARRIAGE

environment—that there were too many royal Dukes and other aristocrats hanging round the stage-door, with intentions which were not, strictly speaking, honourable. The girl had talent, and he wished to see her properly trained for the stage, without the protection of Princes. To that end he took her to America, where she made her *début* in opera at New York. Presently she accepted an engagement to appear at the San Carlos Theatre, in Lisbon; and there she captured the heart of Ferdinand, while playing the part of the page Oscar, in Verdi's *Un Ballo in Maschera*.

His recent bereavements—for this was soon after the death of Dom Pedro—had left Ferdinand in sore need of consolation. He thought that the beautiful girl with the beautiful voice could comfort him by singing to him; and he sent for her, and told her to sing. The comfort of song, he soon discovered, was not all the comfort that he needed; but the rest was easily arranged. His intentions, he explained, if not honourable in the narrowest and most literal sense of the word, were at least as honourable as circumstance permitted them to be. He could offer Mlle. Hensler, if not his hand, at least his heart, the devotion of a lifetime, and satisfactory settlements. She, on her part, asked, for the moment, nothing more; and she was openly established under his protection: a queer sequel truly to her father's prudential withdrawal of her from another Coburg environment—though whether a climax or an anti-climax one hardly likes to say.

THE ROYAL HOUSE OF PORTUGAL

In any case, however, there was a climax to come; and Ferdinand was, after the lapse of a few years, to give his hand to the lady who had not only accepted but retained his heart—a consummation in which we find romance and politics curiously confused.

It was at the time when, Queen Isabella having been turned out of Spain, Prim was looking for a King. Ferdinand was one of those to whom Prim's thoughts turned; and the Duc de Montpensier was another of the candidates for the vacant throne. Though Ferdinand was reluctant to come forward, Montpensier wished to make quite sure that he would not do. He therefore took two steps: causing hints to be conveyed to Mlle. Hensler that her lover, if he became King of Spain, would probably marry again, and dismiss her; pointing out to the Papal Nuncio at Lisbon that Ferdinand's relations with Mlle. Hensler were scandalous, and ought to be rebuked. The rebuke was duly administered, and Ferdinand put an end at once to the scandal and to his own eligibility to the Spanish throne by marrying his mistress on June 10th, 1869.

Even then, of course, it was not everybody who was pleased. Duke Ernest, anxious as ever to do his cousin a good turn, gave the bride a Saxe-Gotha peerage, in which she figured as Countess of Edla; but there were serious attempts at the Portuguese Court to make her position as uncomfortable as possible. There was a new Queen in Portugal now—Maria Pia, the consort of Dom Luiz, and the daughter of the great Victor Emmanuel. She was

THE COUNTESS OF EDLA

a Queen of a terrifying grandeur—so much so that even Queen Amélie is said to have been, at first, afraid of her. Her father-in-law's second wife was to her merely "that person"—a person on whom she would always turn her back; and, of course, the Court took its cue from her. The typical scene is graphically described by Mr. D'Auvergne:—

"On the occasion of some festival the Countess found herself waiting in some ante-chamber of the Palace, with a crowd of diplomatists, functionaries, and courtiers. When the doors were thrown open, no one offered an arm to King Ferdinand's wife. Seeing this, the Spanish Ambassador politely offered his escort, and led the lady into the hall. Every seat was occupied, according to instructions issued overnight. The Portuguese snobs stuck fast to their chairs and grinned. The Ambassador motioned to his wife, who at once surrendered her seat to the Countess; whereupon, to make the insult still more marked, a number of courtiers sprang to their feet, offering their places to her Spanish Excellency."

The Countess of Edla, in short, was treated almost as rudely by the aristocracy of Portugal as Maria Pia's cousin, King Amadeo, was, a little while afterwards, treated by the aristocracy of Spain. The defence would probably be—at all events, one can think of no other—that if charming actresses were not thus humiliated when they obtained matrimonial promotion, they would obtain it too often, and that Princesses who, like Queen Maria Pia, were more formidable than attractive, would too frequently be left as old maids on the shelf. Whether the end justifies the means—whether bad manners are the best sanction of good morals—is another question which must, for the moment, be left unconsidered; though it seems likely that it will be long before ladies who have appeared on the stage in tights are accepted as equals by royal ladies who are conscious that their own appearance in tights would achieve at the best only a success of curiosity.

So that the fight was hard. The Countess of Edla fought it bravely, to the best of her ability, and Ferdinand did his best for her by always taking her with him when he attended a Court function; but one may nevertheless suspect that both he and she were glad when, having demonstrated sufficiently for honour, they were free to withdraw to that private life which they both preferred, and in which they were both qualified to shine. In due course they did withdraw to it, and—neither of them doing anything which gave calumny a handle—the mass of the people came to love them, even if the Court did not.

One trait of pride, it is said—acquired in Portugal—lingered with Ferdinand rather unnecessarily long. Though he was a private person, he still, instead of shaking hands with persons of lower station when he met them in social intercourse, held out his own hand to be kissed; but that method of patronising salutation was terminated by the tact and self-possession of the Minister Plenipotentiary of the French Republic. He affected to misunderstand—to suppose that the hand had been stretched

FERDINAND

out in order that he might examine and admire the rings; and he reviewed the rings, one by one, with suitable exclamations. What a diamond! What a ruby! What an emerald! And what a privilege to be permitted to inspect such precious stones at such close quarters!

It was the most subtle and delicate of rebuffs, proving that Republicans, as well as Kings, are capable of supercilious irony; and it served its purpose. Dom Luiz himself, soon afterwards, abolished the ceremony of hand-kissing; while Ferdinand realised that, when Kings become private persons, the world expects them to behave as such. He did thenceforward behave as such, devoting himself to the luxurious life of a wealthy *dilettante*, who delighted not only in patronising the arts, but in practising them. The magnificent Zoological Gardens at Lisbon were laid out at his initiative; and he learnt how to paint on porcelain.

The worst that could be said against him in those days was that he was rather extravagant. In a poor country, which knew not only deficits but defaults, he spent no less than £320,000 in embellishing his country seat at Cintra. That—like the offering of his hand to be kissed—was a trait, not so much of his own house, as of the house into which he had married; and we shall see, as we proceed, that the contrast between royal opulence and public indigence was one of the considerations which eventually made the House of Braganza impossible. But the Palace was at any rate magnificent—built in imitation of a mediæval castle, with turrets, crenelated walls, machicolations, and all other appropriate embellishments; and the interior, besides being replete with modern comfort, was a valuable art museum.

For Ferdinand, in his later years, was a great traveller and a great collector. Everywhere, from Italy to England, he ransacked the shops of the dealers in pictures and curiosities to enrich his home, described, in Russell Young's *Round the World with Grant*, as "one of the most interesting houses in Europe." When visitors came to him with suitable introductions, he personally escorted them through the galleries and gardens—his pet parrot following him about as faithfully as a dog, and so bearing silent witness—if it did, in fact, remain silent—to the amiability of his character. And when the visitors returned from their tour of inspection, they found tea prepared for them—tea with tea-cakes which Ferdinand had taught the Countess of Edla to make. Those tea-cakes proved, in the opinion of Mrs. Grant, that, whatever might have been her levity at one period of her career, she must be of a character fundamentally serious and virtuous—as no doubt she was.

It must have been a happy life; and the happiness lasted for about fifteen years. The warning that the end was near came when a sore on Ferdinand's face developed into a disfiguring cancer. His interest in the arts continued in spite of his illness; and he had a *grille* placed in front of his box at the Opera, so that he might still go there and see without being seen. The hopes, however,

DEATH OF FERDINAND

which the physicians at first held out were illusory; and he died, with his family about him—his royal family as well as his actress wife—on December 15th, 1885.

The world had so far forgotten him that the papers hardly gave his death more than a paragraph. For years he had lived quite apart from the main current of Portuguese politics; and it is to that stream that we must now return.

CHAPTER XXV

Queen Victoria's praise of Stéphanie of Hohenzollern—And of Dom Luiz—Simple character of Dom Luiz—His marriage to Maria Pia, daughter of Victor Emmanuel—Anti-Clericalism of Dom Luiz—His failure to govern Portugal—Saldanha's last revolution—His treatment of Maria Pia—Her severe rebuke—Death of Dom Luiz and accession of Dom Carlos—The problem which faced Dom Carlos.

WHOEVER might think ill of the members of the Portuguese Royal family, Queen Victoria and the Prince Consort thought highly of them, and were fond of them: not of Dom Pedro only, but of his wife and brother too. Stéphanie of Hohenzollern delighted the Queen, as she told the King of the Belgians, by the "inexpressibly dear and pure and good expression of her dear eyes"; and Prince Albert wrote in much the same strain to the late Empress Frederick:—

"She is so good, simple, and unassuming, and has an expression in her eyes which I do not remember to have seen in those of anyone else—a kind of wistfulness and trustful entreaty, to which one would fain tender every knightly service and protection. She will be sure to please Pedro."

DOM LUIZ

The brief reference to Dom Luiz in Queen Victoria's correspondence with the King of the Belgians runs thus:—

"You ask me if Louis Oporto is grown? He is, and his figure much improved. He is a good, kind, amiable boy whom one must like."

He had not grown to any great size, however, and the improvement in his figure was not permanent. He developed, with the years, into a blonde and podgy little man, who looked rather odd in the Admiral's uniform which he always wore—a comic opera Admiral, one would have said, if one did not know, rather than an actual mariner of the House of Henry the Navigator—a King in piquant contrast with his Queen, Maria Pia, the daughter of the great Victor Emmanuel, who looked her part with more dumfoundering dignity, even as a girl, than any other Queen of the period. The contrast, it must be added, was one of character as well as outward appearance.

Simplicity is often the note of a sailor; and Dom Luiz was simplicity incarnate. Perhaps he had nautical interests—the constant wearing of the naval uniform gave that impression, and may have been meant to give it; but his deepest interests—in middle age, at all events—were literary, artistic, and scientific. He combined the Braganza melancholy with the Coburg accomplishments, and went through life with a sad smile, making the French language fashionable by his example in speaking it, translating the works of Shakespeare into Portuguese, and playing that sorrowful instrument the violoncello—sufficiently well to win a compliment from Rossini. And so the time passed until he was overtaken by sciatica and dropsy—complaints which he aggravated by eating huge plates of meat in the mistaken belief that he needed them to keep his strength up.

Maria Pia, on the other hand, cared little for any of the arts, save that of living magnificently and reigning proudly and devoutly. The royal life, she conceived, ought to be a pious pageant. She longed with an equal longing for more monks and more footmen; and Dom Luiz, though firm in the matter of the monks, gave way in the matter of the flunkeys. It might almost be said that, for every monk suppressed, he allowed a flunkey to be added to the royal establishment. Their scarlet liveries helped to make the Court gorgeous; while the anti-clericalism, mild though it was, diminished the number of idlers who battened on the resources of a poor country. Maria Pia, submitting to the anti-clericalism which she could not prevent, redressed the balance by bringing up her sons on pious lines and exhorting Dom Carlos in particular to become a better Catholic than his father, as he did.

Dom Luiz, at any rate, was anti-clerical enough for all immediate purposes; but unfortunately, though anti-clericalism is the beginning of wisdom, it is not the whole of wisdom; and Dom Luiz, with the Coburg virtues, continued to display the Braganza inadequacy. People, as Queen Victoria said, "could not help liking him"; and the stories

Queen Maria Pia.

of attempts to poison him do not seem to be true. One story related that a fellow-guest who accidentally drank from the King's glass instead of his own fell dead in his place in the banqueting-hall; another that a cigar which he had accidentally thrown away instead of smoking had been analysed and found to contain arsenic. Probably both stories were anti-clerical inventions designed to throw suspicion upon Miguelitish monks. In any case, Dom Luiz was popular—even when revolutions were going on; for it was evident to all that, if he did little good, at least he meant no harm.

But he could not govern Portugal, and can hardly even be said to have tried to do so; and Portugal is one of those Latin countries in which tradition counts for little against logic, and the view prevails that whatever is useless should be abolished. People began to wonder whether it was worth while paying a King a large stipend for doing nothing except look on while the professional politicians took it in turn to bleed the taxpayers white, and debts were piled up, and deficits were the order of the day. There were eight Ministers of Finance in two years —each of them more incompetent than the others; and a Deputy summed up the situation thus:—

"We have a deficit equal to half the amount of the revenue; we have a public debt which absorbs half of that revenue; the people refuse to pay more taxes; we have no fortified towns, nor artillery, nor cavalry capable of charging, nor infantry capable of marching, nor arms of modern type, nor soldiers who know how to fire the arms they have, nor a national militia, nor a navy, nor colonies, nor allies."

He went on, putting certain dots on certain "i's":—

"The desires of the people are for a Republic, as being the form of government most in accordance with their principles: the only one which can save the country from the dangers which threaten it."

There, it will be seen, as far back as 1870, we get our first hint of that Republican movement which was, in the end, to sweep everything before it. It was not as yet powerful enough to be taken seriously; but the feeling was unquestionably once more in the air that, as a long time—as time counted in Portugal—had elapsed since the last revolution, another revolution was due. Any revolution would serve provided that there was a revolution of some sort; and the best way to avert a grave revolution would be to inaugurate a mild one. So, at all events, thought Saldanha, the fire-eater, who, though now an octogenarian, was anxious to eat fire once more before he died.

Of the kind of revolution which the extremists were then threatening we may form some idea from the following incendiary appeal which was being circulated in Lisbon:—

"Citizens! A duty of national honour calls us to arms. To arms against the Palace! To arms against the Crown! To arms against the King! Let us rush to arms, and let our war-cry be: 'Down with the King! Long live the Republic!'"

SALDANHA

It was by no means a revolution of that sort which Saldanha had in mind. He desired, as has been said, a mild revolution which would avert a grave one, much as inoculation with smallpox used to be believed to prevent a fatal attack of the malady. It is characteristic of the old Portuguese way of doing things that he unfolded his programme to the King himself, first suggesting that he should dismiss his Ministers, and then adding, by way of explanation of his attitude :—

"Sire, I am unwilling to be considered ambitious or disloyal to the Crown; but I might appear so if I did not endeavour to prevent a revolution which would oblige me to become the Regent. I will therefore put myself at the head of a revolution such as I know I shall be able to guide and control for Your Majesty's advantage. Your Majesty may rest assured that I shall not, in my old age, dishonour my steadfast principles of loyalty."

It would have been an amazing programme for any other statesman in any other country; but Saldanha was, as it were, a chartered revolutionist —one with whom it was almost a matter of routine to rebel against a King for his good. Indeed, he hardly regarded himself as rebelling in such cases, any more than a nurse regards herself as rebelling when she stands a naughty child of noble birth in the corner. When he had administered such discipline to Maria da Gloria, she had thanked him for it, and invited him to take a comfortable chair by the fire, and tell her of her faults. He may have expected Dom Luiz and Maria Pia to do the same.

THE ROYAL HOUSE OF PORTUGAL

Dom Luiz, left to himself, was quite capable of doing so. His attitude towards revolutions was not unlike the attitude of the man who said that he did not believe in ghosts because he had seen too many of them. He had seen revolution after revolution blow by like a gust of wind; he had no particular objection to any revolution which left him free to translate Shakespeare and play the violoncello. But Maria Pia was cast in a different mould, being the daughter of a King who took himself seriously as a great man, and stood no nonsense. She also proposed to stand no nonsense; and she brought Italian standards to bear on Portuguese affairs, and made a scene which must have caused Saldanha some amazement.

The Marshal had done his work and got his way. Everything had gone off well—and almost quietly—in accordance with his programme. He had risen before dawn, taken an early cup of tea, marched to the Palace, and upset the Government between breakfast and lunch. The few shots which had been fired had been fired by mistake. The people killed had been killed by accident, and were too few to matter and too unimportant to be missed. He had taken the seals of office with little more ado than if he had been sweeping up the stakes after a game of cards. Finally, by way of ending the morning's business with an act of courtesy, he craved an audience of the Queen, in order that he might kiss her hand and present his homage. She sent for him, and spoke her mind. These were her words:—

MARIA PIA

"Marshal, I have sent for you to say that, if I were the King, I should have you shot to-morrow in a public square. Now you can go. I have told you what I think of your behaviour."

It must have been a dramatic scene. We must remember, in order to realise it, that Maria Pia was little more than a girl—just twenty-three years of age—and that Saldanha was an octogenarian warrior, with a venerable bald head, flashing eyes, a ferocious white moustache, and a military reputation which stood as high in Portugal as that of the Duke of Wellington in the past, or Earl Kitchener at the present time, in England. And Maria Pia spoke to him as a headmaster might have spoken to an impertinent schoolboy summoned to his presence to be reprimanded.

He was, of course, in no danger. All his precautions had been taken, and he had the army behind him. It would have been much easier for him to have Maria Pia shot in a public square than for her to have that treatment meted out to him. But that fact, equally of course, only stimulates our admiration for her nerve. It is another of our many proofs that, in the House of Braganza, the women have nearly always been the best men. The young woman had the *beau rôle* at the interview, and the fire-eater knew it. He only held office for a few months, and then accepted the honourable post of Ambassador at the Court of St. James's—a preferment which many regarded as a kind of honourable banishment.

That was the end of that revolution—the only

THE ROYAL HOUSE OF PORTUGAL

one which really mattered in the reign. It occurred early in the reign; and the reign, on the whole, was tranquil. One might, for that reason, call it a success—but not for any other reason. Only minor problems were solved; and major problems were, all the time, demanding a solution. The chief problem was that raised by the proceedings of the professional politicians—the two parties of the self-styled Progressives and Regenerators who, completely out of touch with the laborious Portuguese taxpayers, conducted a mimic battle, the bitterness of which was tempered by the tacit understanding that they would take it in turns to enjoy the sweets of office, cut up the pie, and distribute the slices generously among their supporters. That is the problem which we shall see coming to a head in the reign of Dom Carlos, who inherited as much of his mother's arbitrary disposition as of his father's artistic tastes—whose guiding maxim may be said to have been that of M. Prudhomme :—

"My sword shall defend the Constitution, and even, if need be, overthrow it."

CHAPTER XXVI

Anecdotes of Dom Carlos's boyhood—His achievements as artist, sportsman, and athlete—His feats in the Mall and in the bull-ring—His search for a wife—Incidents of his courtship—Anecdotes of the wedding—Great qualities of his wife, Princess Amélie—Her rescue of a fisherman from drowning—Dom Carlos as a reformer—His desire to be a benevolent dictator—His failure to conciliate the rival reformers of Coimbra.

A STORY told of a nursery quarrel between Dom Carlos and his brother Affonso, Duke of Oporto, may help us to see what manner of man the future King was growing up to be.

Affonso, who was presently to become an officer in the scientific branch of the service, took a precocious interest in mechanics and engineering—matters which left Dom Carlos cold, if not contemptuous. Making scientific experiments with his toys, Affonso constructed a toy bridge out of pieces of string and slabs of wood. Dom Carlos inspected it with scorn, and kicked it over. Whereupon there was an outburst of wrath, and a mutual punching of heads, terminated by the mediation of the Nursery Powers. Inquiry having been made, Dom Carlos was punished, and ordered to apologise. He accepted his punishment, since no other course was open to him; but in lieu of tendering an apology, he put out his tongue. It is a story of no particular importance, but of a certain symbolic interest, illustrating the eternal quarrel between the utilitarian and the artistic temperaments.

Dom Carlos, whatever he might not be, was at least an artist: not only by temperament, but also in virtue of his accomplishments. He knew intimately as many as seven languages, and assisted his father in his translation of the works of Shakespeare. He loved the drama, and patronised its exponents—particularly its female exponents—presenting Mme. Réjane with that team of cream-coloured mules which was, for a while, the admiration of Paris. He was a better sculptor and painter than most amateurs, frequently exhibiting his water-colours at the Lisbon Salon, and even winning a silver medal at one of the Paris Exhibitions. If some people praised his work too highly because he was a King, others depreciated it unduly for the same reason. It was good enough to have counted if he had been a painter and nothing else.

There were several sports, too, in which Dom Carlos excelled. Innumerable stories are told of his skill as a marksman. He would toss a stone into the air, split it with a shot from his revolver, and then split one of the fragments with a second shot before it reached the ground—an exploit which marks him out as a worthy rival of Dr. Carver and certain performers in Buffalo Bill's Wild West Show. He used to stand on the shores of the Lake

DOM CARLOS

of Obidos, and pot the fish as they rose to the surface. He hit a running deer at a distance of a hundred yards while himself sitting behind a fast-trotting pony. He brought down an eagle with a vertical shot at a distance of eighty yards.

Moreover, he was athlete as well as sportsman. On a visit to London he once made himself the idol of the populace by stopping a runaway horse in the Mall; and in Portugal he once thrashed a footpad on the high road, and often entered the bull-ring to show what he could do.

The ordinary Portuguese bull-fight, of course, is a mild affair, for the horns of the bull are padded; but when a Court beauty challenged Dom Carlos to face a bull with unpadded horns, he accepted the challenge without hesitation. The adventure nearly cost him his life; but he escaped, and the Portuguese were wildly enthusiastic. He had every reason—or, at any rate, a good many reasons—to believe that they loved him; and he moved about among them fearlessly, unprotected and almost unescorted. He was the sort of man, in short, of whom one would be really glad to be able to add that he was also a good King. He certainly meant to be one; but he had his limitations, to which we will come after we have spoken of his marriage, which was concluded while he was still heir-apparent.

His choice was naturally limited to Catholic Princesses; and he went on his travels to look for one, as Princes do. It was uncertain, when he

THE ROYAL HOUSE OF PORTUGAL

started, whether he would find one in Vienna, in Dresden, or in Paris. The name of Princess Amélie, daughter of the Comte de Paris, had been mentioned, and Dom Carlos had admired her portrait; but it was by no means certain that the Comte de Paris would look favourably on the suit. The Duc d'Aumale, indeed, invited him to meet the Comte de Paris and his daughter at Chantilly; but there was a doubt whether the Comte de Paris would keep the appointment. He did not know very much about the Duke of Braganza, and desired further information before committing himself; so he sent a messenger before his face.

The messenger was to call on the Duke of Braganza at the Hotel Bristol, and inspect him. If he was favourably impressed by him, he was to say that the Comte de Paris looked forward to the pleasure of making his acquaintance at Chantilly on the following day. If he was unfavourably impressed, he was to say that it was a great disappointment to the Comte de Paris that he would not have the pleasure of meeting him at Chantilly, but that he had unfortunately made his arrangements for starting that very evening for Cannes. It was a slight thread on which to hang a great decision; but the decision was what we know it to have been. In little more than twenty-four hours' time the Duke of Braganza was sitting next to Princess Amélie at the Duc d'Aumale's dinner-table; and, in the course of the following day, the Duke of Braganza demanded the Embassy cipher in order that he might telegraph to Lisbon to say that his journey in search

MARRIAGE OF DOM CARLOS

of a wife had come to a prosperous termination at Chantilly.

He had chosen happily, and he had also chosen well. Not only did Princess Amélie "present" well, as members of her family have generally done, even when the dignity of their exterior has covered cold hearts and empty heads. She was also brilliantly clever, exceedingly accomplished, and endowed with the indefinable charm which causes people to be styled "sympathetic." Born two years before the battle of Sedan, she grew up in a Royalist circle which really believed that the Orleanist bubble could be inflated after the Napoleonic bubble had been pricked. She was given a strenuous education, and took kindly to the strenuous life, combining, as one might say, the knowledge and accomplishments of an Amazon, a Girton girl, and a hospital nurse; while, at the same time, she displayed the shyness and timidity generally evinced by young people of superior merit in the presence of those who are at once grandiose and commonplace. At Vienna she blushed scarlet when the Grand Master of the Teutonic Order teased her, and lost her appetite when the Emperor Francis Joseph stared at her. Moreover, she was too patriotic to marry a German, though the suit of a Bavarian Prince was proposed.

At her wedding, many little incidents showed that in France even Republicans loved her. A workman in his blue blouse protested that he could "never be a real Republican" after she had done him the honour of shaking hands with him. A wealthy retired manufacturer offered her an interesting wedding gift—a twenty-franc piece with a history attached to it:—

"Years ago, in 1844," he said, "when I was a simple working man, the Duchesse d'Orléans, accompanied by the Comte de Paris, paid a visit of inspection to the workshop in which I was employed. His Royal Highness gave me this coin. I did not spend it, but kept it as a *porte-bonheur*; and from that day to this there has been no backward step in my career. May I now be allowed to return it in the hope that it may continue its good work and bring Your Royal Highness the same good luck that it has brought to me!"

And so to Portugal, where the people soon began to realise that, just as the influx of Saxe-Coburg blood had given them Kings of a new type, so a Queen of a new type had been introduced from France—a type most essentially different from that so majestically presented by Queen Maria Pia, who had a poor relation of President Grévy's wife for her dressmaker, and whom a French visitor to Lisbon summed up thus:—

"Elegant, extravagantly dressed, and always haughty and distant in her manner, Queen Maria Pia figured in the eyes of a populace which was almost Oriental in its view of life as the characteristic Queen of the Fairy Stories—the Queen depicted as the incarnation of pride, always seated on a golden throne, with a golden sceptre in her hand."

Queen Amélie preferred to live a simpler life of greater practical utility. She was not too dignified

QUEEN AMÉLIE

to leap her horse over those pebble walls which are the Portuguese equivalent of our five-bar gates. She roamed on the sea-shore with her husband, who amused her by making ducks and drakes with porcelain plates which he smashed with shots from his rifle before they had finished skimming over the surface of the water. She had the most gracious manner of conferring favours—too gracious for some of the old-fashioned Portuguese who had such exaggerated ideas of dignity as have sometimes prevailed at the negro Court of Haiti—and she exhorted her intimate correspondents to put "a little less Majesty and third person" into their letters. She visited hospitals—even the smallpox hospital at a time when an epidemic was raging. She organised—not merely patronised but actually organised—a great many charitable institutions—and seemed to understand them as well as the doctors and directors. Among other things she founded a tuberculosis dispensary and Pasteur Institute, and herself conveyed from Paris to Lisbon the first phials of anti-diphtheritic serum introduced into the country. And there is also, of course, the story of the courageous feat by which she earned the Medals of Royal Humane Societies. It is told in M. Lucien Corpechot's *Souvenirs sur la Reine Amélie:*—

"It was a rough day. She was walking on the beach enjoying the sensation of the spray whipping her cheeks. A short distance from the shore a fisherman, up to his waist in water, was trying to bring his boat to land. The boat itself, tossed about by

THE ROYAL HOUSE OF PORTUGAL

the waves, was in imminent danger of being dashed against the rocks. Suddenly the cable broke. The man fell, and, being injured, did not get up again. The Queen, without an instant's hesitation, rushed into the water with her clothes on, got out of her depth, swam, reached the fisherman, seized hold of him, and dragged him to land. Returning home, dripping wet, she simply said in response to the exclamations of the King and Court: 'Still, I thank Heaven that I did go out and get wet.' The fisherman, however, told the story. It was soon known to everyone, and both the German Emperor and the King of Sweden sent the Queen the medals of their respective countries for saving life from drowning."

One could go on, almost indefinitely, telling stories which thus redound to Queen Amélie's honour. If the Portuguese monarchy could have been saved by a gallant bearing and a resolute and intelligent devotion to self-imposed duties, she assuredly would have saved it. Indeed, it seems that gratitude for her services, not completely extinguished even at the hour of her unpopularity, was the chief reason why the revolution, when it came, was not conducted entirely without consideration for royal feelings. But unpopularity—widespread, though not universal—did, in the end, overtake her; and there were reasons for it.

Some of the reasons were ridiculous enough—reasons which only weighed with those uncivilised Portuguese who had negro blood in their veins. The reason, for instance, assigned by the blackamoor buck who protested that the Queen "had not even the spirit to take a lover," may be dismissed with the sentiments which it merits. Other reasons, though they will not seem equally important to everyone, were better founded. Queen Amélie, according to some austere and high-principled critics, was as extravagant as she was charitable, and as bigoted as she was clever. Her faults, that is to say, stood in the way of her virtues, and her religious fanaticism, while compatible with minor reforms, obstructed major ones. It will be well to illustrate the point by placing side by side examples of her good and evil influence. Here is a characteristic story told of her by the Marchioness of Rio Mayor :—

"One day a man whose breast was covered with medals given to him for saving life at sea by the Humane Societies of nearly every country in Europe presented himself to the Queen and handed her a petition. He was a cobbler from Oporto, who had saved seventeen lives at the risk of his own. He asked for employment in the Customs House. 'If I can get that,' he said, 'my daily bread will be assured, and, as I shall always be near the shore, I may have the chance of rescuing still more people from drowning. Every year, for a long time, I have made this same request, but I have always been told that there is no vacancy for me.' The Queen, in great indignation, took the matter in hand, and demanded, day after day, that this humble hero should be rewarded. He died, however, before she was able to get him the post which he desired."

That is both admirable and characteristic. It shows us Queen Amélie eager to do good, and prevented from doing it by the passive resistance of the professional politicians, who wanted all the plums in all the branches of the civil service for the purposes of bribery and corruption, and insisted upon rewarding party services in preference to merit. On the other hand, however, the Queen encouraged the re-establishment of the religious orders in Portugal; and there is unhappily only too much evidence to show that, when religious orders come in at the door, all prospects of thorough-going reform fly out of the window. Or that, at all events, was the view of the new school of reformers then arising in Portugal: the earnest and clean-handed anti-clericals from the University of Coimbra—men in whose eyes the buzzing monks and cackling nuns were like a plague of flies settling on a carcase.

There were, therefore, two simultaneous currents of reform in the country: currents which could not be fused, but were bound in the end to clash. It is only, indeed, through her clerical influence that Queen Amélie counts in this matter; but Dom Carlos unquestionably had what the French call "*velléités*" for reform. He once threshed the matter out at a French dinner-party, explaining at once his aspirations and his difficulties:—

"It is an inextricable tangle," he said, "and you, in France, must have the greatest difficulty in understanding it. Our people demand reforms, and they are right. Reform is necessary, urgent—but impracticable. Impracticable because members of Parliament will not have it. Reform would strike at the root of their own privileges—privileges which they

Queen Amélie and the late King Carlos.
(when Duke & Duchess of Braganza)

POLITICS

have grasped, and which will be the ruin of my unhappy country."

He went on to explain that Portuguese political system which had come to be called "rotative": the system whereby two groups of politicians maintained a sham fight in the Chamber, and took it in turns to cut up the pie and enjoy the slices. He enlarged on that system with great eloquence, and, after speaking of his present helplessness, outlined the programme which he faintly hoped some day to be able to execute :—

"I can change nothing in this condition of things, for no responsible Minister and no Parliament which one could get elected would lend itself to the revolutionary measures required to put an end to the scandal. Ah! if only I could find a really honest man—a patriot who would put the honour and interest of Portugal before his personal interests and those of his adherents! How gladly and gratefully would I support such a man with all the power at my command! How willingly would I delegate to him all the authority which I have in order that he might introduce the era of reform which I and the Portuguese people equally desire. But though I am always looking for that man, I have not yet been able to find him."

It sounds a noble utterance; and there is no question whatever that it was nobly meant. It sounds like a passionate and conscientious paraphrase of that saying of M. Prudhomme's which we have already quoted: "My sword shall defend the Constitution, and even, if need be, overthrow it." We need to have it before us in order to make out

THE ROYAL HOUSE OF PORTUGAL

as good a case as we can for Dom Carlos in the relation which is to follow. There are still those who maintain that he was, at that time, the only patriot in Portugal, and that his eventual assassination entitles him to the halo of the martyr who lays down his life for his country; and that is a contention which will have to be examined closely.

It is not quite a true contention, and yet there is something in it. Most likely Dom Carlos meant it to be true when he talked to his French friends across the dinner-table; most likely he was still in the same mind when he found—or fancied that he had found—the patriot whom he was seeking in the person of Joao Franco. But—there are a good many buts. For one thing, Dom Carlos did not really possess the monopoly of patriotism which he claimed, but had forgotten Coimbra—that ancient seat of learning which had taken up with modern ideas, and was turning out so many new brooms, bent upon making a clean sweep in the interest of clean politics. In the second place, Don Carlos forgot that those who live in glass houses can only throw stones at their risk and peril.

His own house was not entirely of glass—far from it; but there was a good deal too much glass about it for the exercise of throwing stones to be a safe one for its inhabitants. In particular the financial wing of the house was made of glass. There had been, that is to say—and there still were and continued to be—certain little financial transactions which it is impossible for a financial purist to defend. We will go into those transactions with

POLITICS

such detail as is necessary in a moment. At present it will be enough to insist, at the risk of repetition, that the main causes of his failure were twofold :—

1. He made enemies instead of friends of the Republicans of the Coimbra School.

2. He gave those honest Republicans a handle by using the absolute powers with which he armed himself to execute and shield some very shady jobs for the replenishing of his privy purse.

CHAPTER XXVII

The rise of the Coimbra School—Attempt to define their philosophical standpoint.—Their anti-clericalism and their "Sebastiamism"—Their Republican aspirations develop into a Republican policy—Dictatorship of Joao Franco—Franco's devices for extricating Dom Carlos from financial embarrassments—"Suspicious" transactions—Dom Carlos's touching faith in France—His premonition of catastrophe.

THERE has been nothing more important in modern Portugal than the rise of the Coimbra School—a case, if there ever was one, of the greatest historical events happening in the intellect.

For how much of the "direct action" which changed the face of things the Scholars were responsible is, indeed, still dubious, and may long remain so, and matters comparatively little. What is certain, and does matter, is that, whether the Scholars were or were not, in the physical sense, behind the more violent manifestations, the School was metaphysically at the back of them, supplying the idea, if not the weapons. Previously, though revolutions had been, as it were, the daily bread of Portuguese politicians, those revolutions had only occurred as unco-ordinated spasms. One has the

THE COIMBRA MEN

impression, as one reads them, of revolution for revolution's sake—or, at the most, of revolution for the sake of the aggrandisement of individuals; but now the aspect changes. With the advent of the Coimbra men we begin to detect progressive purpose in what, without them, would have seemed purposeless explosions: a force of intellect and a settled policy making it possible for something practical to be done after the dust of the explosions had settled or been blown away.

The ideas of the School are not very easy to puzzle out; and the names of the leaders of thought which it has produced are not very familiar to English readers. Magalhaes Lima, Theophilo Braga, Oliveira Martins—these are not precisely names to conjure with in the realm of philosophy; and a Portuguese survey of the contributions of the bearers of those names to abstract thought is apt to begin and end in a rhetorical whirlwind. Still, one can find a meaning in the rhetoric if one searches for it; and the quest brings us to this generalisation: that, from the point of view of the world, the Coimbra School is nothing, but that, from the point of view of Portugal, it is nearly everything.

The Coimbra men, that is to say, have not been original thinkers, but interpreters. Their English, French, and German critics have nothing to learn from them, but have taught them all that they know. Judged merely as thinkers, they have been Æolian harps, responsive to all the winds of doctrine which blew on them—uttering responses of purely local application receiving and passing on influences of a perfectly amazing diversity. Hegel, Comte, Herbert Spencer, Michelet, Victor Hugo, to say nothing of Modernists and Higher Critics—the teachings of all these miscellaneous teachers have been fused in their minds into an amalgam which defies analysis. They have taken what they wanted of the philosophical provender, leaving the rest untouched; their Hegelianism which failed to make them Tories, and their Comtism which failed to make them Feminists, being coloured by that vague local Portuguese emotion called Sebastiamism.

We must insist upon Sebastiamism. It began, as we have seen, as the popular fancy that this, that, or the other Pretender was Dom Sebastiam, whom the Moors had not really killed, but who had come back, after biding his time, to deliver Portugal from servitude to Spain. Pretender after Pretender perished on the scaffold; and the definite faith declined into a symbolic superstition. Ignorant people continued to talk about Dom Sebastiam coming again, and educated people let them talk, because the educated and the ignorant had a sentiment in common—both looking back on the days when Portugal had been glorious, and both looking forward to a day when the glory which had departed would be restored. There was, that is to say, all through the ages a national consciousness trying to find itself; and it was through the Coimbra men that that aspiration began, towards the end of the nineteenth century, to be articulate.

Their revolt, to begin with, was largely an intellectual revolt—a throwing off of outgrown intel-

THE COIMBRA MEN

lectual shackles. There was a certain "official" theology and philosophy—a relic of the evil predominance of ecclesiastics, who, after the evil manner of ecclesiastics, especially those who have obtained preferment—had placed opinion on the pedestal which belongs to truth. This had to be got rid of; but that task was comparatively easy. The only intellectuals in Portugal dominated the only University in Portugal. They taught what they were required to teach, with their tongues in their cheeks, but they treated the official body of doctrine with good-natured contempt, and at the same time taught other doctrines incompatible with it. In that way the tone was set; and unintelligent orthodoxy, however reputable elsewhere, came to be classed at Coimbra as obsolete and absurd—unworthy of anyone but a King, a courtier, a priest, or a professional politician.

That was the first stage; the second came when the Coimbra men began to look upon the real life of their own times through their idealist glasses, and asked themselves and each other what could be done to elevate and purify it. It was the same question which we have seen Dom Carlos himself asking—the King and the Republicans being agreed that the body politic was cankered with a disease which called for drastic remedies. But they did not, and perhaps could not, work together to find and apply those remedies, or even understand and appreciate each other. The Republicans had diagnosed the disease while the King was merely trying to make himself agreeable. The King, when he did discover

THE ROYAL HOUSE OF PORTUGAL

it, saw himself as a zealous reformer helplessly entangled in the net of a complicated Constitution; but the Republicans saw him otherwise. To them he was a sort of head conspirator: the impartial but profuse president of a gang of thieves—those Rotatives who played at politics for stakes provided by the taxpayers.

There was an element of truth in both pictures; but neither party could place itself at the other's point of view. It was the more impossible because the Coimbra men were anti-clericals, while Dom Carlos, though he did not set up for being more saintly than his neighbours, at least loved the pious when he saw it, and had a wife whose piety was exceptional and sincere. So the Coimbra conclusion was in favour of a clean sweep, in which the sweeping away of the King was to be the first step. Their Republican aspiration became a Republican policy, envenomed by the brutality with which a Republican rising at Oporto was suppressed; while prominent Republicans, driven into exile, and there able to talk freely, proclaimed aloud that if they could not gain their ends by pacific propagandism, they should not shrink from "direct action."

Those were the conditions in which conspiracy began. But no one knows exactly how, or to what extent, the assassins were affiliated to the professors; and long before that affiliation was complete, Dom Carlos had begun to try his own experiments in reform, with the unhappy result—unhappy for him, at all events—of bringing the conspiracy to a head.

JOAO FRANCO

We left him, a little while back, looking for a strong man who would stand by him while he defied and scattered the Rotatives and introduced the reforms which he and the Coimbra men agreed to be desirable. We now see him flattering himself that he had found such a man in Joao Franco. But he had not, though there seemed, to superficial observers, to be a good deal to be said for Franco.

He was a Coimbra man, though not of the Coimbra School—not infected, that is to say, by the Coimbra politics, though influenced by the best of the Coimbra ideals. Having spent his life in the public service instead of at the University, he brought the right experience to bear upon his task. He had sufficient private means to be independent of public plunder, and a reputation for incorruptibility, energy, and courage. He certainly meant well enough to deserve to succeed; and no doubt it seemed a simple matter to Dom Carlos, with such a Minister standing at his side, to pack the Cortes about its business when it proved recalcitrant, and govern the country as a benevolent dictator by issuing benevolent decrees. The making of a nation, he might have argued, is sometimes only possible through hard discipline; and he might have cited the education of Bulgaria by the brutal methods of Stambouloff as a case in point.

But there was a difference—the difference between success and failure resulting from the difference between strength and weakness. Franco lacked Stambouloff's nerve; and his enemies were cleverer

THE ROYAL HOUSE OF PORTUGAL

than Stambouloff's enemies, and had no need to submit to a domestic dictator for fear of a foreign foe. Neither he nor the King was quite friendless; but their friends were feeble. They soon found that they had alienated the party hacks without conciliating the real reformers. To both of them, consequently, the dictatorship proved a slippery slope. Its opportunities presented them with two temptations, neither of which they resisted : the temptation to violence, and the temptation to financial sharp practice. We will take the charges of sharp practice first.

One might define Franco as a fiscal reformer who engaged in corrupt practices; and the inevitable result of this dual activity was that he made two sets of enemies—the one by his corruption, and the other by his economies. In particular, he appears to have given equal offence to the royal family and to the taxpayers. He exhorted Dom Carlos to save money by drinking the waters which his system required at a Portuguese Spa instead of going to Carlsbad. He refused to decree supplies for a pleasure trip to Italy projected by Queen Maria Pia; and he further refused to pay for the extravagant entertainment of Queen Amélie at the Portuguese Embassy in Paris. Naturally, the King and the two Queens were all displeased; but when Franco tried to put himself right with them by a little bit of financial jugglery, he put himself wrong with the country.

Dom Carlos's Civil List had been £112,000 a

DICTATORSHIP

year; and he had failed to make both ends meet on it. The party hacks, admitting that he had as good a right as they to share in what plunder was going, had allowed him to overdraw his account; and he had overdrawn it to the extent of £154,000, at a time when the external debt of the country was increasing by leaps and bounds. What Franco proposed was to find a means of wiping out the King's indebtedness to the Treasury; and his device was to arrange—by decree and not by Act of Parliament—that the King should sell the country some of its own property at his own valuation. There was the royal yacht, and there were some old Palaces, long since transformed into barracks and public offices. A fancy price was put upon them, and they were solemnly transferred to the nation. It was merely a piece of book-keeping—for no property, and no rights in any property, really changed hands—but a decree set forth that the transaction had discharged the royal liability. And then, to obviate the accumulation of further liabilities, a second decree increased the King's annual allowance by £32,000.

The transaction has been called "suspicious"; but that is too mild a word. It was, in fact, grossly and flagrantly dishonest, though it is improbable that Dom Carlos realised its dishonesty. Kings, doubtless, have the same difficulty in thinking the thoughts of chartered accountants that chartered accountants would have in thinking the thoughts of Kings. They are brought up, in a good many countries, in the doctrine that everything belongs to them, and that other people must be content with what they leave. But this particular act of dishonesty was a blunder as well as a crime. It gave a handle which the Coimbra men laid hold of. Affonso Costa—the first Minister of Justice under the Republic—went so far as to say that "Louis XVI. lost his head for less." His words were punished, but not confuted; and the monarchy and the dictatorship were, in consequence, involved in a common odium.

And the reply to the odium was violence; and the violence of the dictator was regarded as a challenge to violence on the part of his enemies.

He had no more meant to be violent, at the beginning of his career, than he had meant to be dishonest—he simply could not help himself. He had meant his dictatorship to be benevolent; and no doubt it would have remained benevolent to the last if it had not been resisted. It was resisted, however; and Franco did what weak men always do when they find themselves in positions by which the strength even of strong men would be strained. Reluctant, at first, to oppress anybody, he ended by oppressing everybody, because oppression came to seem to him the only means of self-defence; and stories were told of the oppression which recalled the worst days of the Miguelite tyranny. The Press was gagged; the prisons were filled; prominent men, known to be opposed to the dictatorship, disappeared mysteriously.

DICTATORSHIP

The event showed, as we shall see, that Franco had lost all his friends, with the sole exception of Dom Carlos. The masses might have forgiven him for depriving them of their liberty if he had, at the same time, reduced their taxes; but he had not reduced them, and so the masses were hostile. The two Queens and the Duke of Oporto did not like him, for various reasons: partly because they regretted the good old times when they were all free to overdraw their accounts without fear that anyone would ask awkward questions; partly because of the publication in the *Officiel* of a tactless memorandum which, by way of justifying the new financial measures, had pictured them all as reduced to desperate financial straits, compelled to pawn their jewellery and deposit their title-deeds and scrip with their bankers as "collateral"; chiefly, perhaps, because they had no confidence that he would see them through their difficulties, and felt that they were encamped in the crater of a volcano which might burst into eruption at any moment.

Dom Carlos, on the contrary, preserved to the last a touching faith in the man of his choice: partly, no doubt, because he felt that the man who had enabled him to pay his debts must be capable of anything; partly, it may also be, on other grounds. He probably believed in his own mission to be the saviour of the country which he had plundered—there was enough of the Saxe-Coburg blood in him for that. He certainly was not afraid—he had all the courage which one looks for from a sovereign related to the House of Savoy. "Courage is a matter of temperament," he said to a friend who ventured to point out that his position needed courage; and he took no precautions, whatever threatenings were breathed, but continued to go about without an escort, phlegmatically puffing a fat cigar in the face of danger. He also let himself be interviewed, and talked as if all were for the best in the best of all possible Portugals, and Franco were a heaven-sent coadjutor:—

"He and I are quite of one mind," he said to the representative of *Le Temps*. "We work together, and he is completely in my confidence. Those people are mistaken who think that I do not mean to keep him in power. I am quite satisfied with him. Everything is going on satisfactorily. The present state of things must continue—the interest of the country requires it. . . .

"Whatever the future lot of my country may be, Franco's work will not be sterile; for the destiny of a nation can never be unaffected by the fact that it has had working for it a man whose good intentions and talents are supported by robust energy and incontestable force of character."

A sanguine utterance truly! But Dom Carlos was the only optimist in a camp of pessimists; and it was the predictions of the pessimists which were to be fulfilled. Indeed, he himself was to arrive at something very like pessimism before the end, when Franco requested his signature to a decree even more arbitrary than usual. "I shouldn't wonder," he said, "if I were signing my death-warrant; but

THE DEATH-WARRANT

it is no great matter." Evidently he was, at last, tiring of the burden; and it was soon to be shaken from his shoulders. The decree which drew the exclamation from him was the last that he was to have the chance of signing. The assassins had laid their plans, and direct action was imminent.

CHAPTER XXVIII

Warnings—Queen Amélie's pessimism—Her French friends' fears for her—Franco becomes an oppressor—Frustrated plot to declare a Republic—Assassination of Dom Carlos and the Crown Prince—Were the Republicans implicated?—Utterances of representative Republicans—Repudiation of Franco by the royal family—Attitude of Queen Amélie—Accession of Dom Manoel—His hopeless prospects.

THERE had been warnings: the abortive Republican rising at Oporto was only one warning among many. Some ill-conditioned person—presumably a lunatic—had attacked Dom Carlos, and pelted him with stones. He had been put away as a lunatic, and an attempt had immediately afterwards been made to blow up the house of one of the physicians who had certified his insanity. The Republicans in exile had openly threatened " direct action," though the Republicans at home said that the Portuguese had not abolished capital punishment for the purpose of reviving it against the King. Queen Amélie had received anonymous threatening letters, which she believed to have been written by disloyal members of her own Court. She showed no fear, and took no precautions; but disgust and pessimism

PESSIMISM

grew upon her. Some utterances belonging to the time of her last journey abroad illustrate the state of affairs and her feelings toward them:—

"What an ugly business life is! What baseness surrounds us on every side! The very people who fawn upon us in our presence go out and besmirch us and try to injure us. . . . Still, the people of Lisbon will not be the dupes of their coarse calumnies."

"Now I must go back to Portugal to resume the collar of my miserable task."

"Franco is in the right, I suppose, but he is very clumsy in his methods."

One may feel that monarchy had failed in Portugal and yet find the situation pathetic. It is pathetic that Queen Amélie, having meant so well, should have failed so completely to strike root; it is not less pathetic to see her leaning on piety as on a broken reed; it is perhaps most pathetic of all to see her suffering in popularity because her husband was so blunderingly dishonest—dishonest, that is to say, only because he needed money, and considered that he ought to have it, and was incapable of thinking the thoughts of chartered accountants when settling his debt to the nation. However much importance one attaches to honesty —however strongly one feels that anti-clericalism is the beginning of wisdom—one still finds Queen Amélie a very innocent victim, and feels that it was through the faults of the monarchists far more than through those of the monarch that the monarchy was doomed.

THE ROYAL HOUSE OF PORTUGAL

Their friends in France trembled for them; and it is perhaps a further proof of their limitations—which spelt inadequacy—that all their French friends belonged to that royalist faction which is always intriguing against the French Republic. When they visited Paris, they merely paid a "duty call" at the Elysée, and then returned to the circle in which incense was burnt on the altar of a dethroned dynasty, and Republicans were regarded pretty much as the criminal classes are regarded by the police. They found none there to tell them that, even if individual Republicans were objectionable, the Republican ranks included practically all the disinterested and intelligent men in Portugal. They only found frivolous, priest-ridden people to whom Republicanism, wherever encountered, was the enemy.

But these at least knew something of the state of Portugal; and it seemed to them that Queen Amélie, in returning there, was putting her head into the lion's mouth. They said farewell to her in that spirit at the Château de Dampierre, with the same chivalry in their hearts that their ancestors had felt for Marie-Antoinette. They dared not implore her to stay—for they knew that she would not have stayed; but they felt as if, in letting her go, they were abandoning her to a dreadful doom. When the château gates closed on her, it was almost as if they had seen a judge put on the black cap. One of her friends told her what the others were whispering, and she tried to reassure them. "I shouldn't be here," she said, "if I had anything to worry about." But she added the opinion already quoted that Franco was "clumsy in his methods"; and she presently wrote from Lisbon to the Duc de Luynes:—

"My heart was full of emotions during the day that I spent at Dampierre. I should have liked to tell you all about it at the station on the morning of my departure; but my emotions were too much for me. It always pains me to leave France again, and so I was stiff with you for fear lest I should break down."

The catastrophe was very near when she wrote that, though there was no obvious reason for expecting it on one day rather than another. From Lisbon the Court went, in January, to Villa-Viçosa —that ancient seat of the House of Braganza, in which John IV. had knelt in prayer while waiting for news of the success of the revolution which was to free Portugal from Spain and raise him to the throne. A very different revolution was in contemplation now. Rumours had been heard of it—Dom Carlos may be supposed to have had those rumours in mind when he spoke of the signing of a decree as probably equivalent to the signing of his own death-warrant; but precautions had been taken in the light of the information received, and it was thought that the plans of the revolutionists had been nipped in the bud.

They had, in fact, been checked, but only to be diverted into a fresh channel. The original intention, it is believed, was merely to seize the Ministry of the Interior, where all the threads of government were centred, and improvise a Republic by means of telegraphic and telephonic messages. That was prevented; and then the thoughts of the conspirators turned to assassination, in the hope that a Republic would spring up in the subsequent confusion; but they trusted too much to luck, and reckoned without the army—and also without the shock to public sentiment. Franco, knowing that he might need the army, had corrupted it by an increase of pay; and there was a limit to Dom Carlos's unpopularity. He was a sportsman, and everything that the word implies: jolly as a sandboy, and cool as a cucumber—not a bundle of nerves as Franco had come to be.

Franco, indeed, having made terror the order of the day, was himself the principal victim of terror—realising, it may be, from the secret reports of his police, that he had unchained more devils than he would be able to control. Warned that assassins dogged his footsteps, he slept every night in a different house, in order to deceive them. His nerves, in short, were giving way—weakening in preparation for their ultimate catastrophic collapse; while Dom Carlos practised the arts of despotism with a jolly *insouciance* which made him friends even with people who disapproved of him. Though Republican leaders had called to him to "abdicate or be deposed," he could not be shot down with impunity. Nor was he.

He returned to Lisbon by boat; and he, and the Queen, and the two Princes got into an open car-

ASSASSINATION OF DOM CARLOS

riage and drove off. Franco, so careful for himself, had provided no adequate guard for them, though it is quite likely that Dom Carlos desired none. Of a sudden, without warning, a fusillade rained upon them, from quite close quarters. The first bullet struck the King in the nape of the neck, and passed out through the throat, cutting the carotid artery. The Duke of Braganza, who was also wounded, felt for his revolver, but was shot in the face before he could draw it. A third barrel was pointed at Dom Manoel. Queen Amélie threw herself in front of him, looking down the muzzle at imminent death; but that shot was never fired. A passer-by had seized the assassin; and an officer ran him through while he was held helpless.

Even then the danger was not over. Other assassins, posted elsewhere, continued to take aim and fire—one of the bullets hitting Dom Manoel on the arm. Countess Figueiro, Queen Amélie's lady-in-waiting, sprang into the carriage, so as to be at the post of duty. "Get away! Get away! I don't want you to be killed too," Queen Amélie called to her; and the coachman meanwhile whipped up the horses and guided them round a corner to a place of safety. The Duke of Oporto, and sundry *aides-de-camp*, galloped up with drawn sabres. Every assassin who was caught was cut down where he stood; and it is believed that at least one innocent man was cut down by mistake.

So that public opinion was, for the moment, sufficiently shocked by the outrage to upset the Republican plans. That was its tribute, for what it might be worth, to Dom Carlos's personal qualities. He had shown such confidence in his people's patience, even while he oppressed them, that the mean advantage taken of him provoked an outburst of indignation and sympathy for his widow and orphan. But that sentiment swelled like a wave, and passed like one; and then the Portuguese people relapsed into an amazing apathy. As Señor Magalhaes Lima put it: "An ordinary newspaper paragraph about the murder of a woman by her lover would have made more stir than the disappearance of His Most Faithful Majesty." He went on to set forth the Republican view of the incident:—

"The people, exasperated by crushing servitude, naturally revolted. . . . There was a prospect of civil war, with all its consequences.

"One must not be surprised that the red terror of the oppressed has been opposed to the white terror of the oppressors. Logic is inflexible. What has happened at Lisbon is one among many steps towards emancipation.

"From the beginning of time political insurrection has been proclaimed as a right when the question at issue has been the liberation of an oppressed people.

"Certainly I should have preferred the revolution, for which preparations were being made, to a personal attack due to the initiative of an individual. But we must insist upon this: If no political party is responsible for what has happened, it is none the less true that the men involved in it have given a rare proof of courage and self-sacrifice. One cannot but respect the victims who have thus given their lives for their ideals and their country."

FRANCO

So much for the past: he went on to speak of Franco and of the future:—

"Franco is a degenerate who conforms to the laws of atavism. He thought that the monarchy could only be saved by violence and tyrannical repression.

"What is true is that the monarchy can get no men to do its work because all the intellectuals have joined the Republican party. For that very sufficient reason the monarchy is nearing its end. The question at issue in Portugal is not a Cabinet question but a question of *régime*. It is a question which can be solved in no other way than by the establishment of a Republic."

The event showed that he was right. The House of Braganza was doomed because it was inadequate and unadaptable: because, even when, inspired by the better conceptions of royal duty which came in with the Coburg marriage, it set out to cleanse the Augean stable, it mistook low cunning for statesmanship, and sought its instruments from the ranks of the old gang—stupid men who played at being intelligent, and weak men who played at being strong. Queen Amélie herself had evidently had an inkling of that fact when, on the eve of the tragedy, she criticised Franco for the clumsiness of his methods; and the divination of the mistake may account for the way in which the whole royal family turned on Franco on the morrow of the assassination.

Dom Manoel's attitude, of course, does not matter, as he was too young to say or do anything except what he was told to do and say; but the King's widow, and his mother, and his brother, instead of calling upon Franco to continue his bold work and save the country and the dynasty, treated him as a Jonah, to be pitched overboard with curses and contempt. One after the other, if the gossip be true, they set upon him. "There—you see your handiwork," said Queen Amélie. "You promised to release the monarchy from its tomb, and all that you have done has been to dig the graves of my son and my grandson," said Queen Maria Pia. "Franco, Franco, what have you done with my brother?" demanded the Duke of Oporto. And there are those who say that the Duke of Oporto struck Franco in the face, that Franco hit back, and that they would have rolled fighting on the floor of the Council Chamber, if they had not been forcibly separated and held back.

So rumour ran; though whether things actually happened just like that no one will ever know for certain, even if all the witnesses should speak. They might deceive us—they might deceive themselves; they would assuredly contradict each other. The horror was so great and the excitement so tense that no one's recollection of any of the passionate scenes can be trusted. Still, if the details are doubtful, the outcome at least is clear. Franco had long been a bundle of nerves; and now the bundle had burst, and the nerves had given way. When he left the Palace he was a broken man, sobbing like a child; and he left it only to take to flight in a swift motor, and disappear from public life. The interviewers who waylaid him when he reached France got no information from him. He had nothing to

DOM MANOEL

say to them except to beg them to leave him alone, so that he might seek a refuge and end his days in such peace as was still possible. His last message was to the effect that no doubt all the monarchical elements in the country would rally round the throne.

They did so—indeed, they could hardly help doing so. The shock to public sentiment and the expressions of disgust which poured in from the whole civilised world really seemed to have revived loyalty in Portugal, and to have given the House of Braganza a fresh lease of life. Queen Amélie took charge of the situation with a courage and a presence of mind for which no praise could be too high. A ministry was formed, and order seemed secure. Dom Manoel began well by repudiating those of his father's actions which had given most offence and faithfully promising that he would appropriate no money which the Parliament did not vote to him. His mother turned a deaf ear to the advice of those who urged her to leave the country and live abroad on her ample private fortune. She hoped, she said, to be worthy of France and of her family. Portugal was the post of duty, and she should remain at it.

It is a sentiment which has a fine ring in spite of the confusion of ideas which it involves. Queen Amélie's eyes, one cannot doubt, were blinded by the delusion which is common to royal personages: that kingship is a trust, not from their subjects, but from a Higher Power; that their interests are identical with those of their country to such a degree that,

THE ROYAL HOUSE OF PORTUGAL

in defending their own position, they are defending their country's cause. The argument will not stand examination—least of all will it stand it in a country in which inadequate kings have made such a mess of the art of government that all men of acute intelligence and high ideals have become Republicans; but we need not go into that. Queen Amélie has a right to be judged from her own point of view; and, judged from that point of view, her conduct, at the most trying of crises, was sublime. It was admiration for it, more than anything else, which gained the dynasty a respite.

But the doom of the dynasty had been pronounced; and there was no prospect that Dom Manoel would succeed in doing what Dom Carlos had failed to do. If Portugal was to be saved, the Portuguese must work out their own salvation; and the first step towards that end would have to be to clear the House of Braganza out.

CHAPTER XXIX

The royal point of view of monarchy—Queen Amélie's approval of the institution—Extracts from her letters—Her programme for Dom Manoel—His inability to execute it—His trip to Paris—The sowing of wild oats—The King and the dancing-girl—How the friendship helped the lady—How it harmed the King—Increasing power of the Republicans—Their mysterious conspiracy.

THERE is what one may call a royal point of view of monarchy, commonly taken by good Kings and Queens as well as by bad ones. One discovers it in those spontaneous exclamations which reveal the secrets of the soul; and it will be useful to listen to such a royal utterance at this stage. Princess Waldemar of Denmark—Queen Amélie's sister—shall contribute it:—

"Amélie is the man of the family. I have just been paying her a visit at Lisbon, together with my eldest son. She compelled my admiration. If the throne can be saved, she will save it. You will remember that, a few years ago, she plunged into the water to rescue a drowning fisherman. That was a symbolic act."

Nothing is actually said in that letter which all

THE ROYAL HOUSE OF PORTUGAL

the world cannot perfectly well endorse; but there are underlying implications in it on which it is instructive to dwell. It suggests that thrones are ends in themselves, and that it is more important to save the throne than to serve the country; but that is a doctrine of Courts and suburban tea-parties which does not stand examination. The duty of loyalty must, after all, be subordinated to the duty of loving the highest when one sees it; and the throne, far from being necessary in the sense in which the Army, the Navy, the Civil Service, and the Judiciary are necessary, is, in fact, the one part of the complicated machinery of government for which an adequate substitute can at any time be improvised.

Thrones, that is to say, are not ends, but means. If the end of good government is not achieved through the means, they are merely pieces of furniture fit to be pitched out of window. That is what the Portuguese had come to feel at the end of the reign of Dom Carlos. He had used the usurped position of benevolent despot to increase his own income by royal decree and pay his debt to the Exchequer by compelling his subjects to buy their own property from him at a price fixed by himself, and so had failed to justify the existence of the throne. Queen Maria Pia had been, in a minor way, associated with the failure by neglecting to pay the gas rates—her indebtedness under that head being, at the time of the Revolution, about £12,000. Our admiration for Queen Amélie's personal qualities must not blind us to the fact that she failed too.

QUEEN AMÉLIE

Her claim to distinction must be that she did not fail for want of trying.

The root of the trouble, in her case, lay in her divided allegiance: her fluctuation between the desire to do good and the desire to serve the Church and save the dynasty for a son whose public record has not proved him to be a young man of any special value. The men whose ability and reforming zeal were equal to her own were anti-clericals and Republicans: consequently, she could not lean on them. The men through whom she tried to do such good as she could were simply the old gang—men who had no real desire for reform, but only wished to continue to play the old political game for the usual stakes. After a very brief respite, the Rotative System re-established itself, with the result that the renascence of loyalty brought about by the assassination was short-lived, and the Coimbra men who meant rotativism and royalism to go out together did not disarm.

Either Queen Amélie did not understand what was going on, or else she deceived herself: some of her letters to the Duc de Luynes struck quite a sanguine note. In October, 1909, for instance, she wrote:—

"Here, thank God, we are all in good health, and everything is going well. In spite of many difficulties, the atmosphere is quite different from what it was. On the 8th of November my son is to start on an official tour through the northern provinces. I shall join him, and make Oporto my headquarters. I expect great things from this journey."

THE ROYAL HOUSE OF PORTUGAL

The journey was, at any rate, well stage-managed. The right people were got together, and the right cries were raised in the right tone of voice. Queen Amélie received the impression which she desired; and she found herself writing about the principle of hereditary monarchy in the style of a political philosopher.

"The essence of it is" (she confided to the Duc de Luynes) "to conciliate the parties and living forces of the State, instead of playing them off against each other as the party politicians want to do, and, by one's very egotism, to work for the well-being of the people."

She also wrote that Dom Manoel's task must be to "put himself forward as the originator and director of the radical reforms which the salvation of Portugal necessitated"; and Dom Manoel himself was induced to talk as if he had got into the skin of the part proposed for him. He was to open some "works" somewhere; and he allowed himself to be interviewed by a reporter on the staff of the Republican newspaper, *El Mundo*:—

"Our opposed political ideas," he said, "need not prevent us from engaging in amicable conversation. At a festival of national labour, we are, every one of us, patriots, and nothing else. I respect all opinions. I am myself no more than a patriot who most ardently desires the benefit of his country."

Nothing could have been better in a world in which soft words buttered parsnips—or even in a world in which the abstractions of political philosophy buttered them; but Queen Amélie and Dom Manoel did not live in such a world. They lived in a world in which it was imperatively urgent to do things as well as to say them—a world in which nearly all the men who were honest enough to want to do things for the good of Portugal, and clever enough to be able to get them done, were anti-clericals and Republicans. The battle for reform was bound, therefore, to be complicated by a battle between the reformers; and one searches the chronicles of the time in vain for any convincing reason why the personality of Dom Manoel should have damped down the fires of Republican enthusiasm. The religion of loyalty degenerates into superstition when the attempt is made seriously to picture him as "the originator and director" of such reforms as Portugal required.

He was too young, and he was in the wrong hands. One surmises, too, that he had been unnerved by the tragedy which brought him to the throne. His few recorded public utterances do not suggest that he was very sure of himself; and one feels it more likely that the Rotatives would have been a match for him than that he would have been a match for them. That trial of strength, however, never came to a head. There were forces at work beneath the surface which were to blow the King and the Rotatives into the air together; and, while they were fermenting, Dom Manoel went on his travels, to complete his education and enjoy himself. One has a letter written by Queen Amélie to the Duc de Luynes on his return.

THE ROYAL HOUSE OF PORTUGAL

"My grief has dug a deeper place in my heart for those old and loyal affections which are at once my delight and my consolation. It was a great pleasure to me to talk about you yesterday to my son. He has returned from Paris, very happy, and very much touched; and I too was touched and grateful and proud at the thought of the welcome which he had received."

Let us all, by all means, share in that emotion; but we must not commit the error of assuming the trip to Paris to have been exclusively devoted to a debauch of family affection. It came out afterwards —and, indeed, it was whispered at the time—that the visit had also been the occasion of a certain sowing of wild oats which the historian cannot ignore because it had consequences which belong to history. This is the stage at which the dancing-girl enters into—one might even say forces her way into—the narrative.

There is no need for the historian to be extravagantly censorious. There is a great deal of human nature in royal princes as well as in their subjects; and Dom Manoel's susceptibility did not violate the laws of human nature, but conformed to them. He might have quoted—perhaps he did quote—Virgil's:—

Omnia vincit amor: nos et cedamus amori.

Such things, at any rate, do sometimes happen in royal circles; and, as a rule, princes find it possible to arrange matters so that no great harm results to them, or to the ladies, or to the

THE DANCING-GIRL

State, or to public modesty. The prevalent public feeling in such a case is that the dancing-girl herself has probably not been backward in coming forward, but has conceived herself to be fulfilling one of the functions of dancing-girls; and that feeling generally facilitates the adjustment of such difficulties as arise. So that few people were shocked, or suspected that anything was being done out of which political capital could be made, when rumour spoke of a certain party, whereat dancing-girls had been presented to Dom Manoel and one of them had supped with him. That the measure did, as a matter of fact, entail consequences was due to accidents which he could not reasonably have been expected to foresee.

The most important accident was, no doubt, the dancing-girl herself. She came of a class in which no code, either written or unwritten, imposes reticence with regard to intimate affairs. No one had schooled her in those virtues, and she did not invent them for herself. On the contrary, she is said to have combined with a certain kittenish vivacity an instinctive feeling for advertisement which is considered excessive, even in the theatrical walks of life in which she moved. She did not ask her royal lover to respect her secret, and she showed herself no respecter of his. She understood that his favour was, in itself, an advertisement of greater value even than his presents : that the presents themselves would be pearls of still greater price if she displayed them as trophies of her artistic gifts. Whence the frequent exhibition, in theatrical dressing-rooms, and such places, of letters, of portraits, and even, it is said, of garters.

Such things may have happened before; but not in the same way or to the same extent. There was a new twentieth century note in the display; a new pride of vulgarity and a new vulgarity of pride. The thing was happening, too, in a new world in which the envy of rivals was resourceful and unscrupulous. What was easier than for any bold girl to acquire a garter and declare that it had been given to her as a pledge of the undying affection of the King of Portugal and the Algarves? This seems to have been rather freely done—Society newspapers of a certain stamp assisting in the publicity—and the impression was thus gradually created of a gay Bohemia full of jewelled garters presented to the show girls of opera bouffe by His Most Faithful Majesty. And that, unhappily, at the very time when Queen Amélie was claiming eulogies for her son as "the originator and director of the radical reforms which the salvation of Portugal necessitated."

It is not necessary to be a Republican to perceive that the two conceptions do not dove-tail; and it would be unjust to charge Dom Manoel with any hypocritical attempt to make them do so. His temper, so far as one can judge, was simply that of an undergraduate seeing life. He was hot-blooded, infatuated, and quite incapable of perceiving—what he must since have realised—that, when he supposed himself merely to be conferring marks of royal favour, he was, in fact, allowing an ambitious

THE DANCING-GIRL

théâtreuse to make use of him for advertising purposes. Assuredly he made a great mistake when he entertained her at the Necessidades Palace, and a mistake of equal magnitude when he engaged in correspondence with her. That sort of thing always makes talk; and it made more talk than usual in this case, because the lady herself had a turn for loquacity, and liked nothing better than to have a Court of reporters at her feet gathering up the crumbs of her conversation.

The result of the "friendship"—the word is of the lady's choosing—was entirely to the lady's advantage. It gave her the advertisement which was of more value to her than many garters, and launched her on a career which has, no doubt, been as prosperous as it is notorious. But it launched the King's barque on much stormier waters, and sped it in a very different direction. For the Republicans of Coimbra were, in their way, Puritans. Some of them, perhaps, were only professional Puritans, but others were real Puritans; and here was a challenge to their Puritanism which it suited them to take up. It provoked indignant rhetorical questions to which no adequate answer could have been given even if they had waited for one. So that the attempt to analyse the conditions of the last days of the monarchy in Portugal shows us the clash of irreconcilable ideals.

On the one hand there was Queen Amélie's ideal: monarchy as an institution to be defended to the last gasp, because of the admirable programme which she herself was capable of drafting for a King.

THE ROYAL HOUSE OF PORTUGAL

On the other hand there was the ideal of the Coimbra men : a Republic to be substituted for the monarchy because, whatever good it might in theory be possible for Kings to do, the actual King was doing no good at all, was powerless to stop the plundering of the country by the Rotatives, and did not even seem to be trying to stop it, but preferred the apolaustic to the strenuous life. That is why it is true—in part if not entirely—to say that the fall of the House of Braganza was brought about by the sowing of wild oats.

It must be added that the conflicting ideals were maintained with as much passionate intensity as if they had been opposed religions. There were in Portugal, as there are everywhere, men with whom loyalty to the monarch, irrespectively of his personal qualities, is a primary obligation against which there is no appeal. On the other hand there were people in Portugal with whom the Republican ideal incarnated the old Sebastiamism—the aspiration of the Portuguese people to "find themselves" and live their own national life. Only by Republicanism, they maintained, could they, like Lazarus, "get up and walk." And these—especially after the elections of August, 1910—spoke quite openly and boldly of their aims....

"It needs must be confessed," wrote Senhor Rodrigo Pequito, who had held office under the monarchy, "that the country has lost the indifference to politics which distinguished it fifteen or twenty years ago. The Republican propagandism

DOM MANOEL

has given the masses an interest in politics. That fact is both clear and suggestive."

"Let us have done with illusions," wrote the Lisbon *O Dia*. "The democratic idea is growing like the waves of the ocean. . . . To-day's elections are significant. The next elections will be still more so."

"And now," said Affonso Costa—the same Affonso Costa who protested that Louis XVI. had been guillotined for less offences than Dom Carlos had committed—"at the very first threat to our liberties, the Republican party must effect the Revolution. The Republican party has proved that it is the only possible organ of public opinion for the defence of the liberties of all. So obvious is this that, if the King were not, alike by character and by education, the first reactionary of his country, he would already himself have realised that that was the road to be followed."

But Dom Manoel did not realise it, and therefore the Republicans conspired.

CHAPTER XXX

Conspiracy and constitutional opposition—Their points of contact—Denunciation of the House of Braganza by Théophilo Braga—The writing on the wall—Queen Amélie's hopes and fears—Intricate organisation of the conspiracy—Impossibility of discovering who belonged to it and who did not.

THE conspiracy was spun all over Portugal like a spider's web. One knows that there must have been elaborate organisation; but the impression given is one of quick, spontaneous growth, akin to that of the parasitic plant which envelops, grips, and kills a mighty tree. Such details of its conduct as can be discovered shall be set forth presently; but the case is one of those in which the full truth can never be revealed, because there will never be any means of checking any statement which may be made. The complicated precautions taken to prevent betrayal operate also as a barrier to inquiry. Deliberate lies and vainglorious boasts cannot be disentangled from the truthful depositions of those who were in the secret; and there is no witness whatsoever whose testimony is quite above suspicion.

Happily it does not matter; for nothing of importance hinges upon the portion of the story which has to be left obscure. The broad lines and the visible result of the mysterious movement are all that need concern us; and these are first curious and finally sensational. It is not a case of conspiracy driven underground because constitutional opposition was tyrannically oppressed. It is a case of conspiracy deliberately burrowing underground and there working in conjunction with constitutional opposition. The points of contact between the two things cannot be fixed, though they must have been numerous; but it is at least clear that constitutional opposition, in the brief reign of Dom Manoel, enjoyed chances which it had not enjoyed under the benevolent despotism of Dom Carlos. The Coimbra men seem now, at last, to have felt it in their bones that the House of Braganza and its rotative satellites were afraid of them; and they lifted up their voices accordingly. In particular, Théophilo Braga spoke out.

He was a Coimbra man, as important at Coimbra as Jowett was, in his time, at Oxford. He also had a double reputation as a man of letters and a political thinker akin to that enjoyed by Lord Morley when he edited the *Fortnightly Review* and was recognised as one of our most eminent Radicals out of Parliament. He had further, like Lord Morley, political ambitions; and he came forward as a Republican candidate at Lisbon. In that character he addressed mass meetings, and said, with impunity, what he thought of the King, and the royal house, and the methods by which Portugal was governed in their name. He declined to distinguish the faults of the system from those of the dynasty, and he was specially indignant at the suggestion of certain foreign newspapers, freely echoed in the country, that, if the House of Braganza fell, Portugal's colonies would be taken from her and divided between England and Germany.

As a matter of fact, that partition has been contemplated in Foreign Offices as well as in newspaper offices. There exists a secret treaty on the subject, which is not quite so secret as it was meant to be, for various people were told a little about it at the time, and the sundry items, when added together, make a solid mass of information. A very full, if not an absolutely complete, version of it was published by the well-informed "Diplomaticus" in the *Fortnightly Review*; and there has not been, and is not likely to be, any official contradiction of what was there revealed. Whether Dr. Théophilo Braga knew all that "Diplomaticus" knew is doubtful; but of one thing he was quite sure—that the House of Braganza was a broken reed for Portugal to lean upon for the preservation of her colonial Empire. The whole course of Portuguese history proved that; and it was at the bar of history that he arraigned the House :—

"With a dynasty which dismembered our country, as in the cases of Bombay, Tangier, and Brazil, which deserted us in the face of the enemy, as in the time of Napoleon, which invites foreign intervention in Portugal, in order that it may be sustained by the force of foreign arms, and hands us over,

THÉOPHILO BRAGA

bound hand and foot, to the greed of money-lenders for a debt of 800,000 contos—with an egoistic family which is the hybrid product of Bourbon blood, diluted with the blood of the Houses of Coburg, Savoy, and Orleans, and which has no sympathy for our country, but only a desire to enjoy it and exploit it—how, in such conditions, shall Portugal continue to exist? The suggestion that it should try to do so trenches on the absurd."

And then, in a later passage of the same speech:—

"The whole nation shudders with a nausea of disgust at the political system which is ruining us. It is the awakening of the national self-consciousness. A new generation has grown up, and means to serve the national cause in preference to the interests of a family; and that generation has placed its confidence in the Republic, for the Republic means the direction of the people's destinies by the people for the people."

And finally:—

"A country such as ours, in order to remain strong and independent, only needs to be conscious of its own value, its own past, and its own potential energies. All that it requires is to bring the men of character to the front."

It has since brought them to the front—with what eventual result the world still waits to see; but that is not our present theme. To the historian Théophilo Braga's speech is valuable, not as an array of arguments, but as a revelation of atmosphere. It was as if the writing on the wall were being shouted in the streets by the town crier, or flamed on the forehead of the evening newspaper posters: MENE, MENE, TEKEL, UPHARSIN—the House of Braganza weighed in the balances and found wanting! When such things happened, the royal family must have felt a strong suspicion that the end was imminent. Queen Amélie did, albeit thinking of the King of Portugal not as a functionary but as a proprietor, she also regarded herself as the slave of duty who must continue the struggle to keep him on the throne on which no disinterested person wished him to remain, and on which he was, most obviously, doing no good to any one. As her biographer, M. Lucien Corpechot, writes:—

"For a moment, at Oporto, the cheers with which her son was received alleviated her grief and revived her hopes; but, at the Necessidades, she found herself once more in the midst of intrigues, cabals, ambuscades, and conspiracies. It was clear to her that none of her enemies had disarmed, and that there was no chance that the truce which the Spanish people had imposed on their politicians during the minority of their King would be extended to her own kingdom. She strained her will to the breaking point. She resolved not to disarm, but to watch over her son's crown."

Against constitutional opposition, even though Théophilo Braga led it, the crown was com-

CARBONARISM

paratively safe. By trickery, by intimidation, by corruption, the party in power could always, in Portugal, "make the elections." But the conspiracy—that was a different matter. It was one of the most bafflingly mysterious conspiracies that the world had ever seen. It was felt everywhere, but could be discovered nowhere. Everybody was suspected of belonging to it; but no one seemed to know who actually did belong to it—not even the conspirators themselves. Carbonarism was the name it went by; and some remarkable particulars of its intricate organisation were given by M. Jules Sauerwein in the *Matin* on January 22nd, 1910:—

"The association differs widely from that of the freemasons in that it is purely national, and that only the Portuguese are admitted to it. The initiated are divided into four grades, called respectively: 'the wood-cutters,' 'the aspirants,' 'the master,' and 'the grand master.' The unity is the 'work-shop,' which is composed of four 'wood-cutters,' who only know their three companions and their chief. Four 'work-shops' make a 'lodging-house'; four 'lodging-houses' make a 'shanty'; four 'shanties' make a 'shop'; and all the 'shops' in Portugal are affiliated to a 'central shop,' which constitutes, as it were, a sort of Council of the Order. But the supreme direction of the Society is in the hands of the Mystic Lodge known as 'Young Portugal,' whose identity is unknown to anyone.

"During the two and a half years which preceded the Revolution, initiations were multiplied with unheard of rapidity. The Portuguese people are naturally inclined to obey orders, if the orders are meant to subserve a higher end. It would be difficult, in any other country in Europe, with the possible exception of Russia, to find so many men prepared to devote themselves, without reserve, to an ideal undertaking, with unknown comrades, under a mysterious chief whose identity they cannot even guess. But all these precautions were necessary, in order to put justice off the track. The meetings of four or five conspirators took place in the most various localities: in the main streets, in the open country, on board ship, or at the public baths. The simple initiations took place at the conspirators' own homes. Seven or eight persons turned up there; and the candidate was conducted to the indicated spot with every circumstance of mystery. A monk's cowl shrouded the participants from head to foot; and the veils were not lifted even when the ceremony was over. After having taken the oath, and sworn to observe the draconian code of the Association, the novice only knew the three 'wood-cutters' with whom he was thenceforward to work. And yet, on the appointed day, a few hours sufficed for mobilisation."

There is much here which reminds one of those remarkable Secret Societies which flourish among the West African Negroes, for the practice of cannibalism and other horrid rites, under the very noses of the military police; and it may have been the negro blood in the veins of the Portuguese which made the organisation so natural to them. But there were differences as well as resemblances, of greater importance than the resemblances. In West Africa the Secret Societies begin in low cunning and end in savagery and the thirst for blood. In Portugal the low cunning was directed by intelligence of a high order, and was inspired by devotion to a genuine ideal.

That was what made the conspiracy formidable from the first, and at the last invincible. It had its ramifications everywhere—in the Court, in the Army, in the Navy, in the Civil Administration, and among the personal friends of the King. Dom Manoel, after his flight, was amazed to discover how many of his most trusted servants and most intimate associates had been manœuvring for his overthrow. A typical case was that of a colonel commanding a regiment in the North of Portugal, who had warned him of impending trouble, and had asked to be summoned to Lisbon because that would be the post of danger. A French friend of the King's was shown the letter, and commented on it.

"At any rate," the Frenchman exclaimed, "your Majesty had in the army men of stout heart, ready for any act of devotion."

"Yes," replied Dom Manoel, "I have happily had some proof of that. But not in the case of this particular officer. I did summon him to Lisbon, and he seized the opportunity to take a leading part in the *coup d'état*."

Even the police—even the highest functionaries of the police—were infected by the sedition, to the point of refusing to take notice of "information received." It was a mistake—the country was quite quiet, they told the Marquis of Lavradio who laid the information before them. No special measures were called for.

That on the very eve of the outbreak which alone remains to be related.

CHAPTER XXXI

The collapse of the House of Braganza—Shelling of the Necessidades Palace—Plans of resistance—Their impossibility—Flight of the royal family—The dancing-girl held responsible—What she said to the reporter—Dom Manoel at Richmond.

THE end came in October, 1910, when the world woke up, one morning, to the news that the House of Braganza had collapsed like a house of cards. It is so recent a story, so thoroughly threshed out in the newspapers at the time, that the recapitulation of the particulars seems superfluous; and it is not, as such stories go, exciting. One might call the Revolution, as some historians have called the French Revolution of 1848, "a revolution of contempt." No member of the royal party was hurt, except as regards the wounding of their feelings; and the sole question which has worried the searchers after truth is this: Did Dom Manoel funk? Might he not have triumphed over his enemies if he had faced them resolutely with a corporal's guard?

Though the question itself was not asked ironic-

THE ROYAL HOUSE OF PORTUGAL

ally, there is irony in the fact that it should have been raised. When a King has obviously stayed too long, one should not reproach him for departing in a hurry; and that error of judgment shall not be committed here. The precepts of morality no more require a King to fight for his crown than they require a Prime Minister to fight for his portfolio; it is the business of the one as of the other to withdraw with dignity but without fuss when confronted with the proof that he has ceased to attract. The fact that Kings, as a rule, will not do so, but cling to their crowns as a dog clings to a bone—while spectators applaud them for doing so—is no evidence that their characters are noble. It is a proof, rather, that the primitive and passionate selfishness of barbarous ages has lingered in royal bosoms after its eradication from the hearts of mere statesmen.

It seems to have lingered, on this occasion, in the bosom of Queen Amélie. We have already seen her acclaimed as "the man of the family," and commended for the solicitude with which she had watched over her son's crown. We see her, at the last, striking those attitudes to which the world can never refuse its admiration, in whatever cause they may be struck. M. Lucien Corpechot, whose admiration is whole-hearted, records several of them; and we may go to his pages for the few facts which seem to matter. But, in truth, hardly anything matters except that Dom Manoel, after a night of apprehension spent at the telephone, inquiring what might be expected to happen next, was, in the early

THE REVOLUTION

morning, shelled out of the Necessidades Palace by his own ships of war.

It was the Palace in which, on a very different occasion, it had been his privilege to entertain the dancing-girl. Those had been merry times, and the recollection of them was recent, so that the sense of contrast must have been impressive. For now there came a series of disturbing telephonic messages—each more disturbing than the other—about the movements and proceedings of the troops; and then there was silence because the wires were cut. Supper was mentioned; but there was no supper to be had, because all the Palace servants, from the Chief Butler to the junior pages and scullions, had run away from the Palace to join the Republicans. Except for a few personal adherents, Dom Manoel was now alone there; and the projectiles of the big guns were knocking over the chimney-pots. In the midst of the bombardment a letter arrived from his Prime Minister, who exhorted him to leave. The words attributed to him are these:—

"You others can go, if you like. For my own part, since the Constitution assigns me no *rôle* except to let myself be killed, I will try to fulfil my part decently."

But that was not how things were to fall out. Nobody wanted to kill Dom Manoel. All that was required of him was that he should go. He yielded to persuasion and went, taking refuge at Mafra,

THE ROYAL HOUSE OF PORTUGAL

where Queen Amélie and Queen Maria Pia joined him; and there a hasty family counsel was held:

"It was recognised," said the Marquis of Lavradio, who now writes letters to the papers as Dom Manoel's secretary, "that an immediate landing in the northern provinces, which we were deluded into regarding as a Portuguese Vendée, would furnish us with the starting-point of an effective, though tardy, resistance. The success of the plan was a question of hours. It was necessary to get there before the Revolution. It was decided, therefore, to set out instantly, without waiting for either provisions or baggage."

Queen Amélie, according to her biographer, "applauded the decision"; and he on his part applauds her:—

"It is her view," he writes, "that a sovereign, the legitimate inheritor of such a throne as that of Lisbon, owes it to his people to keep his crown at any price, even though he must have recourse to 'those mysterious forces which give mortal men life and take it from them.' Already she sees the King at the head of loyal regiments, putting down the revolt. She will not abandon him. She will follow him in the midst of the risks which await him, happy to sacrifice her own existence to the glory of this well-beloved son."

But that was another of the things which were not to be. It was impossible for the royal party to go to the northern provinces by land because the revolutionary army held the roads. It was equally impossible for them to go there by sea because the

THE REVOLUTION

revolutionary navy blocked the way. As the commander of the royal yacht ventured to point out, the only road open was the road to exile. And then came the *beau geste*:—

"That," replied Queen Amélie, "is the only road which it is impossible for us to take. The King cannot run away: he much prefers to die."

It was like Cambronne's great saying—"The Guard dies, but does not surrender"—which was declared to have saved the honour of French arms on the disastrous day of Waterloo. The brave soldier is now believed to have been incorrectly reported; and it is quite possible that Queen Amélie has been incorrectly reported too. In any case, there is a difference to be remarked. The cause for which Cambronne announced that the Guard would die was greater than either the Guard or its commanding officer. The cause for which Queen Amélie thought it well for Dom Manoel to die was precisely co-extensive with himself. The utterance was magnificent, but wrong-headed: how wrong-headed we may realise if we try to picture Mrs. Asquith calling upon Mr. Asquith to die rather than submit to be ousted from office by the myrmidons of Mr. Bonar Law—a thing which it is impossible to picture, in spite of the fact that Mr. Asquith is so much more obviously the right man for the office which he holds.

One admires the utterance, of course, in spite of its impropriety when examined in the light of pure reason, because it called for, and exhibited, a fine character and a high courage. There is something melodramatic about it which appeals, and is sure of applause. The appeal, however, is not to our better selves, but to certain barbarous instincts which we know, at hours of sober reflection, that we ought to have outgrown. Queen Amélie's doctrine that a King owes it to his people to do the best that he can for himself at their expense, even though he has to sabre them in order to do it, is not, after all, a noble doctrine, but has its root in that selfishness which we have seen Théophilo Braga denouncing as characteristic of the House of Braganza. Let none, therefore, speak disdainfully of Dom Manoel because, instead of acting on it, he sailed, with his mother and his grandmother, from Ericeira, first to Gibraltar, and thence to England. Whatever reasons we may think we have for speaking disdainfully of him, that particular reason must be rejected. This is his farewell letter:—

"My Dear Texeira de Sousa,
"Constrained by circumstances over which I have no control, I find myself obliged to embark on the yacht *Amelia*. I am Portuguese, and I shall always be so. It is my conviction that I have always, and in all circumstances, done my duty as a King, and placed my person and my life at the service of my country. I hope the country, persuaded of my affection and my devotion, will recognise that fact. Long live Portugal!
"Pray give this letter all possible publicity.
"Always yours affectionately,
"Manoel."

It was the right attitude—if one may assume that

THE REVOLUTION

it was sincere: much more correct than that of Queen Amélie, whose heroic call to arms, in spite of its splendid melodramatic ring, resolves itself, on analysis, into an expression of affection for the country akin to that of the miser for his gold. Whether it actually was sincere is another question, and one to which one cannot confidently, in the light of subsequent events, give an affirmative answer. Dom Manoel's friends, as we all know, formed a base of operations on Spanish soil, and thence conducted a raid into Portugal on his behalf. Though he did not pay with his person, one cannot help suspecting that he was cognisant of these proceedings and in sympathy with them: that he could have stopped them, if he had chosen, but simply did not choose.

If that be so, then certain inferences follow: that Dom Manoel did, in fact—and perhaps does still—in spite of the Coburg constitutionalism, cling to the antique view that a King is a proprietor, and that his kingdom is his appanage which he is entitled to defend as a householder defends his effects against burglars; that he would have accepted blood and slaughter with smiling equanimity, if only he could have waded back through it to his throne. And, if those inferences are well-founded, then Dom Manoel's place is outside the moral pale—though he may have wandered outside it without knowing exactly where he was going, and may be persuaded by the courtesies of the municipality and suburban residents of Richmond that he is still within it: a point which it is important to make, in the interest of truth and morality, even at the risk of seeming to speak with disrespect of one who has occupied an exalted station.

These considerations are obviously of more importance than any considerations connected with the dancing-girl; but those considerations also are significant as well as picturesque. The dancing-girl herself took care that they should be so. Someone printed somewhere the scandalous statement that the fall of the dynasty was due to her: that the King's extravagance in presenting her with jewelled garters and other tokens of affection had been the last straw which broke the back of a patient people. She saw in that calumny the chance of a life-time, and she seized it. Her beckoning finger summoned the interviewers of all nations, and they assembled, with the result that her view of the matter was proclaimed *urbi et orbi* wherever newspapers are printed.

All the uncontrollable pride of the footlights flashed out in that memorable proclamation. The dancing-girl reminded the world that she, as well as the King, was a public character, in a great position—a position, in fact, more stable than the King's, and quite as well remunerated. His presents, therefore—such presents as she had had from him—were of no material moment to her, but only valuable on sentimental grounds. Of course, she treasured his portrait and his letters; but if she wanted jewelled garters, she could perfectly well afford to buy them for herself. The King of Portugal, in short, was a very good friend of hers—she hoped he would long continue to be so; but the

FLIGHT

friendship did not rest upon a monetary basis—perish the thought of such a thing! It was on equal terms, as became equal potentates, that he and she were accustomed to meet and correspond.

That, too, was magnificent—a sign of the times which compelled the admiration of the modern world. Never before had the claims of art—and such an art!—been asserted with such a supreme degree of self-assurance. One may regard it as a case of Nemesis overtaking a world which has latterly been disposed to make too much of artists —and of such artists; or one may take it as a manifesto in support of Princess Louisa of Tuscany's indignation at the great wrong done when artists who contribute, in whatever way, to the relaxation of Courts, are simply "paid their fees and dismissed." Assuredly, this particular dancing-girl was not to be got rid of in that particular way; and one admires her demonstration for the same reason for which one admires Queen Amélie's demonstration—as a stout blow struck for personal dignity in embarrassing circumstances—the sort of thing that brings the apple to the throats of the gallery in a Lyceum melodrama.

The curtain may fall on it; for there is nothing more to be said. We have seen the House of Braganza declining because it was inadequate, and falling because it had become ridiculous. Latin countries take the logical view that monarchical institutions, like other institutions, must either justify themselves or disappear. The House of Braganza has failed to justify itself, and therefore it has, once more, "ceased to reign." The municipality of Richmond, and the pillars of suburban society in that interesting borough may, if they choose, accord Dom Manoel that title of Majesty which is no longer currently given to the claimants to the Kingdom of France and the Empire of Brazil; but the probability of his actual recall to the throne of his ancestors is sufficiently remote to be negligible. The cinematograph, of which he is said to be so fond, may have to be kingdom large enough for him in the years to come.

THE END.

INDEX

INDEX

Acunha, Tristan d', 17
Adalbert, Prince of Prussia, 173, 174
Æschylus, 32
Affonso I., King of Portugal, 11, 13
Affonso V., 27, 34
Affonso VI. (the Victorious), 58–69, 72
Affonso, Duke of Oporto, see Oporto, Duke of
Affonso, Pedro, 40, 41
Agassiz, Louis, 173
Albert, Prince of Saxe-Coburg, afterwards Prince Consort of England, 195, 211, 220, 234, 238, 246
Albuquerque, 17, 18, 39
Alcacer-Kebir, 22, 39
Alcantara, Pedro d', 206
Alcobaca, 15
Algarves, 162
Aljubarrota, 12, 13
Almanza, Battle of, 80
Almazan, Dr., 20
Almeida, Francisco d', 17, 25
Almeida, Miguel d', 51
Amélie, Queen, 44, 240, 258–264, 274, 277, 280–285, 287–296, 298, 299, 306, 312, 314–317, 319
Alvares, Matheus, 40
Amadeo, King, 241
Ameiscial, Battle of, 72
Andrada, Jose Bonifacio da, 168
Anna, Donna, 42
Anne of Austria, 53
Antonio o Crato, 44
Assis, Dom Francisco d', 58
Atháide, Dona Catharina d', 27

Augustus of Saxe-Coburg, 193, 194
Aumale, Duc d', 258
Aumale, Mademoiselle d', see Maria Francisca, Queen of Portugal
Auvergne, Edmund B. d', 211, 212, 241
Azores, 155–157

Badcock, Lieut.-Col. Lovell, 159
Barcellos, Count of, 34
Barthou, M., 187
Bates, D., of Philadelphia, 170
Bavaria, 2
Beauharnais, Eugène de, 210
Beeching, Canon, 16
Beira, Prince of, 104
Belem, 218
Beresford, Marshal, 111, 129
Berry, Duchesse de, 162
Berwick, Duke of, 80
Bollaert, William, 121, 155, 226
Bombay, Island of, 71, 304
Bom Retiro, Viscount of, 188
Bourmont, Marshal, 162
Braga, Théophilo, 269, 303, 304, 305, 316
Braganza, Duchess of, widow of John I., 44, 45
Braganza, Duchess of, Donna Luiza de Gusman, wife of John II., 46
Braganza, Duke of, 285
Brazil, History of, 76, 80, 106, 108, 112–120, 123, 138, 154, 166–169, 171–180, 190–199, 203
Broussonet, 98
Brugère, General, 205
Bulgaria, Ferdinand of, 7

INDEX

Bulwer, Sir Henry, 220
Burgundy, Affonso Henriques of, 11, 12
Busaco, 111

Calmette, Gaston, 184
Camoens, 24–33, 37
Cannes, 168, 202, 258
Canning, Lord, 124, 141, 154
Capet, Hugues, 34
Carignan, Prince of, 210
Carlos, King of Portugal, 3, 14, 213, 248, 255–259, 264–267, 271–280, 283–286, 292, 301
Carlota Joaquina, Donna, daughter of Charles IV. of Spain, and Consort of John VI. of Portugal, 100, 113, 122–125, 127, 130, 135–137, 146
Carlsbad, 274
Carnota, Conde, 119
Carver, Dr., 256
Castelmelhor, Count of, 60, 63, 64
Castile, 11, 50
Castlemaine, Lady, 73
Castro, Inez de, 14
Catalonia, 50
Cathelineau, 162
Catherine of Braganza, daughter of John IV., 57, 58, 71–76, 79
Chantilly, 258, 259
Charles II. of England, 71–74
Charles IV. of Spain, 104
Charles, Prince of Naples, 209
Charlotte, Princess of Belgium, 230–233
Chartres, Duke of, 208
Cintra, 67, 243
Civil War in Portugal, The, 123
Clarendon, Lord, 73
Cochrane, Lord, 119
Coimbra, 14, 15, 26, 37, 94, 152, 264, 266, 267, 268–273, 276, 293, 298, 299, 303
Colbatch, Chaplain at Lisbon, 78
Comte, Auguste, 191, 270
Constant, Benjamin, 191
Constantine of Braganza, 27, 30, 35
Constantine, King of Greece, 4
Conti, Antonio, 59, 60
Corpechot, Lucien, 261, 306, 312
Costa, Affonso, 276, 301
Crato, Dom Antonio, o, 44, 45

Dampierre, 282, 283
Darwin, Charles, 181
Davidson, Miss Lillias Campbell, 73
Dearborn, General, 127
Devaux, J., 238
Dieppe, 76
Dietz, Herr, Tutor to Ferdinand of Saxe-Coburg, 218, 223, 230
Disraeli, B., 185
Dobrzencz, Countess Dobrzensky de, 206
Dom Miguel: Ses aventures Scandaleuses, 146
Doyle, Sir J. M., 155, 160
Drake, Sir F., 45
Dresden, 258
Dugay-Trouin, General, 80
Dumas, the younger, 183

Edla, Countess of, 238–240
Elizabeth, Queen of England, 13
Ericeira, 40, 316
Ernest, Duke of Saxe-Gotha, 220, 221, 233, 238, 240
Espinosa, Gabriel de, 42
Esterhazy, Princess Thérèse, 143
Eu, d' Comte, 192–196, 198
Evora, 162

Fénelon, 226
Ferdinand I., Duke of Braganza, 12, 34
Ferdinand II., Duke of Braganza, 34, 35
Ferdinand VII. of Spain, 124, 136
Ferdinand, King of Bavaria, 7, 8
Ferdinand, Prince of Saxe-Coburg, Consort of Maria Gloria, Queen of Portugal, 210–230, 234, 236–245
Feversham, Lord, 74
Figueiro, Countess, 285
Flammarion, Camille, 202, 204
Flashman, 150
Fletcher, Rev. James C., 174, 176
Fontainebleau, Treaty of, 104
Francis Joseph, Emperor, 259
Franco, Joao, 266, 273–278, 281, 283–285, 287, 288
Frank, M., 183
Frederick, German Emperor, 232
Frederick, Empress, 246

INDEX

Galicia, 11
Galippe, Dr., 20
Gama, Vasco da, 17, 26
George, Prince of Saxony, 231
George IV. of England, 126, 208
Gibraltar, 76, 316
Gladstone, W. E., 181
Goa, 17, 18
Godoy, French Minister, 104
Grant, Mrs., 244
Greece, Constantin, King of, 4
Greville, Charles, 144, 208, 209
Gusman, Donna Luiza de, 48

Haakon, King of Norway, 4
Hegel, 270
Henri I. of France, 34
Henri III. of France, 37
Henry III. of England, 12
Henry, King of Portugal (the Cardinal), 11, 13, 22, 23, 36, 42
Henry, Prince (the Navigator), 8, 13, 17, 247
Hensler, Mlle. Elise Frederica, see Edla, Countess of
Hodges, Captain, 155, 157
Hooker, Sir Joseph, 181
Houssaye, Arsène, 181, 184
Hugo, Victor, 151, 186–188, 199, 270
Hunt, Colonel, 72

Indes, Joseph, Carmelite Friar, 24
Isabel, Princess of Brazil, 191–195, 201, 204, 205
Isabella, Queen of Spain, 2, 3, 5, 58, 220, 240
Isandula, 22
Islington, 75

James II. of England, 74, 75
James, Duke of Braganza, 34, 35
John I., Duke of Braganza (the Constable), 8, 14, 17, 27, 34, 36
John II., Duke of Braganza, see John IV., King of Portugal
John of Austria, Don, 42
John III. (the Pious) of Portugal, 27, 36
John IV., King of Portugal (the fortunate), 14, 34–36, 46–58, 283
John V., King of Portugal (the Dilettante), 79–84

John VI., Prince of Brazil, afterwards King of Portugal (the Runaway), 97, 99–118, 120–140, 146, 147
John of Gaunt, 13
Jordâo, Telles, 153
Joseph, King of Portugal, 84, 85, 87, 89, 92–95
Joseph, Dom, elder brother of John VI. of Portugal, 100
Josephine, Empress, 210
Junot, Marshal, 98, 104, 107, 110

Kidder, Rev. Dr., 174

Lafôes, Duke of, 98
Lamartine, 175, 185, 188
Lannes, Marshal, 103, 104
Larochejacquelain, 162
Lavradio, Marquis of, 310, 314
Leon, 11
Leopold I., King of the Belgians, 210, 211, 230, 234, 238, 246
Leopold II., King of the Belgians, 212, 238
Leopoldina, Archduchess, Consort of Pedro I. of Brazil, 167, 208–210
Leopoldina, Doña, daughter of Pedro of Brazil, 193, 204
Leuchtenberg, Duke of, 209, 210
Lima, Magalhaes, 269, 286
Linch's *Travels in Portugal,* 101
Lisbon, 12, 19, 28, 40, 41, 45, 48, 54, 55, 69, 72, 77, 78, 83, 84, 85, 90, 98, 101, 103, 105–109, 115, 125, 126, 128, 131, 141, 151, 162, 201, 208, 211, 221, 224, 225, 233, 238, 239, 243, 250, 256, 258, 260, 261, 283, 284, 286, 291, 303, 309, 314
Longfellow, 175, 177
Longueville, Duc de, 57
Louis XIV. of France, 75, 87
Louis XVI. of France, 276, 301
Louis XVIII. of France, 165
Louis-Philippe of France, 209
Louisa, Princess of Tuscany, 319
Loulé, Marquis of, 125
Ludwig II., King of Bavaria, 2, 3
Luis, Duke of Oporto, King of Portugal, 14, 213, 233, 234, 236, 240, 243, 247–252
Luynes, Duc de, 283, 293–295

325

INDEX

Macao, 17
Macdonell, 162
Mackail, Mr., 16
Madeira, 201
Madrid, 32, 48, 49
Mafra Convent and Palace, 81, 82, 102, 312
Magellan, 17
Maintenon, Mme. de, 226
Manoel I., King of Portugal (the Fortunate), 19, 35
Manoel II., King of Portugal, 1, 3, 4, 5, 7, 8, 10, 14, 202, 213, 285, 287, 289, 290, 294, 298–301, 303, 309, 311–318, 320
Mantua, Duchess of, 51
Marcos, Father, Confessor to Ferdinand of Saxe-Coburg, 218, 223
Margate, 76
Maria I., Queen of Portugal, 95–98
Maria Francisca, Queen of Portugal, Consort of Alfonso VI., 62–67
Maria Gloria, daughter of Pedro I., Emperor of Brazil, 139–143, 145, 148, 154, 156, 166, 207–228, 251
Maria Isabel, daughter of John VI., and Regent of Portugal, 140
Maria Pia, Princess, 206, 240–241, 247, 248, 251–253, 260, 274, 277, 288, 292, 314
Marie-Sophie of Pfalz Neuburg, Consort of Pedro II., 77
Martins, Oliveira, 269
Mary II. of England, 75, 76
Massena, 162
Maximilian, Emperor of Mexico, 24, 232
Mazarin, Cardinal, 57
Medina Sidonia, Duke of, 48
Methuen Treaty, 76
Metternich, 138, 142, 143, 150, 151, 181
Michelet, 270
Miguel, Infant Dom, son of John VI. of Portugal, 5, 14, 121–128, 130–135, 137–163, 207, 208, 210, 215
Miguel, Prince of Braganza, 163
Mistral, Frederic, 183, 184
Monmouth, Duke of, 74
Montez, Lola, 2
Montpensier, Duc de, 240
Morley, Lord, 303

Morton, Dr., 176
Mosse, M., 182
Mozambique, 17

Napier, Captain, 155, 160, 162
Napoleon I., 98, 103–106, 109, 110, 113, 160, 162, 164, 304
Nemours, Duc de, 61, 193, 204, 209, 210
Neuville, Hyde de, 126–130, 136, 137
Neuville, Mme. Hyde de, 126
New York, 239
Nichols, Mr. John Bower Buchanan, 15, 16
Nicholson, John, 18
Norris, 45

Otto of Bavaria, King of Greece, 237
Oates, Titus, 72
Odivelas, Convent of, 90
O'Donnell, Marshal, 195
Olivares, 53
Oporto, 141, 153, 155, 158, 159, 162, 263, 272, 280, 293, 306
Oporto, Duke of, 277; son of King Luis, 255, 285, 288
Orléans, Duke of, 208
Orléans, Duchesse d', 260
Orth, John, 24

Padua, 43
Palmella, 143
Palmerston, Lord, 220
Paris, 135, 137, 148, 169, 204, 211, 256, 258, 261, 274, 282, 296
Paris, Comte de, 258, 260
Pedro, Duke of Coimbra, 34
Pedro I., Emperor of Brazil, 118, 119, 138–141, 143, 154–167, 169, 207–209, 224, 230
Pedro II., Emperor of Brazil, 166–205
Pedro II., King of Portugal (the Glum), 14, 15, 58, 63–67, 70, 75–79
Pedro III., King Consort of Maria I. of Portugal, 95, 97
Pedro IV., King of Portugal, see Pedro I., Emperor of Brazil
Pedro V., King of Portugal, 213, 229–234, 236, 246
Penamaçor, 39

INDEX

Pequito, Rodrigo, 300
Perez, Inez, 34
Peter of Saxe-Coburg, 203
Petropolis, 196
Philip II., King of Spain and Portugal, 13, 20-23, 32, 36, 37
Philip III., 42-46
Philip IV., King of Spain and Portugal, 49-56
Philippa of Lancaster, 13
Pitt, William, 136
Pius IX., 5
Pombal, Marquis of, 84-90, 92, 94, 95, 136
Ponte, Countess da, 120
Potsdam, 186
Prim, General, 240
Prudhomme, M., 254, 265
Punjaub, 18

Queluz, 136

Reinhardt, Dr., 174
Réjane, Mme., 256
Renduffe, Baron de, 149
Richard II., of England, 12
Richelieu, Cardinal, 135
Richmond, 1, 320
Rio de Janeiro, 107, 109, 147, 176, 179, 195
Rio Mayor, Marchioness of, 263
Ristori, Mme., 180
Robert I. of Burgundy, 34
Roberts, Earl, 253
Rome, 163
Rooke, Sir George, 76
Rossini, 248
Rouen, 182
Russia, 135

Saint Goard, Vivonne de, 37
Saldanha, Field Marshal the Duke of, 119, 120, 140, 141, 160, 161, 164, 223-226, 231, 250-253
San Christovao, 174
Sandwich, Lord, 72
San Lorenço, Count of, 89
Santarem, 162
Santos, Marchioness of, 167
Sartorius, Captain, 155, 160
Sauerwein, Jules, 307
Savoy, Duchess of, 67
Schomberg, General, 69

Sebastian, King of Portugal, 20, 21, 23, 30, 31, 270
— Impostors posing as, 38-43
Shakespeare, 256
Shaw, Captain, 155
Simon, Jules, 186
Smith, James Henry, 163
Smith, Sir Sidney, 107, 108
Sobieski, John, 69
Solignac, General, 160, 161
Southey, Robert, *Letters from Spain and Portugal,* 102, 107, 108
Spencer, Herbert, 270
Stambouloff, 273, 274
Stéphanie, Princess of Hohenzollern-Sigmaringen, 233, 234, 246
Stewart, Anita, 163
Stewart, William, Rhinelander, 163
Strathfieldsaye, 143
Subserra, Countess of, 126
Swinburne, Algernon Charles, 16

Tangier, 71, 304
Terceira, Duke of, 162
Terceira, Island of, 67
Texeira de Sousa, 316
Theodosius I., Duke of Braganza, 34, 36, 45
Theodosius II., Duke of Braganza, 34
Thornton, Sir Edward, 127
Torres Vedras, 162
Torres Vedras, Marquis of, 41
Trafalgar, 104
Trieste, 24
Tullio, Marco, 42
Tuscany, Duke of, 43
Twiss, Richard, 90

Venice, 42, 43
Versailles, 204
Victor Emmanuel, King of Italy, 240, **247**
Victoria, Queen of England, 154, 195, 208, 223, 230-232, 234, 246-248
Viegas, Antonio Paes, 49
Vienna, 69, 138, 142, 148, 163, 258, 259
Villa novia da Rainha, Viscount de la, **129**
Villa-Viçosa, 47, 50, 283
Ville, Jesuit Father, 68
Villèle, 137

INDEX

Visea, Duchess of, 163
Visea, Duke of, 163
Voltaire, 83, 84, 186

Waldemar, Princess, of Denmark, 291
Walpole, the British Ambassador, 95, 96
Waterloo, Battle of, 111, 162, 315

Wellington, Duke of, 111, 143, 154, 162, 164, 208, 253
Weyer, Sylvian Van der, 214
William, Prince of Orange, afterwards King of England, 43, 74, 75
William IV. of England, 154, 209
Windsor, Treaty of, 12

Young, Russell, 244